CRAZY LOVE

Dealing With Your Partner's Problem Personality

W. Brad Johnson, Ph.D.
Kelly Murray, Ph.D.

RebuildingBooks™
Relationships – Divorce – and Beyond

Impact Publishers®
ATASCADERO, CALIFORNIA

ATTENTION ORGANIZATIONS AND CORPORATIONS:
This book is available at quantity discounts on bulk purchases for educational, business, or sales promotional use. For further information, please contact Impact Publishers, P.O. Box 6016, Atascadero, California 93423-6016.
Phone: 805-466-5917, e-mail: info@impactpublishers.com

Library of Congress Cataloging-in-Publication Data

Johnson, W. Brad.
    Crazy love : dealing with your partner's problem personality / W. Brad Johnson, Kelly Murray
        p. cm. — (The rebuilding book series)
    Includes bibliographical references and index.
    ISBN 978-1-886230-80-4 (alk. paper)
 1. Personality. 2. Interpersonal relations. I. Murray, Kelly. II. Title.
    BF698.J58 2007
    616.85'81—dc22

                                                                    2007000613

Publisher's Note
This publication is designed to provide accurate and authoritative information in regard to the subject matter covered. It is sold with the understanding that the publisher is not engaged in rendering psychological, medical, or other professional services. If expert assistance or counseling is needed, the services of a competent professional should be sought.

Impact Publishers and colophon are registered trademarks of Impact Publishers, Inc.

Cover design by Gayle Downs, Gayle Force Design, Atascadero, California
Composition by UB Communications, Parsippany, New Jersey
Printed in the United States of America on acid-free, recycled paper
Published by **Impact 🕸 Publishers®**
POST OFFICE BOX 6016
ATASCADERO, CALIFORNIA 93423-6016
www.impactpublishers.com

To Dr. Shannon Jill Johnson,
the best little sister on the planet.

WBJ

To the members of my family
who have held and continue
to hold me:

My parents and sister,
and now my husband, Sean,
and our five little ladies:
Jillian, Meghan, Sloane, Maeve,
and Catherine Quinn.

KMM

Contents

1. Crazy Love: The Weird Partner Detection
   and Survival Guide   1
2. Personality Disorders 101: Understanding Weird Partners . .   7
3. How Could I Be Attracted to PDPs? Let Me Count
   the (top Nine) Ways! 17

Cluster A: Odd, Eccentric, and Weird Partners

4. The Doubting Partner: The Paranoid Personality 31
5. The Detached Partner: The Schizoid Personality 45
6. The Odd Partner: The Schizotypal Personality 61

Cluster B: Dramatic, Erratic, and Dangerous Partners

7. The Dangerous Partner: The Antisocial Personality 77
8. The Stormy Partner: The Borderline Personality 95
9. The Theatrical Partner: The Histrionic Personality 113
10. The Self-Absorbed Partner: The Narcissistic Personality 127
11. The Undermining Partner: The Passive-Aggressive
    Personality 143

Cluster C: Anxious, Withdrawn, and Needy Partners

12. The Scared Partner: The Avoidant Personality 161
13. The Sticky Partner: The Dependent Personality 175
14. The Rigid Partner: The Obsessive-Compulsive Personality . . 189
15. The Glum Partner: The Depressive Personality 207

Some Final Thoughts

16. What If I'm Married to a Personality-Disordered Partner? . . ̄

Bibliography . . . .

Index . . . .

CHAPTER 1

CRAZY LOVE

The Weird Partner Detection and Survival Guide

The scenario is all too common. Girl meets guy (or guy meets girl). Guy is smart, charming, and maybe even endearing. Girl falls in love. As the relationship progresses, guy's serious personality problems begin to surface. She gets longer and more vivid glimpses of habits and tendencies she didn't notice at first:

- He seems to "need" her attention all the time; she feels smothered.
- He seems increasingly possessive and suspicious.
- He is detached and uninterested in socializing.
- He is exploitive and manipulative.
- He seems to expect abandonment.
- He is rigidly organized and humor challenged.

She becomes increasingly frustrated and insecure; she even starts to feel like she's going a little bit crazy. How could she have missed the signs? Where did this guy come from anyway? How could she have fallen for him in the first place? Why does she always seem to end up with weird guys? Is he even aware of how his unusual behavior impacts others? Can he, and more important, *will* he change?

If this scenario is all too familiar to you, if you find yourself dating or living with a person whose everyday behavior — behavior that he finds perfectly normal — causes you frequent distress, you may be involved with a personality-disordered partner (our shorthand in this book will be "PDP"). What's more, you may have a track record of involvement with partners who are detached, erratic, dangerous, or just too clingy. Looking back, you may see some alarming similarities in these lovers and wonder what it is about you (and them) that keeps you coming back for more. In chapter 3, we'll explore the "why" of repeated involvement with PDPs. For now, recognize that PDPs have personality characteristics that are almost always weird, high maintenance, difficult, and toxic to genuine and enduring love. Whenever possible, we'll recommend that you detect PDPs early and that you steer clear of them as potential partners.

Does Your Partner Have a Personality Disorder?

For just a moment, sit back and think honestly about your former partners and your former love relationships. Some of these connections may have faded away with hardly a whimper while others ended loudly and in dramatic fashion. Think about the behaviors and traits of these partners. If you are currently in a relationship — perhaps even married — think about your current partner too. Now, thinking about specific partners, ask yourself these questions:

- Did things start off wonderfully but then come to a screeching halt for some reason?

- Does your partner appear to be completely unaware of his impact on others and the effects of his behavior?

- Is your partner "OK" with behaviors you find quite inappropriate — perhaps even disturbing?

- When you make efforts to correct the problem, does your partner fail to respond or follow through (suggesting little motivation to change)?

- Is your partner frequently in intense conflict with you, other people, or even institutions and employers?

- Does your partner create a positive first impression on people, only to later display problems with anger, poor social interaction, or manipulation?

- Is your partner "odd" and "eccentric" to the point that it causes him rejection?

- Does your partner seem to feel most comfortable when he is the primary focus and you are diminished by comparison?

- Does your partner have such profound needs for your attention or adulation that you feel exhausted managing the relationship?

- Is your partner so rigid and regimented that changes to the routine provoke anxiety or anger?
- Did you notice something weird about this person and decide to proceed with the relationship anyway?

Behavior that provokes a yes answer to any of these questions is a red flag and means you should be concerned about the health of your partner's personality. While no single item is alone diagnostic of a disorder, each is a warning sign indicating further exploration is in order. More than one red flag should increase your level of concern. Personality disorders are psychiatric disorders characterized by long-standing and long-lasting patterns of disordered behavior. The disordered behavior seriously impairs a person's ability to perform optimally in society — and especially in relationships. Personality disorders are enduring patterns of seeing, relating to, and thinking about both the world and oneself that are rigid and that ultimately sabotage relationships. A landmark survey conducted by the National Institutes of Health (2004) revealed that about 15 percent of the adult population suffers from one or more personality disorders — that's over 16 million potential relationship partners. Among adults in counseling or therapy, the percentage is much higher — about 50 percent.

Think about those numbers for a minute. Even if you are looking for love in a relatively healthy environment (e.g., church, college, work), chances are that nearly one of five potential partners has some serious personality problem. And, when you consider the fact that many people have strong features of a personality disorder — even if they are not severe enough to be diagnosed — that figure probably increases. But wait, it gets worse: If you are seeking relationships in singles bars or online dating services — settings that appeal to those who have had trouble finding love elsewhere — then the probability of encountering weird personalities escalates even more.

Finding the right partner and maintaining a healthy love relationship is hard work in the best of circumstances. It is much harder when your partner has a personality disorder. In this book, we shed light on these odd but surprisingly common disorders of character so that readers can become better informed and more careful when entering or continuing a relationship. We also draw attention to the reasons many of us are so attracted to PDPs and offer strategies for detecting and avoiding PDPs. Although in most cases it is better to become good at detecting and staying away from PDPs, we also understand that many reading this book are already in committed relationships with a personality-impaired partner — perhaps someone you genuinely love. In this case, we offer hope in the form of survival strategies and tips for making the relationship more livable; life is just too short to spend most of it walking on eggshells.

Why a Guide to Detecting Weird Personalities?

The story is all too familiar. We sit across from a new client — often an attractive and successful man or woman who has done well in life. He or she has a good career, supportive friends, and ample resources. Our new client has good judgment in most areas of life and is clearly above average in the realm of intelligence. He or she enjoys a healthy self-esteem and exudes the kind of confidence one expects from an up-and-coming young professional. In those first moments of consultation, we may wonder: *What could possibly be wrong in this person's life?*

Then, a familiar story begins to unfold — sometimes slowly through a haze of confused bewilderment, and sometimes abruptly — accompanied by tears or anger. The focus of each story is a love partner. Sometimes it is a person our client has only recently begun dating. Sometimes it is a long-term partner or a fiancée. As the relationship stories tumble out, a consistent theme begins to emerge. At times, the symptoms are like neon signs accompanied by sirens. At other times the telltale markers are more subtle and deceptively nested in the client's own confused narrative.

But here is the consistent piece. By the end of that very first fifty-minute session with our new client, we have a pretty good idea that the problem lurks in her partner's basic personality. Maybe the partner's subtle doubting and chronic suspicion have begun to make our client doubt herself. Or perhaps the partner's unpredictable fluctuations between seductive flirtation and angry withdrawal have the client mesmerized but shaking her head and wondering how the relationship ever got this far. Unaware that the partner suffers from a personality disorder, our client has come to us in genuine distress. She may be anxious and depressed; she may wonder what has gone wrong and if she is to blame. Unaccustomed to failure and used to relying on keen perception and solid judgment, the current relationship has destabilized her and perhaps even begun to undermine her confidence and self-esteem.

Once the story is told and our client looks to us for answers, we must often begin the work of helping her understand that she has probably hooked up with someone suffering from one of many personality disorders. It can be difficult to tell a person that she has fallen for a PDP, but understanding the nature of personality disorders is often the first step in regaining control of one's life.

As psychologists who have seen the above scenario play out time and time again in our own practices, we have written this guide to help you detect and avoid PDPs before they wreak havoc in your life. In reading this guide, we hope that you will

- learn to quickly recognize the symptoms of the twelve personality disorders.

- correctly "diagnose" personality impairment before a relationship goes too far.

- make better choices about the partners you date and eventually commit to.

- learn from previous relationship mistakes.

- make an informed and deliberate decision about staying or leaving if you find yourself involved with a PDP.

- be honest and sober in accurately appraising a partner's personality disturbance.

How to Use This Guide

PDPs are chronically maladaptive in their behavior, likely to cause you distress and disappointment, and sometimes they can be dangerous. If you are single and "in the market" for a partner, we hope you will use this guide to actively and assertively detect and avoid PDPs. Think of the guide as equipping you with internal weird partner vision goggles; don't leave home, or at least don't date, without them.

By becoming familiar with the varieties of problem personalities, you will become increasingly inoculated to the charms and spells these partners can initially weave. By detecting impairment up front, you will be in a position of considerable power with regard to screening out PDPs and avoiding the heartache that can accompany relationships with them.

If you have a history of hooking up with PDPs, it's time to look carefully at your own patterns of attraction and do something about them. If you are currently involved with a partner who shows all the signs of having one of the personality syndromes covered in this guide, you have some hard choices to make. At some point, you have to decide either to acclimate to a love interest's personality disorder — to commit in spite of the problems rampant in your relationship — or to leave. Although we cannot ultimately make this call for you, we hope this guide gives you the tools to make an informed decision. If you do decide to move on — a healthy choice in many circumstances — then it will be important to consider how to exit the relationship with as much grace and kindness as possible while ensuring your own health and safety.

If in reading this book you come to the conclusion that you are characterized by one or more of the personality patterns described, we encourage you to acknowledge and own your own contribution to failed or dysfunctional relationships, seek professional help, and work to help your partner better understand your disorder.

Finally, a word of warning: On rare occasions a PDP may become so impaired that hospitalization or incarceration is required. If someone you are dating or involved with begins to express suicidal thoughts, begins to have very disorganized thinking, or becomes threatening to you or others, it is time to seek professional help or call the police. Avoid the trap of trying to "rescue" this partner on your own — it will seldom work.

CHAPTER 2

PERSONALITY DISORDERS 101
Understanding Weird Partners

W hat are personality disorders and why are we devoting a book to helping you ferret them out and understand your attraction to people who have them? A certain proportion of people in every country and community show signs of personality disturbance. As early as 400 BC, Greek physician Hippocrates noted a wide range in fundamental personality dispositions, which he called the *temperaments*, and that some temperament mixes were prone to causing difficulty. Body makeup, diet, and even climate were thought to influence the development of these personality types. Although psychiatry and psychology have referred to problem personalities for years, it was not until 1980 that the American Psychiatric Association's diagnostic manual began to separate personality disorders into an entirely separate diagnostic domain. What was the reason for this differentiation? In contrast to other psychiatric disorders (e.g., depression, phobias, schizophrenia), personality disorders were noted to begin relatively early in life, to be inextricably entwined with the person's basic personality or character, and to be very difficult to change. In contrast to many other psychiatric problems, personality disorders have no clear date of onset, no specific cause, and no clear resolution. They are pervasive and, in many cases, permanent.

How are people with personality disorders different from the rest of us? Think of most personality traits as existing on a continuum from barely notable to extreme — present to a significant degree in every situation. For example, while many of us have some measure of caution and self-protection in new relationships, a few of us are at the extreme end of this spectrum and become downright suspicious in every new situation and relationship — expecting to be wronged and accusing our partners of duplicity or unfaithfulness even when there is not a shred of evidence to support these claims. This person has the Paranoid Personality Disorder (the one we call the *doubting partner* and discuss in chapter 4) and is rigidly suspicious in all relationships and begins to suffer socially and occupationally as a result. In a nutshell, people with personality disorders evidence consistent patterns of thinking about, relating to, and experiencing the world and love relationships that are profoundly consistent across time and situation and nearly always correlate with dysfunction.

What causes someone to develop a personality disorder? On that question, the scientific jury is still out. Here is one thing you can bank on: There is never a simple cause-effect relationship in the creation of a personality disorder. There are numerous genetic, biological, psychological, and social causative factors creating pathways to personality disturbance. Attempting to disentangle this web of factors will probably not be very helpful when it comes to understanding your own personality-impaired partner; your time and energy will be better spent considering what to do here and now and why this partner was so attractive to you in the first place. In most cases, we'll recommend that you make a graceful exit; in other instances, we'll recommend that you run for it! But if you choose to stay, we'll encourage you to take good care of yourself along the bumpy road you most certainly have ahead of you in this relationship.

Even the professional diagnostician engages in a certain amount of guesswork and speculation when he or she attempts to understand the complex network of developmental influences in the early lives of persons with personality disorders. Also, remember that some personality disorders (e.g., the antisocial) are prone to lying about their history, and the childhood memories of many PDPs must be considered dubious in light of the fact that they now interpret their life experiences through the distorted lens of a character disorder.

It does appear that both genetic and environmental factors play a part in the development of personality impairment. We know that genetic contribution to fundamental personality dimensions such as introversion and extraversion is close to 50 percent, so it is safe to assume a strong genetic loading for various personality disorders. But even if genes play a role, it is also true that developmental experiences — especially those with parents — are profoundly important in contributing to the development of a personality disorder. (American Psychiatric Association, 2000; Millon, 1996; Sperry, 2003).

Many personality impairments have their roots in childhood experiences characterized by neglect, conflict, emotional abuse, or the modeling of disordered behavior by adults. Relationship researchers have linked relationship attachment style with the development of personality disorders. When an infant's caregivers are engaged, responsive, and attentive to the infant's needs and when the caregivers react with consistent soothing to the infant's discomfort, fear, or rage, the infant learns to trust at a fundamental level. The young child expects important others to be reliable and trustworthy and sees the world as predictable and safe. However, when such caregiver responses are not forthcoming, the infant may be insecurely attached. Later in life, this adult is vulnerable to rigid defensiveness, emotional detachment, suspicious distrust, or rage-filled reactivity to perceived discounting or abandonment. The personality-disordered adult cannot effectively regulate emotions or self-soothe; trusting others relationally may be a monumental challenge.

Keep in mind that the formation of secure attachments occurs very early in life — during what might be called a *critical period* of personality and brain development. Attachment habits — either secure or insecure — form neural pathways in the brain that become automatically stimulated in subsequent relational situations. Thus, the insecurely attached adult responds instantly with rage, fear, or sullen disengagement because the brain is habituated to respond this way. In contrast, the brain of a securely attached adult has the capacity for more responses — depending on the context and the appropriateness of the situation — and neural pathways that allow self-soothing and effective management of emotional experiences.

Consider for a moment the schizoid (detached and withdrawn) personality (you'll meet "Roy" in chapter 5). Beyond genes, what might lead a child to adopt a strategy for relating or surviving that involved thorough detachment and disconnection from other human beings? We would not be surprised to discover that the schizoid adult was neglected or ignored as a child. Alternatively, the schizoid may have weathered a high-conflict or otherwise disturbed childhood environment — he found the comfort of solitude to be an antidote. By the time the schizoid reaches adulthood, this once adaptive strategy has become a permanent or calcified facet of the personality. Cut off and entirely uninterested in relationships, the adult with Schizoid Personality Disorder now alienates co-workers and avoids all personal relationships. This coping style, however, is no longer adaptive as an adult and now causes the schizoid to have impaired relationships with others.

Perhaps the most salient facet of a child's parental experience is his sense of acceptance versus rejection by parents. Research on this powerful perception indicates that the child who feels rejected is considerably more likely to develop personality disturbance by adulthood; feeling unwanted or unloved places the child at considerable risk for either hostility or indifference. It is also important to remember that many PDPs used strategies to deal with childhood abuse or neglect that made terrific sense at the time. So, the emotionally abused child who adopts a strategy of guardedness, defensiveness, or detachment should be applauded for adapting to a terrible situation; however, as the child becomes an adult and exits the abusive situation, his defensive strategies are so inextricably entwined with his core personality that they have become rigid and inflexible. The adaptive child has, thus, become a personality-disordered adult. As we discuss each personality disorder in this book, we will address some of the most prevalent experiences with parents and caregivers.

Key Features of Personality Disorders

In order to help you better understand the personality disorders, we now list some of the common fundamental elements of disordered personalities. These essential features are consistent across each of the disorders covered in this book. Whether your partner is narcissistic, dependent, or obsessive-compulsive, each of the following personality disorder components remains constant. Of course, these components only form the bedrock of the disordered personality; in later chapters, we consider the unique and defining elements that are specific to each disorder. According to the American Psychiatric Association's diagnostic manual (DSM-IV) and other research bearing on personality problems, essential qualities of any personality disorder include the following:

- The way the person experiences the world, handles emotions, and behaves is rigid and deeply etched. It is quite different from the experience and behavior of most others.

- This pattern of unusual experience and behavior is evident in the person's way of thinking, emotional expression, interpersonal relationships, and impulse control.

- This personality pattern is rigid and inflexible; you will see it across a broad range of personal and social situations. Unlike most of us, the personality-disordered adult can't change or flex her demeanor or behavior to appropriately fit different situations.

- These chronic and enduring patterns lead to significant personal distress (e.g., anxiety, depression, anger) or clear impairment in social relationships, occupational success, or other important areas of functioning.

- The personality pattern is stable and of long duration; its onset can often be traced back at least to adolescence or early adulthood.

- Although the disordered personality pattern may become less obvious and troublesome with old age, it often remains in some form throughout life.

- The maladaptive personality patterns are self-sustaining in that the person's style often creates stressors, conflict, and dysfunction — she then has maladaptive responses to these very stressors.

- The enduring pattern is not the result of a mental disorder but is a unique expression of personality.

- The experiences and behaviors that define a personality disorder are paradoxically experienced by the person as normal — even comfortable and integral to her identity.

- The pattern of behavior is extremely resistant to change, and there is often low motivation to pursue change in self.

Detecting PDPs

By now you may be wondering how you will know if the person you are involved with suffers from a personality disorder — or perhaps whether several of the "train wreck" relationships from your past might fit into the PDP category. There are several aspects to personality disorders that make their detection a challenge early on in a relationship. First, people with certain personality disorders may initially come across as not only behaving appropriately but also gregarious and socially skilled. They may do alright at work and in some social circumstances and yet, over time, those closest to them begin to suffer. Take the Antisocial Personality Disorder for instance. Although prone to exploit and manipulate everyone he relates to, the antisocial often creates a very positive first impression; the word *smooth* comes to mind here. It may only be on the third date or even further into a relationship that evidence of exploitation, deceit, disregard for societal norms, and a willingness to make only superficial commitments come into full view. Further, PDPs can be just as physically attractive and intellectually gifted as any other partner — initial evidence of impairment is not always readily recognized. Whatever you do, don't blame yourself for this. personality disorders are radically underdiagnosed in clinical settings precisely because psychologists and psychiatrists often miss signs of personality impairment during initial therapy sessions.

A second contributor to difficulty in detecting personality disorders early on is the fact that accurate information about the person's past behavior is crucial to making an early diagnosis. Remember, diagnosing personality disorders requires evidence of a history — an enduring pattern — of bad interpersonal experiences and problem behavior. In the early phases of a relationship, it is understandably difficult to gain this kind of background and perspective on a potential partner. Conducting the kind of interview required to glean this information (and personality disorders are prone to cover up or downplay evidence of previous problems in relationships) is not exactly romantic or appropriate on a first date. Imagine this first date dinner dialog:

"So, tell me some more about yourself."

"Well, I'm from Cincinnati and my folks still live there. I have a younger sister. I'm working in sales right now. And...I love to backpack."

"That's a great start [she pulls a steno pad from under the table]. Now, let's get real here. I'd like to go through your romantic relationships one by one and hear about why each one ended, what behaviors seem to consistently get in the way, and how your partners end up feeling about you and themselves; and I'd like to get names and contact information for each so I can get another perspective. Care for more coffee?"

Clearly, most of us would find this more than a little odd and intrusive. But you get the idea; accurately detecting personality disturbance is often no easy task early in a relationship.

Finally, it is frequently hard to see evidence — even rather transparent evidence — of personality disturbance when we happen to be attracted to that very behavior! Yes, many of us find certain elements of personality-disturbed behavior intriguing, exciting, endearing, or even erotic. If you have been or are currently involved with a PDP, ask yourself honestly what first attracted you to him or her? Was it a propensity to make things exciting and take risks? Was it an endearing shyness that tugged at your caretaking strings? Did you feel flattered by your partner's wish to spend all of his or her time with you? Was it a larger-than-life persona and an ability to regale you with stories of accomplishment and connection to important people? Whatever the specific draw, it is possible that something about one (or more) of the personality disorders is subtly or overtly appealing to you — this is especially likely to be the case if you keep ending up in relationships with this type. It isn't until time passes and you have a better handle on the many facets of your partner's personality traits that you may begin to notice that the sum of your partner's personality overrides the parts that initially attracted you. It may only be in retrospect -- after you or your partner have fled the relationship — that the evidence of a personality disorder will become clear. Evidence suggests that spouses, partners, and close friends of PDPs can typically diagnose their condition reliably and accurately — after sufficient time and experience.

And remember, many of us are attracted to people with impaired personalities — regardless of the specific type. Thus, as you read this book, you may discover a trail of relationship turmoil with a variety of different types of PDPs. Perhaps some of your partners have been sticky and needy but you occasionally find yourself connected to a self-absorbed narcissist as well. In this case, there may be something about caring for malignant personalities that draws you in. See chapter 3 for more information on patterns of relationships with PDPs.

PDPs Have Other Problems

One of the very consistent strands of research on persons with personality pathology shows that they often have coexisting mental, social, and job-related problems. (American Psychiatric Association, 2000; Millon & Davis, 1996; Widiger & Costa, 1994). For example, a partner with Borderline Personality Disorder is more likely than other people to be clinically depressed, a partner with Antisocial Personality Disorder is more likely than most to abuse drugs and alcohol, and a partner with Paranoid Personality Disorder is more inclined to have a history of disputes with and simmering anger toward co-workers and love partners. This is why some estimates suggest that about half of all people going into treatment for outpatient psychiatric reasons have coexisting personality disorders (Millon & Davis, 2000; National Institutes of Health, 2004). Personality disorders tend to cause additional psychiatric problems, legal difficulties, occupational failures, and a perpetual trail of broken relationships. Trust us on this one: If you become involved — and stay involved — with a PDP, you can expect him or her to have a number of problems beyond odd behavior, and you can expect your partner to create a whole host of problems for you!

Prospects for Change: Poor

One of the most disheartening things about PDPs is the very low probability that they will change significantly. Although mental health practitioners and love partners often make earnest attempts to help these persons to "get over" their long-standing patterns of behavior, evidence suggests these disorders are particularly resistant to any "cure." Without being too cavalier or pessimistic, we offer this principle regarding the chances of substantial change in your partner's personality: *What you see is what you get*. That is, persons with personality disorders by early adulthood often continue to evidence personality disorder patterns throughout life. Not only are the perceptual, thought, and behavioral habits that define personality disorders thoroughly ingrained by adulthood, they are comfortable and familiar to the PDP. He is likely to simply say, "But that's just the way I am!" when confronted with a problematic behavior pattern. In fairness, we acknowledge that very few adults make significant changes in personality after they reach adulthood. The dye is cast, as it were. In fact, trying to change your personality in adulthood would be a great deal like trying to learn to walk backward everywhere or navigate life with your eyes closed — these things would make you feel distressed and disoriented and you would quickly return to your previous habits of walking forward and using your eyes.

The prognosis for personality disorders is also poor because these persons rarely seek therapy or counseling for their condition. Typically, they will only darken the door of a mental health professional's office when a lover threatens them with separation or divorce, when the legal system threatens them with incarceration or monetary damage, or when an employer threatens to fire them. If it is possible, effective therapy for most personality disorder conditions would require a very lengthy period of time — often several years — and even then, the prognosis for fundamental change in basic personality will remain grim.

Emerging psychotherapy outcome evidence indicates that if a PDP is highly motivated to change and if he has demonstrated an ability to make small changes in behavior in the past, then over time, the prognosis for change is improved (Sperry, 2003; Stone, 1993; Turkat, 1990). Yet, in a dating situation it is unwise to anticipate that your PDP will be motivated to participate in long-term treatment targeting his fundamental personality style. This would be like entering a relationship harboring the expectation that your partner will happily comply with your wish that he undergo extensive plastic surgery. Is it possible? Maybe, but let's admit that it is unlikely, probably unfair to your partner, and raises real questions about the health of the relationship from the start.

And yet, if you are hopelessly committed to a PDP, some hope remains. As one example, a person with Borderline Personality Disorder after an extensive regimen of treatment for which she is quite motivated, may no longer make suicidal gestures, may no longer require occasional inpatient admissions, and may be less likely to interpret her partner's comments or behaviors as evidence of abandonment. As a result, she may enjoy fewer blowups at work and in her relationships and may be capable of maintaining a single romantic relationship for a long period of time. Although she may still be considerably more likely to react with anger in some situations and although she may continue to struggle with a healthy sense of identity, she experiences important improvements and this should be cause for celebration.

What does all of this mean for you? It means you need to understand that the personality-disordered romantic partners you encounter are unlikely to ever make major changes in behavior — especially not without significant professional help. Modifications in specific habits and routines are always possible, but will your partner's fundamental personality change dramatically over time? Probably not.

CHAPTER 3

HOW COULD I
BE ATTRACTED TO PDPS?

Let Me Count the (Top Nine) Ways!

It may seem odd that we are devoting an entire chapter to the question: How could I be attracted to PDPs? After all, it's the PDP who has the weird personality, right? The answer to this question is yes and no. As chapter 2 suggests, personality-disordered adults often create havoc in relationships and they tend to be problem partners no matter how hard you work to help them. But as any marriage therapist will tell you, it will be very difficult to fully understand and appreciate why you seem to hook up with odd characters without first understanding yourself. As psychologists, we have seen countless partners work adamantly at changing each other — usually at the expense of looking honestly at their own part in an unraveling relationship.

Before considering each personality disorder in detail, we ask you to honestly reflect on the characteristics that attracted you to a new love interest — or perhaps a whole string of PDPs. We encourage you to consider the relationship dynamics that tempt and intrigue you so that you get sucked into these relationships time and time again. For instance, consider these difficult questions:

- Are you so enamored by one element of a potential partner's appearance or behavior that you seem to overlook numerous giant red flags?
- Does your disordered partner share one or more traits in common with one of your parents or other family members?
- Does this partner have some characteristic you feel is sorely lacking in yourself?
- Is rescuing or taking care of an impaired person compelling to you?

- Do you feel too guilty to move on even though you know you should?

- Does your "need to be needed" become so strong that you just can't turn your back on a low-functioning partner?

- Are you initially attracted to a partner's' eccentricity, intensity, risk-taking, or smooth talk without considering other important elements of her or his behavior?

- Is your self-esteem so fragile that saying no to someone you view as more powerful or superior to you is very difficult?

- Do you tend to enter and remain in lousy relationships primarily because they beat the alternative — loneliness?

Clearly, none of these questions is easy to answer. Each of them strikes at the very heart of our own vulnerabilities and self-defeating habits. Yet each of these questions can help to shed some light on patterns of relationships with poorly chosen partners. Careful self-examination may open your eyes to what it is about you, your history, and even your past relationships that keeps you choosing PDPs. If the idea of exploring your own role in selecting impaired partners sounds too painful or distressing, we understand the drive to avoid dredging up painful memories — some of them from early in life and others from especially disappointing love relationships. But let us be candid: Unless you accept that your own needs, wishes, habits, and lousy experiences continue to impact current relationships, you may be destined to keep repeating the same relational mistakes over and over. As an illustration of how easy it is to be enamored by someone who is ultimately a terrible match, consider the following relationship scenario.

Judy and Ben's Story

Judy sees Ben in a darkened, crowded, singles bar. They make eye contact across the room and feel an instant attraction to each other. Throughout the evening they engage in a nonverbal dance of mutual flirtation. Eventually they come together, introduce themselves, and over a few drinks begin the volley of disclosing shared bits of their lives. How do they decide which of their millions of life experiences to share with each other? What is it about Ben that Judy finds most attractive and alluring? What is it about Judy that Ben finds intriguing and beguiling? Ben wonders how much of his rocky childhood in an alcoholic home to disclose when Judy asks him to tell her about himself. He decides to avoid any discussion of his abusive father and frequent run-ins with the law and focuses instead on keeping it light with Judy and glossing over his many bad relationships.

Judy wonders whether she should tell Ben right away that her mother died when she was young and that she was raised by her grandparents because her father never really recovered from her mother's death. On some level, she knows she has never come to terms with her father's emotional abandonment. She is still reeling from yet another breakup and is feeling intensely lonely and rejected. But Judy too decides to keep most of these less than happy experiences under wraps for the moment and spends the evening in small talk with Ben. Judy realizes in the course of the evening that it isn't just Ben's blond good looks that bewitched her; it is also his bold confidence, his attentiveness, and a sense that he is strong and "in control." Ben, on the other hand, is taken in by Judy's seductive beauty and shy manner. While soft spoken, she also seems very kind, competent, and independent. They both see traits in the other that they admire and that make them feel good and attractive to the other.

While Judy is a capable woman, she loves to be with other people, and she is at her best when she is socially active and engaged. She craves attention and closeness to men and often feels an overwhelming need to be cared for by a man. Judy also values her relationships with her girlfriends; she is a great listener and her friends come to her with all of their problems. She would love to have a close, emotionally intimate relationship with a man and believes she will be really complete as a woman when she is married with children. She has been planning her wedding since she was ten and has all of the details down to a science. Although she currently has a career in marketing, she plans to stay home and raise her children someday. Ben never finished college as he never discovered his true career calling. He is currently in sales, and while he makes a decent living he doesn't love his job. Although he is a master when it comes to socializing and schmoozing, he despises being accountable to supervisors and resents all the policies and paperwork. He has gotten in trouble at times for cutting corners and telling supervisors off. Further, he finds that he is most successful at work with a few drinks under his belt. He, too, would like to be married someday but is frankly not very excited about the prospect of children; his own role models weren't so hot. He is, however, into Judy and likes being with her.

Ben and Judy progressed in their relationship and initially the attraction was strong. They found each other physically attractive and they were also compatible sexually. They each had traits the other admired and believed that the other could help them meet their relationship goals. Judy was available and willing to help Ben with anything. She loved that he asked things of her and was more than happy to make his life easier so that he was less stressed and had more time to see her. He loved to choose their date locations, and she got to know the good bars and pubs in town. She was carefree and went along happily, which made Ben feel strong and confident. If he couldn't go out with her for some reason, she rarely became angry and he liked that he didn't have to explain himself. He treated her well and was present when they were together, which left her feeling cherished and loved.

Sounds good, right? Now, fast-forward one year.

Ben has changed jobs twice — always to pursue bigger commissions and always without consulting Judy. Although his income has been wildly inconsistent, he seems unmoved and annoyed by Judy's anxiety about finances. He seems to go out more socially with his clients and often overdrinks to get through the night, to feel less stressed and more confident in himself. He spends less time with Judy because of this and she is feeling rejected. Increasingly, she gets upset and tearful about Ben's absences and although she hates the way she sounds, she hears herself pleading with him to stay home with her. This causes Ben to become angry and stay away even more. He finds himself avoiding Judy by not telling her what he is doing or who he is with. Judy tries harder to make Ben pay attention to her but is often left feeling that he is absent and uncaring. One of her friends reports that Ben often spends inordinate amounts of time with female clients. Judy, in turn, doubts herself and her attractiveness and starts to feel more down and desperate.

When Judy tries to discuss her worries with Ben, he adopts his "smooth" persona and trivializes her concerns but Judy gets the sense she's probably not getting the truth about his drinking, his other liaisons, or his impulsive spending. Ben and Judy have had a few explosive fights, and on one occasion Ben became so angry at Judy's neediness and tears that he pushed her down and verbally assaulted her.

Eventually, Judy realizes that her relationship with Ben is not a healthy union for her. She notices that she tends to fall for guys who call the shots in her relationships and who start out being present but eventually become aloof, distant, and rejecting. She realizes she overcommits to relationships quickly and frequently gives too much of herself to men. She hates feeling needy but sees that this is a chronic problem. Ben admits that he has a long track record of relatively short relationships with women and wonders why he tends to pick clingy and dependent women. What initially start out as easy relationships with what seem like independent women turn into relationships with women who want more time and energy than he can offer. He also acknowledges that he ends up with women who have problems with his drinking and socializing and preference for independence. Honestly, he is not too worried about it; he already has his eye on someone new.

The case of Ben and Judy highlights several of the reasons otherwise healthy adults end up in relationships with PDPs. When you look back at the course of your relationship with a disordered partner, you may shake your head and wonder how you could ever have fallen for him or her. But the truth is, it can be quite easy — especially if you have consistent patterns of attraction to one of the personality disorders covered in this guide. In our example, Judy is perpetually attracted to antisocial men while Ben's partners always have a dependent nature.

In the remainder of this chapter, we highlight the top reasons you might be so attracted to people with serious disturbances of personality. If you have a chronic history of bad relationships, consider each of these factors honestly. If you are currently in a dysfunctional relationship, ask yourself what it is that so compels you to remain with a person who seems to undermine you and the relationship. If you are relatively new to the dating scene and purchased this guide to learn which potential partners to avoid, it will be helpful for you to consider your potential vulnerabilities to bad relationship judgment before a serious relationship even begins.

The Top Nine Reasons for Attraction to PDPs

Reason #1: I Seem to Be Fooled by First Impressions

Let's face it: All of us put our best foot forward in new situations — especially those involving the opposite sex. When attempting to lure in a new romantic partner, we become hyperaware of presenting our most polished and appealing front. Blemishes, bad habits, and records of relationship wrecks are carefully concealed. All of us work hard at impression management when courting someone new. The same is true for adults with personality disorders.

Notice that both Ben and Judy were deliberate about screening and suppressing important information about their own histories during the early dating phase of their relationship. Ben conveniently deleted information about his own substance abuse and employment problems, his childhood history of physical abuse, and his frequent run-ins with the law. Needless to say, this information might have assisted Judy early on in deciding whether to enter into the relationship. For her part, Judy was careful to leave out her long history of broken relationships — typically a result of her clingy and needy behavior with men.

Not only do all of us withhold potentially negative information from new partners, we are also prone to focus on one or two very attractive features of a new partner — ignoring everything else until various problems become impossible to ignore any longer. Unless you plan to bring a psychologist along with you on all your first dates to administer diagnostic tests, conduct clinical interviews, and take childhood histories, it is unlikely that you will always be able to easily detect personality pathology in the first — or even the second or third — meeting.

Reading this guide will make you a much more effective diagnostician, but keep in mind that even mental health experts can initially be fooled by sophisticated personality-disordered clients. Psychologists, like romantic partners, sometimes miss evidence of unhealthy traits and behaviors early on; it is only after some time has gone by — allowing the emergence of pathologic behaviors — that clear evidence of a personality problem comes into full view. So, if you have been shocked by your own failure to detect serious character problems in a new partner, give yourself a break. When an adult is somewhat socially skilled, intelligent, and experienced in relationships, he may be able to easily hide pathology — at first.

What can you do? Read the remaining chapters of this guide carefully, become familiar with the different types of personality disturbance, and take plenty of time when it comes to entering into any new relationship. If you are cautious and discerning in the early phase of a new romance, the chances of being unpleasantly surprised later will diminish considerably.

Reason #2: I Seem to Get Tunnel Vision

What is it that first gets you excited about someone? On first encountering a person to whom you are attracted, which traits or behaviors quicken your pulse or make you start imagining a potential future together? Is it raw physical beauty, height, or athleticism? Is it purely extraversion or the ability to regale you with interesting stories? Is it a quiet, solemn, mysterious aura that makes you yearn to know more? Is it the person's apparent lack of interest in you that makes you insistent on getting him to notice you?

All of us have attraction buttons — key features or aspects of appearance, personality, or behavior that turn us on to romantic intrigue while simultaneously blocking our attention to other features that should make us stop and think twice. If a certain physical "look" or one facet of a potential partner's demeanor sends you into an infatuation tailspin, you may be prone to tunnel vision, the tendency to ignore prominent warning signs because you are so preoccupied or smitten by one or two superficial characteristics.

You may be so entranced and impressed by a smooth-talking confident antisocial PDP that you manage to ignore glaring evidence that he is a relationship shark with little genuine regard for laws, relationships, or you. You may be so charmed by a dependent PDP's unreserved attention and desire to be near you that you ignore clear evidence that he is sticky, clingy, and needy. Or, you might be so impressed by the apparent success and achievement of a narcissistic PDP that you forego appropriate doubt that his grandiose list of talents and achievements is legitimate.

If you have a propensity for getting into relationships with problem personalities, ask yourself what your own attraction buttons are. What gets you to suspend your own good judgment early in a dating situation? What characteristics restrict your vision so that you can only see and experience the positive? How can you practice slowing things down and looking at the bigger picture when it comes to potential love interests? Who can you turn to for objective advice before you get in too deep?

Reason #3: I Keep Pursuing the Same Dysfunctional Type

If you grew up in a home in which one of your parents — especially the parent of the opposite sex — had some dysfunctional behaviors and if you grew accustomed to accommodating him or helping to manage his behavior, you could be set up to seek out a partner with this same disordered profile. Although it may sound crazy, you are probably attracted to the very behavior that ultimately ends up undoing your relationships. Most of us are familiar with the saying that "the behavior we loved at the beginning is the behavior we hate at the end." Nowhere is this truer than in the case of falling in love with personality-disordered adults. Her intense life-of-the-party ways soon become exhausting and reveal themselves as superficial efforts to grab attention. His sincere attention to detail and cautious approach to things soon become monotonous, rigid, and deadly to romance. Her unusual appearance and eccentric habits move from novel and intriguing to weird and bizarre over time. His quiet, mysterious demeanor reveals itself as a tedious form of low-level depression; being around him makes you depressed as well.

If you are familiar with a specific personality disorder covered in this book because a parent or other respected caregiver had these same symptoms, you may be especially vulnerable to falling in love with this type — over and over again. Only deliberate effort and hard work will help you to recognize these features early on so that you can change course and find someone who will not keep you reliving a dysfunctional childhood.

Reason #4: I Need to Be Needed

Some reading this guide have a history of seeking out relationship "fixer-uppers." Friends and family members may ask why you always seem to "choose the losers!" It's not that you're not bright, perceptive, or capable of good judgment, you just have a need to rescue and remodel your partners. Think about it. Are you a sucker for someone who seems vulnerable and a little wounded by life or relationships? Or, are you compelled by the need to tone down and tame the bad boy characters? For some, a sense of identity comes through the act of caretaking, healing, and rescuing partners who seem to perpetually get themselves into trouble.

Where does this need come from? Quite often, we need look no further than our culture's approach to socializing men and women to find an answer. Women are generally reinforced for caretaking and it may also be a strong and enduring piece of the feminine genetic code. All too often, we see women clients who leave their antisocial, narcissistic, alcoholic fathers only to run into the arms of an antisocial, narcissistic, alcoholic mate. Again, we seek the familiar and many of us respond almost unconsciously to the caretaking role. And men are not immune to this drive. We have each worked with countless men who have repeatedly taken on dependent or histrionic partners precisely because they are compelled to rescue and protect needy women.

Here is the rub when it comes to nurturing adults with personality disorders: IT WON'T WORK! Sticky, clingy behavior, detachment, acting out against society, suspiciousness, phobic avoidance, and other personality disorder symptoms cannot be nurtured away. Instead, you will find yourself in an endless cycle of caretaking and bailing your partner out of repeated bad decisions, panic about abandonment, or rejection by others. Your work will never be finished. If you live to cure PDPs, you will be chronically frustrated. And if you try to do the tough work of change for your impaired partners, they may just avoid taking responsibility for themselves — you are enabling the very dysfunction you are trying to help them resolve. If you are a compulsive caretaker, you must be especially careful to guard against becoming mired in relationships with PDPs.

Reason #5: I'm Not Worthy of More

It is a sad truth in the world of relationships that people with a poor sense of self-worth often end up settling for partners who cause them misery later on. Is it possible that you choose partners with clear pathology (e.g., self-absorption, violent behavior, dishonesty) because you believe that on some level, that's all you deserve? If you tend to feel chronically inferior to love partners, then even a relationship with someone abusive or neglectful may somehow offer the promise of elevating your own sense of value. This is erroneous thinking of course, but it can be a powerful motivator when it comes to entering and staying in bad relationships.

If you enter relationships with impaired partners because being with someone (anyone) is better than being alone, you may also be somewhat dependent yourself (see chapter 12). Low self-esteem and dependence often go hand in hand. When our self-esteem is paper thin, we can begin to feel more desperate for affirmation through connection to another —

even when that very connection requires that we ignore our own needs, wishes, and rights. If any of this rings true for you, it is time to get busy in counseling. There is a good chance you will continue seeking and finding PDPs unless you can begin to feel confident and self-protective enough to say no to bad matches.

Reason #6: I Keep Trying to Fill a Hole in Myself

At times, we find that the partners of personality-disordered adults got into these relationships in the first place because they are deeply attracted to one aspect of the PDP's personality that they feel is entirely lacking in themselves. All of us can be attracted, at least at first, to what we are not. If you are quite staid and conservative, you may be magnetically pulled toward the loud risk taker. If you are extremely extraverted, you might be charmed by the silent type. And if you are known for caution, rigidity, and organization, there may be something inside you that hungers for someone spontaneous and carefree.

Here is the problem: Decades of research indicate that although opposites can attract, we tend to ultimately be most compatible with those who match us in personality. A partner with a glaring trait or behavior that you admire on some level can be exciting and appealing. But over time, expect this feature to become somewhat less appealing and perhaps even the source of real conflict. What's worse, if this characteristic is one facet of a personality disorder (e.g., the spontaneous partner is actually borderline, the risk-taking partner is actually antisocial, or the silent partner is actually schizoid), then you have gotten yourself into a very difficult relationship all for the sake of trying to find someone who can somehow fill in your own deficits.

It would be far healthier for you to work on these deficits yourself in a supportive environment. How can you expand your own repertoire of interests and behaviors? Can you find good friends with some of these missing features? And when you do find a healthy partner to love, it is likely that he will be interested in supporting your efforts to become more extraverted, more self-reflective, more spontaneous, or whatever you would like to become.

Reason #7: I Feel Too Guilty to Leave

If you tend to linger, or are currently lingering, in a relationship with a severely personality-impaired partner, one question to consider is whether you feel too guilty or ashamed to leave. Too many adults avoid making the break from serious personality disorders because for some reason they believe (1) they are to blame for their partner's problems, and (2) their partner could not go on without them and that would also be their fault. Of course, this is certifiably absurd thinking. Here is one certainty: Your PDP was disordered long before you came on the scene and he will be disordered long after you leave. *Should* you have somehow known in advance that your partner had a personality disorder? Of course not! Remember, even mental health experts are frequently fooled by personality disorders early on in therapy; severe symptoms of these disorders sometimes emerge only after the initial phase of the relationship gets underway.

If you struggle with guilt, shame, and a sense of obligation — especially if you have not married this person already — we encourage you to get counseling and stop taking responsibility for someone else's mental health problem. This will be a good opportunity for you to practice self-care and rational thinking.

Reason #8: Maybe the Problem Is Not Just My Partner

Another reason for attraction to PDPs is the simple possibility that you yourself have some personality disturbance. It may be painful on some level to acknowledge that you too suffer from some personality impairment, but if you find yourself in a pattern of relationships with a specific type of PDP, this is worth considering. As one example, we frequently find in our own practice that dependent men and women frequently end up with very disturbed partners (e.g., antisocial, narcissistic, borderline). Being with someone — even someone who probably cannot ever make them happy — is more important than being healthy.

If any of this rings true for you, it may be time to launch a program of therapy and self-exploration. Keep in mind that many of your personality traits — even those that now get you into trouble — were once highly adaptive and made sense in light of your childhood experience. Unfortunately, as we age, these same tendencies become impediments to healthy functioning and good judgment in relationships. For instance, if you are dependent in relationships, you probably fail to assert yourself, allow yourself to be exploited in various ways, and stay in relationships long after they have ceased being positive or healthy.

Reason #9: Oops! (It Was an Accident)

Sometimes, a relationship with a personality-disordered person is just an aberration and suggests nothing about a pattern of attraction to these types. Generally healthy, you may have ended up dating a very odd character and now wonder, "How did this happen to me? I usually have good radar and can pick out strangeness in a crowd. Now, here I am questioning myself, my own judgment, and my own mental health. Does this mean I'm destined to keep choosing losers?" The answer is: Probably not.

Remember: Personality impairment exists on a continuum of severity. Sometimes more subtle forms of these disorders are hard to detect early on. And don't forget that PDPs are often masters at impression management at first. You may be charmed and taken in by these characters only to wonder later on how you could possibly have missed the warning signs. You may be drawn to the stimulation and intensity of a borderline or histrionic, wooed by the smooth, suave, confident conduct of an antisocial, or attracted to the quirky and novel behavior of a schizotypal. Only later on will it become apparent that these initial features were only the tip of a pathologic iceberg.

What can you do? If you have made a mistake, recognize that it is probably just that — an aberration. Perhaps you let your guard down, perhaps you were a bit too impulsive, perhaps you were overly focused on one particular attractive trait, or perhaps there was no sign of trouble at first. Whatever the cause of any single relationship fiasco, be careful not to overgeneralize or assume you are destined to repeat this mistake. Read this guide carefully, become familiar with the various forms of personality disorder, and resolve to be more vigilant in the future.

Summary

Now that you have soberly considered your own pattern of attraction to PDPs and the various reasons you find these partners so alluring, it is time to look carefully at each of the personality disorder types. In the chapters that follow, we describe each problem personality in detail and offer a case example that highlights how these relationships unfold and why each personality disorder can result in a love relationship tainted by distance, crisis, and dysfunction. We explore some of the reasons otherwise healthy adults fall in love with each type and then offer some tips for managing the relationship while staying healthy as long as you decide to stay.

ODD, ECCENTRIC, AND WEIRD PARTNERS

The Doubting Partner

The Paranoid Personality

The Detached Partner

The Schizoid Personality

The Odd Partner

The Schizotypal Personality

CHAPTER 4

THE DOUBTING PARTNER
The Paranoid Personality

Paranoid Personality Checklist

✔ He suspects that you are harming, exploiting, or somehow deceiving him.

✔ He seems preoccupied with whether you are truly loyal and trustworthy.

✔ He is hesitant to confide in you and is fearful about how personal information will be used.

✔ He reads demeaning or threatening meanings into things you say — even when you sincerely intend to compliment.

✔ When he feels insulted or slighted (which is often), he seems to bear the grudge forever.

✔ He easily feels attacked or wronged and quickly reacts with anger or counterattack.

✔ He seems chronically suspicious about your faithfulness and questions your fidelity.

Are any of these behaviors and habits ringing bells for you? Have you dated a suspicious, distrusting, accusing partner? Is your current partner prone to any of these doubting tendencies? If so, we encourage you to read Julia's story and then consider the warnings later in this chapter. In a nutshell, pervasively doubting partners, people psychologists term "*paranoids*," can be dangerous — if not physically, then certainly on emotional levels. How can you detect and avoid the doubting type? What should you do if you find yourself stuck with a paranoid? Read on!

Julia's Story

When I think about Max now, I am shocked — really shocked — that I fell for him in the first place. He was very handsome and quiet too; quiet in a mysterious and solemn sort of way — not in a weird way. When he was transferred to our branch office, several of my women friends were going gaga over the guy, and I admit I was interested from the start. Still, there were signs early on — like the way he refused to say much about himself or why he had been transferred to our branch. He also seemed "edgy" at times and didn't seem to "get" jokes or humor around the office. Oh, he painted on a smile at the right times, but I think he always wondered if the joke was about him, as if the whole office was sort of in on it — poking fun behind his back. At those times he seemed scared or uncomfortable. He looked hurt and vulnerable. I guess I liked that on some level.

When Max asked me out the first time, he seemed really intense about it, like he was carefully trying to gauge my reaction. Our first few dates were really nice. Max seemed to need a lot of reassurance, and I didn't mind giving it to him. For example, he asked about other men I might be dating and seemed genuinely afraid he could be intruding on another relationship. I realize now that even then he suspected me of being involved with other men. He also seemed genuinely fearful that others around the office disliked him and wanted to know what people said about him. He made some pretty negative comments about some of our co-workers, but I chalked it up to nerves and a wish to impress me. Although I tried to be soothing and reassuring when these questions continued to surface, I began to have my first concerns that the guy was disturbed in some way. I also noticed that our conversations typically revolved almost exclusively around me — not because I wanted to talk about myself, but because Max seemed so intensely interested and continually asked me questions about my history, my thoughts about various subjects, etc. But after a while, it began to dawn on me that I knew almost nothing about Max and that, in fact, he had been purposely evading any genuine discussion about himself. I realized I had been doing all of the disclosing while Max seemed to be making mental files about me and offering very little authentic sharing in return. Needless to say, this began to make me uncomfortable.

Still, Max was quite handsome, and his insecurity touched me somehow. I'm still not sure why, but the fourth time we went out, I allowed myself to sleep with him. Afterward, the strangest thing happened. I tried to give Max some compliments about what a good lover he was, but for some reason it backfired horribly. He became immediately defensive and seemed to think I was teasing him or being sarcastic; the more I tried to persuade him otherwise, the more I sensed he doubted me. And here's the really bizarre thing; I began to feel really guilty about hurting his feelings that way, as though maybe he was right and I was teasing him — I realize now this was all absurd.

Sometime the next day, he walked by my office area and overheard me sharing a laugh with some friends. It had nothing to do with Max, but I could just tell from the look on his face he was hurt and angry — as though I was talking about him behind his back. That night he called and was very odd on the phone, saying things like "So, did your friends get into hearing about us in bed?" and "I only became intimate with you because I thought I could trust you." He also mentioned that another guy in the office, Steve, seemed to be treating him differently — as though he was angry at Max — and by the way he said it, I could tell Max was insinuating that I had told Steve about our lovemaking too. Well, I was pretty shocked and ticked off by this and pretty much gave Max an earful on the phone. He backed off and apologized, but I could tell he still doubted me.

Things were normal for a few more days and I saw Max a few more times, but things really began to go downhill after that. He started calling me at home several times each evening. If the line was ever busy when he called, he questioned me — suggesting that perhaps I had been talking to another man. A couple of times, I would shop in the evening or go out with a girlfriend. Each time I returned there would be a message from Max, and although he tried to sound nonchalant I could sense a suspicious accusation in the tone of his voice. Things like "Where are you, Julia? If we're going to be together, I need to be able to trust you. I need to know you are loyal without question. That's what makes love grow, Julia." Creepy things like that. He also said odd things at work about the guys he was working with and how they wanted to steal his marketing ideas and get credit for them. How he couldn't trust them. Once he even implied that I might be sleeping with one of them.

I soon figured out that I wasn't the only one worried about Max. My own supervisor, Margaret, cautioned me behind closed doors to be careful around him. She said his co-workers were fed up with his suspicious and accusing behavior and two of them had requested transfers — supposedly because Max had said things to them. He said threatening things, sort of vaguely and darkly hinting that if anyone else tried to steal his work, "the price would be far more painful than they imagined." Geez, talking about him now, it's like Max was one of those berserk postal workers or something. He was angry all the time just under the surface. I don't think he really trusted anyone — even me. One morning, Margaret pulled me aside. She looked really worried and I knew it was something about Max. She had called Max's previous supervisor and inquired about the circumstances of his transfer. It was the same story. He had been impossible to work with — blaming co-workers and accusing them of trying to steal his work and ruin his career. He had very subtlety threatened a few of them and had accused his own supervisor of being "out to get him." He was given the option of accepting a transfer or being fired.

Well, this really overwhelmed me and I started avoiding Max completely. He called at all hours and drove by my house at night. I tried to tell him I just didn't want to date him anymore, but he demanded to know why and accused me at different times of "screwing" different guys who were out to get him at work or of sleeping with him only to humiliate him later. I was emotionally drained. I eventually had a girlfriend sleep at my place until he stopped coming around and calling, and I filed a formal complaint at work asking that he not be permitted to come near my workspace. He quit shortly after that. Just vanished. I must say that nobody appeared sad to see him go. In fact, I think our office breathed a collective sigh of relief. I've never heard from Max since that time and I hope I never do. Now and then, I feel sorry for any woman he's involved with today.

The Doubting Partner

Most of us would agree that some degree of caution and appropriate guardedness in the world is wise. After all, naïve people tend to get manipulated and exploited. Healthy human development requires that we develop some self-protective defenses so that we can avoid victimization in life and relationships. But when a partner consistently doubts us and comes across as constantly suspicious and distrusting, she may be suffering from **Paranoid Personality Disorder**. This personality syndrome goes well beyond a healthy level of interpersonal caution and guarded scrutiny. For the paranoid, distrust and fear rule the day. According to the paranoid, people cannot be genuinely trusted and everyone has malevolent and harmful intentions. Thus, the paranoid's dictum for life might be: *Trust Nobody*.

Because their capacity for trust has been destroyed at some point in development, the paranoid type are constantly guarded and mobilized against an endless stream of perceived slights and attacks from the environment. They simply assume, even though there is rarely any good objective evidence, that others mean to exploit and harm them. The world is dangerous. Nobody, including you, in the paranoid's world is immune to accusations of evil intent. The paranoid only feels safe when he is an emotional island.

A paranoid partner will misinterpret good-natured humor or even sincere compliments as putdowns and attacks. They "feel" cold, lacking emotion, and humorless to those who get to know them. Seemingly innocent comments may arouse major hostility, and the paranoid is often quick to counterattack and react with anger to any perceived slight or insult. Their lack of trust will cause them to vigorously resist external influence and control — nobody, not even a lover or spouse, can ever be trustworthy enough. Paranoid people are notorious for bearing grudges. They are unwilling to forgive injuries and insults — even though these are usually imagined or misperceived. Expect paranoids to "stew" and "nurse" perceived wrongs so that their anger over something you see as minor might actually escalate and become unreasonably severe during the ensuing hours and days. Most frustrating for their partners, paranoids see themselves as blameless. Instead of owning their own contribution to problems, they find fault and blame for their own mistakes in others — especially you! They are often described by others as edgy, rigid, angry, accusing, blaming, and very difficult to work with, let alone love.

In terms of thought processes, paranoids are dichotomous thinkers; they see the world in black and white. For example, this person often insists that people are either "for" or "against" him. This, of course, will extend to those he dates; you must constantly affirm your loyalty or be accused of relational treason. In addition, this person will ignore objective data or twist it to confirm his paranoid beliefs; paranoids distort reality to fit their preconceptions that the world and everyone in it is hostile and unreliable. For example, when it comes to a partner's fidelity, overwhelming evidence of trustworthiness may be ignored in favor of a microscopic inconsistency (e.g., "why were you fifteen minutes late coming home from the store tonight?"). Sadly, because of this tendency to pay only selective attention to the truth, it is nearly impossible to out-argue a paranoid — especially if you are relying on logic.

Over time, paranoid people are simply difficult to like and they often find themselves rejected socially — thus confirming their suspicions that others are out to get them. This, of course, is a vicious circle. The paranoid is hostile to others, receives negative reactions or equal hostility in return, and uses this as evidence for the accuracy of his paranoid thoughts. It is hard to love someone who is constantly argumentative and prone to threaten litigation or other retribution. In truth, it is also very hard to feel emotionally close to a paranoid person. He does not easily offer warmth or affection and does not appear especially bonded or sentimental about any relationship.

Be Forewarned!

Here is a sober warning — especially for those in relationships with more severely doubting partners: Paranoid personality disorders are more likely than the other personality disorder types to act out violently. Whenever we see a breaking news story about a tragic shooting — often a murder-suicide — at a place of employment or in a family's home, we first wonder about paranoia as a diagnosis. Remember that the more serious a paranoid's thoughts about persecution become, the closer these thoughts come to real delusions (a psychotic symptom) and the greater the probability that the paranoid will take what he thinks is justified preemptive action to avoid harm. So, if the severe paranoid believes that an employer is about to fire him or that a partner is about to desert him, he thinks why not take action and strike first? You can see how dangerous paranoid thinking can become.

What Makes a Paranoid?

As a child, the paranoid person was typically solitary, hypersensitive, and seen as "odd" by others. The paranoid had few relationships and was likely teased and rejected by other children. In addition, these doubting types often describe at least one parent as cruel, degrading, and controlling. They got the message that they were flawed and deserved punishment. As adults, they have come to expect attack and abuse from everyone they meet. At the same time, paranoids often got the message that they were "different," "special," and "alone." Caregivers were probably perfectionistic, especially harsh when it came to punishment, and likely to communicate that mistakes were intolerable. In order to make sense of the apparent contradiction that they were both special and prone to being ridiculed by others, paranoids assumed that the reason for the constant social attacks was the fact that they were indeed better than others. This disorder is diagnosed more often in men.

The Paranoid as Partner

The paranoid type will be a doubting partner and will be among the most difficult partners described in this book. When you get involved with a paranoid, you'll quickly discover firsthand what is meant by the phrase, *walking on eggshells;* you may soon be humorlessly and gingerly tiptoeing through minefields of suspicion and distrust. Paranoid Personality Disorder often leads to very serious romantic relationship dysfunction. Because the paranoid's primary interpersonal stance is mistrust, he will refuse to disclose much that is authentically personal and will be programmed to fear closeness and intimacy. Attempts at fostering emotional connection and intimacy may be regarded as an attack on his precarious defenses and he will probably respond by either retreating further or angrily rebuffing your efforts. The paranoid will assume that your intimate overtures are actually thinly veiled attempts to expose his vulnerabilities. Regardless of how much time and effort you devote to this relationship, you will find yourself dangling at an emotional arm's length — forever regarded with at least some measure of suspicion and mistrust.

If you find yourself dating a paranoid, you will discover that after the early infatuation phase, the paranoid type becomes especially difficult to love. This person will be chronically suspicious and distrustful of you.

Although your intentions are sincere, the paranoid will interpret them in the most negative light, expecting to find that you are mistreating or deceiving her somehow. You will notice that the paranoid lover is constantly on "high alert" — vigilantly watching for emotional attacks. Paranoids are defensive, fearful of losing control, and preoccupied with the loyalty of those around them. This partner can never seem to figure out that her own hostility is the cause of the hostility received from others. The paranoid's primary defense mechanism is what Freud called *projection:* In utter denial of their own rage and hostility, paranoids "see" or "project" these malevolent attributes onto everyone they meet.

Perhaps more troubling is the fact that the doubting partner may angrily lash out emotionally (and in some cases, physically) for perceived slights and criticisms. The paranoid type will be argumentative, frequently complaining, aloof, and silent as a form of hostility. She may be stubborn, sarcastic, and controlling. When your friends and family members find your partner "impossible," they are probably referring to these features. Your friends and family may question why you are involved with someone who is so hypersensitive and joyless; they may begin avoiding interaction with you and your partner — tired of her edgy argumentativeness and the tension this often creates.

Sadly, paranoid types will have little capacity for sustained intimacy, self-disclosure, or trust. Remember, the paranoid may become threatening when she feels especially vulnerable or ridiculed (which is often). Keep in mind, however, that the source of the hostility is typically fear. The paranoid — despite all of the bravado and beliefs that they must be special — are actually terrified that they are unworthy and therefore highly prone to being rejected and humiliated. In some instances, the paranoid lover will become violent and quite dangerous — vindictively seeking revenge for perceived rejection.

Finally, a word about infidelity: On some level, the paranoid type will expect it — and will probably accuse you of it either overtly or subtly on more than one occasion. Although this may evoke both indignant anger and pain on your part, keep in mind that such assumptions of unfaithfulness are at the very core of paranoia. As the romantic focus of a paranoid, you present profound emotional danger: There is much to be lost when (not if) the person closest to the paranoid abandons him. Expect the paranoid to be angry about this assumed outcome even when you are unquestionably faithful.

Why Am I Attracted to Doubting Partners?

So what if I'm in a relationship with a doubter? And what if I have been involved with more than one doubting partner over the course of my life? By way of review, that means I'm drawn to a partner who

- suspects me of being malicious or deceptive.
- assumes that I'm not loyal or trustworthy.
- avoids really confiding in me.
- reads hidden threats or derogatory meaning in whatever I do or say.
- always seems to be nursing a grudge and stewing about a perceived slight.
- reacts with anger or sullen withdrawal for no apparent reason.
- actually thinks I'm interested in or sleeping with someone else.

So, does this mean I'm crazy?

Beyond sheer physical attraction, there are several facets of a paranoid's demeanor that might draw you in and even keep you coming back for more — even though the relationship is ultimately likely to be quite toxic for you. Some of us might find the solemn, mysterious, nondisclosing aspect of this personality type appealing. We wonder what lies beneath the surface or interpret the withholding as humility. Perhaps we notice the person's discomfort and apparent insecurity about whether we might really like him. This can pull caretaking strings and stimulate endless rounds of kid-gloves reassurance and attempts to sooth the partner's distrust and worry. Some of us are vulnerable to attraction when a new love interest presents as "wounded" or "damaged" and therefore in need of intensive relationship care.

If you find yourself repeatedly attracted to the paranoid type, ask yourself this question: Why am I so drawn to relationships in which I have to walk on eggshells? What is it about my own needs to caretake and "win over" someone who is fundamentally unpredictable, abusive, or accusing? Did I grow up in a home like this? Was one of my parents volatile, distant, alcoholic, or abusive? Did I learn early on to accept the role of placater and pseudoparent? If the answer to any of these questions is yes, then perhaps you are drawn to life with a paranoid because the pathological dance is so familiar on some level; you are oddly at ease when working hard to sooth, reassure, and constantly prove yourself worthy of love. If you recognize this pattern, it's time to get help and time to get over the chronic need to placate.

Some of us may also misinterpret a paranoid's intense interest in our current or former relationships as genuine concern about not intruding on these relationships or just honest curiosity. In fact, the paranoid is already considering who your lover will be when you later betray him. And later, as this partner becomes increasingly obsessive and controlling, you might actually interpret this as deep care and connection. Don't be fooled, this behavior is motivated by fear and paranoid thoughts about infidelity. We know some women who have even interpreted a partner's stalking behavior (e.g., obsessive calling, following them) as love and commitment! "This just shows how much he loves me!" In fact, it shows how much he distrusts you and how much potential danger you are in.

Here is a paradox that leads some otherwise healthy people to stay in relationships with paranoids: You may actually begin to believe you *have* done something wrong and then feel guilty for it! This is an insidious process that is most likely to impact those of us already prone to guilt. Over time, the paranoid partner's constant accusations, wounded demeanor, and apparent pain at our behavior can lead us to assume the stance of guilty party. Before you know it, you're trying to make amends and always apologizing for things you don't really understand. This tendency to own or accept false blame probably says more about you than it does about your paranoid partner.

Finally, doubting partners can be reasonable for short periods between bouts of blaming and sullen withdrawal. We may see glimpses of healthy potential and allow the hope it induces to keep us engaged in these relationships. Even when our family and friends cut off or curtail contact with us in order to avoid our partner, these brief spells of normality convince us that our partner is indeed misunderstood. There can be something alluring and romantic about the "us against the world" isolation that paranoid partners often cause. Also, these short periods of reasonable stability might even convince us that the problem lies not with our partner but with ourselves or the environment. Over time, this thinking will prove erroneous.

Clearly, there are many ways we can be captivated by relationships with doubting partners. And once lured in, there may be things about the paranoid's behavior and more — baggage from our own childhood — that keep us locked in. So, if you are attracted to a man or a woman with strong paranoid features, there are probably some very good reasons. Unfortunately, at the end of the day, the paranoid type will remain paranoid. And it is unwise to expect more.

Living with a Paranoid

What should you do if you find yourself dating someone with a paranoid disorder? Is there any hope for a long-term relationship? Can you ever be above suspicion with a paranoid partner? Are you in danger? These are important and difficult questions — they defy easy answers. As clinical psychologists who have seen our share of paranoid personalities, we offer this advice first and foremost: RUN (and fast). Our gut instincts tell us that a seriously paranoid adult is unlikely to ever make a suitable romantic partner. In nearly every case, we suggest that you cut your losses and move on quickly.

Having warned you, we also recognize that there is a substantial range in severity among paranoid types and that making a decision to leave or stay — especially if you are already married — should be thoughtful. If you decide to remain in a relationship with a paranoid type — even for just a while, here are several suggestions for smoothing the ride and keeping yourself safe and sane.

Be Realistic in Your Expectations

Paranoia is a lifelong pattern; it is slow to change. It may seem that everything you try only makes your partner more hostile, and you can easily become disheartened. Because the roots of paranoia almost always extend back to early childhood experiences, it is very hard to reshape these patterns later on. If you can accept your partner's paranoid view of the world while simultaneously hoping for some change — even if modest — you are in a good position to be tolerant of her inevitable suspicious and hostile behaviors.

Work Patiently at Establishing Trust

Because a paranoid will naturally see both psychotherapists and romantic partners as dangerous, critical, and judgmental, any real growth or bonding will require a very cautious and patient approach to establishing trust. Engaging your partner without pressure and slowly allowing him to see you as consistent and trustworthy seem to be key. Remember that pushing the paranoid to trust you prematurely (e.g., "why can't you just trust me!") will fall flat; this will affirm the expectation of criticism and will raise red flags about your "real" agenda. Whenever possible, let your paranoid partner drive: By giving the paranoid control of the pace with which intimacy is established, you are increasing the chance that your partner can make small gains in trust. Patience is essential.

Although It Is Tempting, Don't Rise to the Bait

Living with a paranoid partner's constant suspiciousness and accusatory behavior can be both unnerving and aggravating. It is natural to respond to a partner's paranoid comments, blaming, and abrasiveness with your own anger. After all, any of us would get sick of consistent provocation and daily arguments — often over frankly silly and unsupportable perceptions. But here is the problem: The paranoid expects you to become hostile and cruel. Your angry retaliations will only confirm what the paranoid always knew — like everyone else, you can't be trusted. This may seem like an unfair burden, but try to avoid responding in kind. Developing a visual image of a paranoid person as a scared and wounded child may help you to resist the urge to lash out.

Engage in "Verbal Holding"

Because the paranoid partner will seldom respond to a direct frontal assault in the form of challenging her paranoid thoughts, wisdom suggests a soft sell approach to becoming better connected. One expert on therapy with paranoids recommends a strategy called *verbal holding:* simply being with a paranoid partner and listening actively without offering anything beyond unconditional regard, acceptance, and empathy. Disputes about details will devolve into arguments and further retraction and isolation by the paranoid. Rather, listen without judgment and affirm your partner's willingness to confide and share. Here is a caveat: You must also avoid joining in or endorsing your partner's paranoid thinking and you must firmly confront behavior that is hostile, demeaning, or threatening.

When It Comes to Your Health (and That of Children) Don't Compromise

Although we have been advocating a nurturing and empathetic approach to paranoid partners, you simply cannot compromise when it comes to health and safety. Living with a paranoid can be depressing and emotionally demeaning. You may be so often accused and criticized that your own self-esteem suffers. More important, there may come a time when your partner threatens you physically or engages in actual assault. To this we say, set firm limits in advance and leave immediately when either threats or actual violence ensue. If children are involved, this becomes even more crucial. Nothing justifies exposing a child to a caustic, hostile, and unpredictable adult. If your paranoid partner's behavior is so severe that either you or any children are suffering, it is time to separate; you need to get away from the paranoid partner — fast.

Therapy Is Unlikely to Be Helpful

Like many of the personality disorder types covered in this book, paranoid personality disorders rarely volunteer for treatment unless threatened with divorce or job loss. At times, they may be willing to talk to a therapist about how others are harming them or about how they have been victimized, but don't expect genuine acceptance of personal contribution to problems. It is wise to assume that the prognosis for change is guarded at best.

When It's Time to Leave

In the end, it is hard to imagine that if your partner chronically doubts and suspects you that you will not eventually decide to move on. In most cases, this will be the healthiest thing you can do — just make sure you follow the departure with some good psychotherapy to address the "why" question about your attraction to this person.

But before you leave or even indicate any intention to do so, please consider your own safety. Earlier in this chapter, we noted that partners with Paranoid Personality Disorder can be dangerous. Perceived disloyalty and actual abandonment will likely trigger some strong reaction, and sadly, this could take the form of stalking, harassment, and even physical violence. When we read about a woman being gunned down by her former boyfriend or husband or when we hear about a murder-suicide in the aftermath of a breakup, one word pops into our minds — paranoid. Get excellent support from friends and family before you leave. If you have any worry about stalking or retribution, please go to the police immediately and take steps to find secure living arrangements before moving on. The paranoid partner's tendency to stalk or act out can also be diminished by a strong, no-nonsense approach — be very clear about why you are leaving and that this is nonnegotiable — and a clear show of force from family, friends, an attorney, and the police. Be careful and take care of yourself and any children first.

Summary

Watch out for the doubting type. Paranoid men and women are prickly, hypersuspicious, and prone to distrust you no matter how loyal you may be. Be alert to subtle indicators of distrust, accusation, and uncomfortable scrutiny of your motives and intent. When it becomes evident that a new or potential partner is the doubting type, cut your losses and move on quickly. The probability of a healthy relationship is low. Worse, the paranoid type can be emotionally toxic and even physically dangerous. You can do better!

CHAPTER 5

THE DETACHED PARTNER
The Schizoid Personality

Schizoid Personality Checklist

- ✔ He neither desires nor enjoys close relationships and may even seem apathetic about your relationship.
- ✔ He normally chooses solitary activities and prefers these to time with you.
- ✔ He shows little or no interest in sex.
- ✔ Very few activities or experiences appear to bring him any pleasure.
- ✔ Other than a family member, he has no close friends or confidants.
- ✔ He appears indifferent to both praise and criticism from others.
- ✔ He is best described as "cold," "detached," and "emotionless."

Have you dated someone like this? Is he or she described by others as "cold" or "indifferent?" Do you end up feeling *alone* even when you are with this person? And do you sometimes wonder if the person you love would even miss you if you were gone? If these detached symptoms fit your current partner or perhaps others you've dated, you may be drawn to partners with Schizoid Personality Disorder. Schizoids are aloof, detached, and largely uninterested in relationships — including a relationship with you. When dating, how can you detect the schizoid? What signals and cues might signal that the person across the table from you is a detached type? What can you expect from a schizoid partner? Let's start with Betty's story.

Betty's Story

I met Roy over a period of a year. I do mean a year, because it took that long to even get him to talk to me. I was working in this small neighborhood grocery store and Roy would come in every Saturday morning when I was working. Oh, he wasn't coming in to see me or anything, that's just the day he did his weekly grocery shopping. He was older than me, about forty-two then. I was thirty-one. Neither of us had ever been married, though I had come close a few times. I later found out that Roy had never even dated anyone! That really shocked me because he was a nice looking man — though he was balding when I met him. He was just really quiet and maybe shy about meeting people.

Roy would come through the checkout line every Saturday morning at the same time and with the same groceries in his cart. He would pick up a newspaper and read it while standing in line so that he didn't have to talk to anyone — including me. When I would try to make small talk with him, he looked confused and unsure of how to respond. He mostly just stared back at me and answered in monotone yes and no replies. I kept waiting for him to initiate some sort of conversation or greeting, but he never did. It was the same every Saturday.

"Hey, Roy, how are you today?"

Long pause . . . "Fine."

"What do you have planned for the weekend?"

"Not much."

"Think we'll get that rain they're predicting?"

"I'm not sure."

He really did seem paralyzed about what to do when I'd start talking to him. He also seemed sad and I wondered if he'd been through some difficult things. Well, it took a year, but he did start to respond a little more in the checkout line. He still never initiated conversation, but he did start talking more and made more eye contact too. He even smiled a few times, which was wonderful because I wasn't even sure he could. I think I just sort of slowly became fond of Roy. I had been through some rather crazy relationships with men who were unpredictable and manipulative. Roy was just the opposite: He was steady, calm, and always the same. I liked that. I also knew that I enjoyed the challenge of getting him to open up every week. When it seemed that he was really starting to enjoy seeing me every week, I think I fell for him.

I finally just asked Roy out one Saturday. I asked him to go with me to an outdoor concert Sunday afternoon. He seemed a bit stunned by the invitation and just stood there staring for a minute. Then he just shrugged his shoulders and said, "OK." Roy was the same outside the store as he was inside. Quiet, calm, and not much for conversation, but he would respond to my questions — at least with his short "yeses" and "nos." He didn't seem wild about the concert, but then he didn't seem wild about much of anything! Well, I kept asking Roy to go places with me and he usually agreed. I have to admit now that I don't think going out with me was ever truly exciting for him. He might have been just as happy staying home and working on one of the cars he restores in his garage. Still, I was lonely, and I enjoyed being with Roy. I felt very safe with him.

Roy worked as a machinist for a small company in town that made prosthetic limbs. He worked in a back room molding and grinding down rubber and plastic materials to form a custom limb for an adult or child who needed one. It seemed like very boring and lonely work to me, but Roy never complained and I think he preferred the solitude. I eventually learned that Roy used to be the person who took measurements from the patients themselves, but that he had been taken out of that job when patients and their families complained about his rudeness. Of course, I don't think Roy was really rude at all; he just isn't very sensitive and can't really read other people very well. Instead of being kind and empathetic, I'm sure he just took the measurements without talking or reassuring or explaining the procedure at all. Roy admitted that he didn't really like talking to customers and was much happier about his job when he was trained as a machinist and allowed to work on his own. He now has a schedule that lets him go in at noon and work into the evening — after most of his co-workers are gone. He prefers it that way.

All the time we were dating, Roy never really initiated anything physical. This surprised me, and for a while, I worried that he didn't find me attractive. I eventually kissed him one evening. Poor guy. He just stood there, eyes open, arms at his side, lips frozen in place. It became clear he had probably never kissed anyone before. I asked him and he just shrugged his shoulders and said he couldn't recall, but didn't think he had. Well, it was like that with anything physical. I initiated and basically had to teach Roy how to respond and what to do. At that time I thought it was rather sweet that he was so naïve, and I enjoyed having more physical contact. I thought that Roy would begin to enjoy a physical relationship as much as I did — like every other man I'd known — but that never really happened.

As with everything else, I eventually took the initiative to propose that we get married. He very unromantically stared at the ground for a while, shrugged his shoulders, and said, "OK." I know that people reading this will shake their heads and wonder what was wrong with me. I just felt so secure and safe with Roy. I always knew what to expect from him and I needed that dependable quality in a man.

Roy and I have been together for three years now. Not much has changed, at least not with Roy. I guess the problem is mine. I suppose I allowed myself to believe that after we were living together, Roy would become closer to me and that if we spent more time together, we'd become more intimate and connected. As the months and years have gone by, I've become more and more lonely and hopeless that Roy will ever really need or want anyone. Roy goes to work every day and will go with me places on the weekend, but he never initiates anything for us to do together. If I don't say anything, he might go a week without anymore than a few grunts or single-syllable sentences. It's not that he doesn't like me, I think he really does. He just doesn't need me. Not at all. In fact, I really think his happiness level would remain the same, as long as he could continue his hobbies. He restores cars out in the garage, and when he's not doing that, he organizes his huge collection of baseball cards. He also spends hours on the Internet checking for baseball card auctions. Roy isn't much interested in sex. I've just about given up on trying very hard in that department. He'll "comply" if I really push him to make love to me, but I don't think he's ever really initiated it. He just doesn't seem to enjoy it all that much.

I've talked to Roy's family a few times. He rarely sees them, and they are a little strange. His brother told me that Roy has always been this way — isolated, quiet, and hermit-like. He's never really had friends and doesn't seem to want any. They were shocked when he actually married someone. As an adolescent, he played Dungeons and Dragons with another boy on the block, but otherwise, there have been no consistent connections. I don't know if I can stay with Roy much longer. I've thought about divorcing and moving on. The sad thing is that I don't think Roy would really care that much. He might protest a little, but I doubt he would authentically miss me. I feel intensely lonely, and I realize now that I need a partner who needs me in return, someone who'll communicate and find pleasure in my company. I know now that Roy can never offer that.

The Detached Personality

The hallmark of the person with a **Schizoid Personality Disorder** is an inability to form attachments to other people. Schizoids often have a history of social isolation and detachment from relationships. They also show a restricted range of emotional expression in their interactions with others (including those they date or marry). The schizoid will come across as lethargic, inattentive, and somehow "vague" and monotone in speech. Their communication may be experienced as unclear or indecisive. The truly unusual — even inhuman — quality of the schizoid is her lack of desire for connection and intimacy with others. In fact, schizoids appear thoroughly apathetic and indifferent to the idea of bonding or enjoying a close relationship with someone else. Not only will this person spurn opportunities to socialize with groups or even her own family members, there will be relatively little authentic and sustained interest in a romantic connection.

The detached person will be a classic "loner," always seeking refuge from the press of interpersonal demands. This is the true hermit; the schizoid is most comfortable and at peace with solitude. Given a choice, this person will gravitate to solitary activities — both occupationally (perhaps seeking such typically solo jobs as night-shift security guard or mail sorter) and recreationally (choosing fantasy games, mechanical tasks, or computers over more social pursuits). As a result of these inclinations, schizoids will seldom have friends and will almost never have close friends. They may interact with one or more family members, but even these connections may be somewhat superficial. The important point here is that the schizoid person does not "miss" closeness with others and is therefore not distressed by isolation and detachment.

The authors of this book were once naval officers and psychologists stationed at various naval bases around the country. As military psychologists, we were often called upon to conduct psychological evaluations of military personnel for a wide variety of reasons (e.g., security clearances, alcohol treatment screening, and forensic evaluations for court martial proceedings). One of the more unusual evaluations we were occasionally asked to perform was the psychological screening of a candidate for one of the Navy's isolated research stations. Military and civilian research personnel wishing to "winter over" in these small, remote, and potentially dangerous research stations were required to show evidence of psychological "fitness" for the extended stress and isolation that characterized life out of touch with civilization. Recreation was limited and many personnel worked in relative solitude — perhaps with only occasional contact with fellow station dwellers. Psychologists learned quickly that very often, a certain personality type performed quite well in these conditions of isolation — the schizoid type. Interpersonally aloof, detached, and generally uninterested in people, schizoids were a strangely good fit. Although we were careful not to select personnel with full-blown personality disorders for service in these stations, those with schizoid traits often performed reasonably well because of their preferred, self-selected wish for solitude. As we show you in this chapter, however, they do not perform so splendidly in relationships or in jobs that require close interaction with others.

Schizoid persons are not interested in sex — or at least not sex with others. This is often hard for other adults to understand. While most human beings seek out and savor physical touch and sexual enjoyment with another, the schizoid person does not. He may masturbate on occasion, but there will be little initiation of sexual bonding with a partner. The experience of physical touch and sexual stimulation are actually muted or diluted for the schizoid, thus these experiences are considerably less important and compelling in daily life.

Because persons with Schizoid Personality Disorder are indifferent to the scrutiny and evaluation of others, they are poor performers — both in relationships and at work. schizoids have abysmally low emotional intelligence, meaning that they are inept at reading other people, interpreting subtle social cues, and discerning the emotional state of another human being. As a result of their indifference and poor social skills, they are often viewed by others as "weird" or as "nerds." Detached persons are often poorly understood by co-workers and are frequently ridiculed, rejected, and even feared. Although no more likely to become violent than anyone else, their aloof and odd behavior may raise worries about mental instability or danger.

The truly schizoid person is best described as emotionally and relationally bland. Schizoids only rarely have episodes of significant emotional expression and have difficulty interpreting and reciprocating the physical gestures and facial expressions of others. For example, the schizoid person may fail to return a smile, understand a wink, or negotiate a handshake or hug. He is often described as a "cold fish" because of this constricted affect and aloof interpersonal behavior. Peers may see him as the social equivalent of molasses. Although he may actually appear clinically depressed, this is unlikely. The schizoid simply lacks positive (or negative) emotionality and is most at home with interpersonal distance and emotional detachment. Because schizoid persons are so unaware emotionally, it is unlikely they would know it if they were depressed. On occasion, a schizoid person may be misdiagnosed as autistic. This is understandable. The schizoid's disengagement, poor eye contact, and apparent absorption with isolative pursuits are reminiscent of the autistic adult in many respects. But there is nothing wrong with the schizoid's brain; this is a problem of fundamental character structure. The schizoid's poorly developed social and interpersonal skills and interests result from a pattern of detachment and lack of concern about others that began early in life. It is important to note that the schizoid is a good example of someone who others realize is "different," or "odd," yet the schizoid has little insight into how others' view him. Schizoids are NOT distressed by their lack of close relationships with others; they do not wish it, nor do they seek it. Others in this person's life may become upset or distressed at the schizoid's distance and apathy; however, the schizoid personality is typically comfortable with his social avoidance and isolation.

What Makes a Schizoid?

Although no specific childhood experience or family background is known to cause Schizoid Personality Disorder, schizoid persons very often have at least one parent with strong schizoid features. Schizoid traits run in families. It is also true that schizoids are more likely to come from families in which there is some history of schizophrenia — a very severe psychiatric disorder characterized by hallucinations and loss of touch with reality. In addition, the childhood of the schizoid may have been characterized by neglect and a deficit in emotional connection and engagement with parents and other family members. The family may have been stiff and cold; silence, solitary activity, and emotional disconnection were the norm. Schizoid behavior may be considered a defensive or self-protective posture. A child growing up in a chaotic or threatening environment might disengage socially as a form of self-protection. Although this schizoid withdrawal is adaptive at the time, when it persists in adolescence or adulthood it begins to create serious problems occupationally and relationally. Schizoid Personality Disorder is diagnosed only slightly more often in men than women.

The Schizoid as Partner

The schizoid personality type will always be a detached partner. If you have managed to become involved romantically with a schizoid man or woman hoping to find a relational partnership, you are no doubt disappointed. The schizoid may make a fine financial associate, roommate (if you like a roommate who seldom makes demands or desires attention), or research associate, but she will *never* meet your needs emotionally or physically. The problem, of course, is that the schizoid person has no real desire for a closely bonded relationship. She is likely to be apathetic about a love relationship and will not be particularly interested in having you near, spending time together, or even talking. Here is the paradox: Your schizoid partner can never really be a partner in the romantic sense of the word. She simply does not have enough interpersonal interest to genuinely bond with you.

It would also not be surprising if you are having difficulty acclimating to your detached partner's lack of sexual interest and desire. Although he may go through the motions or make efforts to please you sexually, this person is considerably less likely than others to initiate and long for sexual connection with you. This disengagement and lack of interest helps explain why schizoid's seldom date and rarely marry. It may be helpful to trace your relationship history with a schizoid partner and ask yourself how the relationship came to be in the first place. Chances are you were the primary initiator and relationship maintainer. Schizoids seldom take such initiative.

Beyond sexual apathy, your schizoid partner probably lacks drive for emotional intimacy. This coldness and relational indifference is often the primary complaint of those in a relationship with a schizoid man or woman. Although most of us harbor wishes for love and connection and fears about rejection and scrutiny, schizoids' have no such wishes or fears. Indifference reigns. Even when a schizoid person marries, the marriage is characterized by separation and a parallel versus intertwined coexistence.

Feeling walled off and ignored by a schizoid partner, romantic partners and spouses may bring a schizoid lover to couples counseling in order to address the traits mentioned in this chapter. Not surprisingly, the schizoid partner will be perplexed about the need for treatment, apathetic about her partner's concerns, and apparently unfazed by threats of a breakup or divorce. Only at this point does it become clear to the therapy-seeking member of the relationship that the schizoid partner truly does not need him!

In summary, if you have become involved with a schizoid type, you are not surprised to hear that he is likely to be extremely emotionally detached and a relationally apathetic loner. He will avoid intimacy and will generally prefer solitary activities. The schizoid owns neither the interest nor capacity for emotional connection, and most people will feel ignored and isolated in such relationships. The prognosis for a healthy, vibrant, and emotionally satisfying union is poor. If you have the notion that you can work harder or smarter to change this partner, you are misleading yourself and probably prolonging your agony.

Why Am I Attracted to Detached Partners?

So, what if I'm in a relationship with a detached type? And what if I have been involved with more than one detached partner over the years? What does this mean about me anyway? If you tend to fall for detached types — schizoid personalities — it means that you are drawn romantically to a person who

- doesn't really care about being close to you or anyone else (even if she says she does).
- nearly always prefers to be alone.
- seems uninterested in sex or physical touch.
- has almost no close friends.
- seems indifferent to your praise or criticism.
- feels cold and emotionless much of the time.

So, why would you actually pursue a schizoid? How could anyone be drawn to someone who seems so uninterested in a real relationship? What elements of the schizoid's behavior pull you in, and what keeps you coming back for more?

By far the most charming and beguiling quality of the schizoid is his quiet aloofness. This person may seem so inexperienced, so unsophisticated, and so unsure of what to do or what to say in any social or relational setting that we want to rush in to care for him. Much like a parent or older sibling, we are drawn to what we perceive is emotional need and social discomfort. We want to make it better. We want to reassure him that somebody is watching out for him. If you have a need to be needed, the schizoid may push all of your attraction buttons. The irony, of course, is that this detached partner doesn't need you at all. The schizoid is perfectly happy alone; his apparent fumbling and discomfort socially is a reflection of both inexperience and disregard for relationships; at a fundamental level, connections to others just don't mean that much.

Given such extreme detachment, you might wonder how schizoid persons ever get married (they do on occasion). Quite often, a rescuing, caretaking, nurturing, soul with a profound need to be needed finds the schizoid so endearing, she takes all the initiative in pushing a relationship and even ends up proposing marriage. The basically indifferent schizoid may agree, but it is with a shrug of the shoulders and a "sure, whatever" — at least on the inside. The decision to become engaged or even marry carries less emotional importance for the schizoid person. And when the relationship ends, the detached partner feels less impact.

Here is a paradox: Some of us only fall in love with partners who appear apathetic or uninterested in us. The schizoid will certainly fill this bill. In our practice, we have seen many clients who report a string of relationships with lovers who are entirely uncommitted and disengaged. Perhaps you seem to really want only the ones who don't really give a damn (at least in their behavior and attitudes) about you!

If you are a chronic caretaker and rescuer, if you find that you only love the ones who don't easily return any affection, if you find yourself connected to a schizoid partner — or perhaps a whole string of the personality-impaired partners covered in this guide — now is the time to sit up, take notice, and ask yourself *why*. Let's face it, schizoids have little to give in a relationship — mostly because they just don't care on any deep and enduring level about relationships. This will not be a mutual and/or reciprocal experience; you will be doing all the work. And getting small tokens of care and appreciation will be a full-time endeavor. If you are drawn to love relationships with aloof and withholding partners, it is time to honestly ask yourself what significant parent was similarly detached. What parent treated you this way? We suspect that at least one parent or significant caregiver was similarly untouchable emotionally — nothing you did ever seemed to rouse this person's interest or cause a genuine show of affection. Unfortunately, this early withholding often leaves us with an insatiable need for what we can never get from a detached personality — overt affection, interest, and a deep connection.

There are some other factors that may spur attraction to a schizoid personality type. Some of us are chronic healers; we need to get to the bottom of what may be troubling a love interest and then — through Herculean love and care on our part — heal him. The schizoid may easily elicit such feelings. He is so quiet, uncomfortable, and inexperienced, we assume some awful background — perhaps abuse, neglect, or poor treatment at the hands of other lovers — and become determined to provide a new or corrective relationship sure to erase the impact of these earlier traumas. Many schizoids also appear depressed (it is easy for mental health practitioners to misdiagnose them with depression initially), and you may even wonder about suicidal risk. Surely, this poor soul just needs some TLC to overcome what ails him. The truth is the schizoid is not depressed, and no matter how loving and supportive you are, no current relationship will refashion his fundamental personality style.

Some of us may find the schizoid's quiet, aloof, nonverbal air alluring. This apparent indifference can appear intriguing — even mysterious. If very attractive, the schizoid's detachment can come across as hypermasculine stoicism in the Clint Eastwood tradition. Of course, the disappointment will be that there is little mystery behind the stoic demeanor — just a guy who doesn't care much about relationships!

Some who end up in relationships with detached types are attracted by the schizoid's inexperience relationally. In a world where sexual involvement seems to happen all too quickly, the schizoid's obvious lack of sexual experience and willingness to easily forgo sex altogether may seem endearing, unique, and traditional. Your partner's sexual naiveté may be sweet and perhaps a refreshing and reassuring change from partners who seem entirely focused on sex early in relationships. But keep in mind, this lack of sexual interest is pervasive and will remain so even after marriage.

There are other motivations for pursuing a schizoid partner. If you have struggled personally with loneliness over the course of your own life, you may easily overidentify with the schizoid's lack of friendships and connections. In trying to alleviate the detached partner's loneliness, you may actually be trying to care for yourself. But don't be fooled. The schizoid is not lonely — you are. Finally, some of us require a challenge in relationships. Drawing out a detached partner might be just the challenge we are seeking. It is a challenge with a low probability of long-term success but a challenge nonetheless.

Many facets of a schizoid partner's behavior can draw us in and keep us working to establish a connection. Quite often, we are replaying the tapes from an earlier relationship — working overtime to secure the affection of an aloof parent. In other cases, we need to be needed and are drawn by the promise of validating ourselves through rescue and caretaking. And some of us simply find the detached personality engaging and loveable. Whatever the motivation, be honest with yourself about one thing: Your schizoid partner will remain detached and distanced as a way of life. If you have strong needs for a reciprocal relationship, life with a schizoid partner will be difficult.

Living with a Schizoid

What should I do if I'm involved with a schizoid personality type? Would therapy help? Is there any hope that she might change? Will I ever get my emotional needs met in this relationship? These are the kinds of questions we routinely hear from men and women who finally realize that their disengaged partner may have a personality disorder.

As the partner of a schizoid person, you need to soberly appreciate the lousy prognosis for change and the startling reality that your partner has little capacity for engaging in a genuine relationship. Like all personality disorders, people with schizoid features range widely when it comes to severity: While some are simply very introverted, others are thoroughly detached and almost entirely arelational. Someone who meets the diagnostic criteria for Schizoid Personality Disorder has difficulty relating to all human beings — including you. It is not that she is unwilling to offer emotional reciprocity; on the contrary, she is quite simply *unable*.

For most human beings, getting serious about or even marrying a schizoid partner is not a great idea — especially if you prefer to be with a lover who is mutually excited to be with you! Nonetheless, some reading this chapter may already feel "stuck" with a schizoid person. Maybe you are married or have young children. In this case, there are a few things you should keep in mind as you work to both accept your partner and make the relationship more livable.

Be Realistic in Your Expectations

Let's be clear: The prognosis for change in your schizoid partner is poor. Schizoids have little or no desire for interpersonal relationships, they are indifferent to both praise and criticism, and they have minimal capacity for emotional life. On the other hand, not all schizoid persons have severe symptoms and some will show more promise when it comes to relational growth. As the partner of a schizoid person, you may feel disappointed and defeated. You may be tempted to believe that if only you could be more empathetic, caring, or engaging your partner would "come around," open up, and become interested in talking, sharing, and disclosing. This is erroneous thinking. Your schizoid partner would be schizoid with ANYONE, not just you. Expect little or no change and celebrate when you discover any at all.

Don't Push Too Hard

Remember that your schizoid partner has accumulated a lifetime of practice when it comes to his aloof and disengaged style. Withdrawing is a primary defense and a well-honed habit. If you constantly push your partner for connection, it is quite likely that you will become a trigger for your partner's isolative behavior. Confronting your schizoid partner about his withdrawal or demanding that he meet your needs are self-defeating strategies. A smarter approach would involve a permissive and tolerant style. Knowing your partner values and needs time alone, why not encourage it? By so doing, your partner may feel better prepared to handle episodic periods of engagement with you. In a nutshell: Badgering schizoids for interaction is a sure-fire way to make them shut you out altogether. For the schizoid, nothing is worse than an emotionally intrusive partner.

Whatever Your Partner Enjoys, Join Him in It!

A person with Schizoid Personality Disorder appears to enjoy relatively few activities in life — at least few activities with social components. Your partner may enjoy watching movies, working on cars, or reading. Why not join him — even if he prefers relatively little verbal exchange? In all probability, there were certain things you initially enjoyed with your partner, why not rekindle some of these? The secret is to get your partner to associate you with moments and activities that he finds pleasurable. Rather than badger and demand, this is a softer approach to gaining a foothold in his emotional world. Over time, the schizoid partner may become more comfortable with your presence and may even begin to prefer it. While there are no guarantees, there is wisdom in luring versus pursuing the schizoid partner.

Reinforce, Don't Punish

Famed behaviorist B. F. Skinner earned his place in history by discovering that reinforcing desired behaviors is always more effective than punishing undesirable behaviors. Rather than chastise or shame your schizoid partner for her disengagement and withdrawal, you are likely to have a much better effect if you praise even tiny flickers of interpersonal interest. Praise and encourage your partner's willingness to allow you to be present during her solitary activities, and then look for opportunities to praise any involvement in social activities or efforts to initiate a conversation or interaction — no matter how brief. This is what Skinner called *shaping*. By rewarding progressive approximations to the desired behavior and tolerating very gradual changes in behavior, you are more likely to nurture the relational conditions conducive to growth in your partner.

Find Ways to Meet Emotional Needs outside the Relationship

If you plan to stay in a long-term relationship with a schizoid partner and if you have emotional needs and relational interests, you will be very wise to seek out and nurture alternative connections. Stay involved with good friends (but don't expect your partner to be happy about couple obligations), join support or social groups, take some classes, and don't lose touch with your family. By getting at least some of your relational needs addressed elsewhere, you will naturally place less demand on your partner and may feel better able to endure and accept his disengagement. Of course, becoming emotionally connected to someone of the opposite sex or to whom you are otherwise attracted may increase the risk of an affair. Remember that significant self-disclosure and frequent interaction naturally increase intimacy. Having an affair is never a helpful solution to problems with your partner.

Therapy Is Unlikely to Help

In the case of full-blown Schizoid Personality Disorder, it is unlikely that sending your partner for professional counseling or psychotherapy will be fruitful. Schizoids are not especially psychologically minded, nor are they prone to significant insight about their own pattern of detachment. Most important, schizoids have little relational motivation for change. Although your partner may like you a great deal, she will just not be adequately motivated by threats of terminating the relationship. You can probably guess that your schizoid partner will be about as detached from her psychotherapist as she is from you. Even though a schizoid person may be comfortable with an intellectual conversation about your relationship, there is unlikely to be a parallel emotional component. In sum, it will be up to you to acclimate, develop modest expectations, and accept small gains in your partner's interpersonal behavior.

When It's Time to Leave

Sooner or later, you may find that life with a schizoid partner is simply not something you can endure over the long haul. The factors that lured you in initially are now exposed as symptoms of a disordered personality style. Not only is your partner unable to reciprocate affection and connection, he has little motivation to do so. Maybe you have undergone some good personal therapy and now have a clearer understanding of your own misguided need to rescue and heal; once exposed, these motivations are no longer powerful enough to keep you pursuing a schizoid partner. Here is the good news: If a relationship with a schizoid partner ends, it is unlikely to be devastating for the schizoid. Remember, this person has a very low capacity for relational connection and is often quite content alone. Of course, each person is different, and the less severe a partner's schizoid traits, the more connected he may feel to you. In most cases, the schizoid will adapt more effectively to the end of a relationship than most of the other personality types we mention in this guide.

Summary

The schizoid personality type will be a detached partner — a "cold fish." This partner has spent a lifetime perfecting the art of disengagement; she is most at home on a perpetual emotional island. Even if you are attracted to this person's mysterious preference for solitude, it is unlikely that she can ever satisfy you emotionally. If you are dating a schizoid partner, you are probably doing all of the work in the "relationship." You will soon discover that staying with this person is a recipe for loneliness, not love.

CHAPTER 6

THE ODD PARTNER

The Schizotypal Personality

Schizotypal Personality Checklist

- ✔ His thoughts are often best described as bizarre — your friends and family call him "weird."
- ✔ He thinks that neutral events or random occurrences hold special meaning or importance for him.
- ✔ He has a strange way of perceiving things, and you sometimes feel confused by what he reports seeing or experiencing.
- ✔ He has a strange way of speaking at times, and you notice that others seem confused or startled by things he says or does.
- ✔ He becomes suspicious at times.
- ✔ His emotions often seem either inappropriate or weird.
- ✔ His clothing and appearance are often strange.
- ✔ He has very few close friends outside of your relationship.
- ✔ He is often very uncomfortable in social situations because of the way that others respond to his odd behavior.

Have you dated someone who is odd, eccentric, or weird in striking ways? Did his or her strange behaviors become more apparent after you began dating? Do these odd traits seem to have the effect of causing social rejection because people you meet think your partner is strange? If so, you may be involved with someone whom mental health professionals might diagnose with **Schizotypal Personality Disorder**. These adults are simply so odd and eccentric that they have trouble finding and maintaining jobs, friendships, and romantic relationships.

As you read this chapter, consider whether your partner has the distinguishing features of schizotypal behavior and also consider what you can do to more effectively spot this type. If you frequently end up with odd types, it may be wise to ask yourself what schizotypal traits appeal to you and lure you in.

Patricia's Story

I doubt I'd have even begun dating Stewart if I'd had more time to actually get to know him first. Don't get me wrong, I still like Stewart a lot and he has many nice qualities. We still keep in touch once in a while by email; there is just no way I could really love the guy in the long run.

I had been divorced for about six years when a friend from work hooked me up with Stewart on a blind double date. I should have been a bit more skeptical from the start; my friend can be a little odd herself. She's very funny but has a preoccupation with unsolved mysteries and ghost stories. I found out she belonged to a "book group" of like-minded mystery sleuths and was intrigued — I was very lonely in those days and with twin ten-year-olds to take care of, I didn't get out much. So, the idea was for me to attend a book club meeting and then go out with my friend, her boyfriend, and his best friend — Stewart.

I liked Stewart right away. Although he was several years younger than me, he didn't seem to care. He was average looking but by that point in my life, I was less interested in looks and more concerned about stability and loyalty (my first marriage was a mess). He had a strange sense of humor and a dry wit that really made me laugh. Because everyone in the book group got so animated about the unsolved mysteries they were discussing, Stewart's intense belief in ghosts and conspiracies to keep ghost sightings covered up didn't seem so odd or excessive at first. I did notice that Stewart seemed rather nervous about talking to me on that first date and I found that rather cute and refreshing — someone was actually nervous about being around *me!*

I enjoyed my time with him enough that I agreed to go out with him again. The next weekend we met for a movie and dinner. I enjoyed Stewart and found him to be funny in an odd kind of way. I did notice, however, that our conversation would always come back around to strange ghost stories, legends, and "evidence" Stewart was aware of that the government had "units" designated to cover up and suppress information about supernatural events. I found this whole idea a little creepy but Stewart obviously took it very seriously. And although he laughed and smiled when he did it, he insisted that I have his email address and phone number in case "anything unusual" happened. His email address had MoonDog in it. He explained that this was the nickname his book club friends gave him because he often spent his evenings with friends exploring ghost stories. That night as he drove off, I noticed his license plate also read MoonDog.

Stewart and I started dating off and on, although our relationship always felt a little more like a curious friendship than an intense romance. He was prone to writing long and sometimes rambling email messages that contained links to all sorts of odd conspiracy theory and unsolved mystery Internet sites. And sometimes, his attempts to crack jokes or be humorous just passed right over my head. I also discovered that Stewart, or MoonDog, had a strong affinity for fantasy role-playing games. Sometimes, he would momentarily lapse into one of his characters when we were talking or eating a meal together and he would find this quite funny. Initially, I found the whole thing novel and interesting, but over time, it became more annoying than anything else.

I found out that Stewart worked in a record store and that he had held a number of different low-level jobs over the years at book stores, game shops, and record stores. He had only a handful of friends — most of whom were equally focused on mysteries and role-playing games. I also began to notice that Stewart could get very "weird" about ghost sightings and supernatural phenomena. For example, he would point out tiny details in newspaper articles or television stories and nod emphatically as if it were perfectly clear that there was evidence of the work of the departed or a government cover-up of some kind. I started to find this too creepy.

The end came when I invited Stewart to a picnic at the park across from my place with several of my neighborhood friends. As I watched Stewart, I realized he was very uncomfortable around strangers and his anxiety seemed to make him behave even more strangely. After interacting with him for only a few hours, each of my friends commented that Stewart was "bizarre," and each of them rolled their eyes while describing something odd Stewart had said or done at the picnic. He even yelled at some poor guy who had laughed (not intending anything mean I'm sure) when Stewart described one of his role-playing characters. I suppose the topper was when my own children became terrified by a story Stewart insisted on telling them about a woman who had supposedly been murdered at the park and how several people had seen her apparition wandering our neighborhood at night.

I broke things off shortly thereafter. Stewart was upset for a while but then admitted women usually just didn't understand him. Even now, I get the rare email message from MoonDog warning me of a ghost sighting in my area or inviting me to a role-playing meeting.

The Odd Personality

The odd dating partner, one suffering from Schizotypal Personality Disorder, is likely to show signs of eccentric appearance, thinking, and behavior fairly early on in your relationship. These adults have just plain whacky thinking characterized by belief in magical powers or abilities, immediate supernatural influence over daily events, and ideas that they are influencing (or is being influenced by) external or otherworld forces. You may discover that the schizotypal person you are dating believes that characters in a movie are uttering lines with specific importance or meaning for him; or your partner might believe fervently in telepathy and become frustrated when you cannot read her thoughts or sense her feelings. Events and occurrences that most of us would attribute to chance are often interpreted by the odd personality as having specific meaning, importance, or personal relevance. This can come across as both bizarre and more than a little unnerving to those around him. A schizotypal partner who is absorbed by a role-playing game or watching *Lord of the Rings* for the fiftieth time may suddenly blurt out lines from the game or movie with such sober intensity that those who do not share his odd thinking about the game or movie can become both confused and frightened.

Schizotypal adults often have poor or haphazard hygiene and grooming habits. This is because they are both out of sync with current trends and conventions and simultaneously distracted and preoccupied with fantasy and bizarre thoughts. This personality type may also have odd speech patterns or strange greetings that other people find bizarre (e.g., "I am Frank, resident of this planet for twenty-eight years"). Imagine the odd high school student sitting largely alone in the cafeteria. His hair is unkempt and his clothing out of style. When another brave student finally sits down at his table one day, this boy stares inappropriately for a while before raising his hand and giving his best Vulcan greeting from *Star Trek*. This is enough to convince the other student he has made a grave error, and the schizotypal kid is quickly left alone. Again.

As you might easily imagine, this personality type is likely to experience a very painful and lonely adolescence and young adulthood. His is a story of rejection and ridicule that only exacerbates his belief that others cannot be fully trusted. He has notable interpersonal skill deficits and is very uncomfortable in social situations — especially around unfamiliar people. Entering into novel settings may make him too anxious to interact or so nervous that he blurts out inappropriate thoughts. The schizotypal person may also ramble from topic to topic in a seemingly incoherent way that makes those around him wonder if he is crazy or using substances. Sadly, these personalities seldom have many friends or confidants other than first-degree relatives. Unlike the detached partner, this person would actually like to have some relationships and probably feels lonely, isolated, and rejected.

As a result of her chronic rejection and isolation, this personality type probably has very poor emotional intelligence, meaning she is very poor at accurately reading others' verbal and nonverbal cues and picking up on social nuances while communicating; she will not understand the implied messages in things people say. Because she has so often been the target of ridicule and humiliation, she is also prone to suspicion and doubt about the intent of others. Sadly, this creates a vicious circle in which the schizotypal person is guarded and suspicious, gets rejected, and then becomes even more withdrawn and suspicious. Of course, this withdrawal further prevents her from developing the social skills she so desperately needs.

In our own teaching, we have often struggled to help our psychology students understand what a genuine schizotypal personality-disordered person might look like. The release of the movie *Napoleon Dynamite* made our job much easier. In this movie, the main character is a severe high school "nerd," who has a preoccupation with magical characters such as unicorns, the Loch Ness monster, and even a fantasy creature of his own creation, the "Liger" (a cross between a tiger and lion but with magical powers). Napoleon has few friends, has trouble communicating appropriately in social situations, and is suspicious of the intentions of peers at school. His clothing is eccentric, he is poorly groomed, and he doesn't seem to "get" the normal banter of his classmates. In his own loveable way, Napoleon Dynamite suffers from Schizotypal Personality Disorder.

Some final thoughts about the odd type: First, this person is likely to have occupational problems. It is very hard to secure or maintain a job when one is extremely anxious around others and prone to bizarre comments and a strange appearance. Customers and co-workers can easily be put off or frightened. Unless this person finds just the right niche (e.g., working alone or in an environment where others share her preoccupations), work may be a trial. Second, be aware that the schizotypal person can become so stressed that her bizarre thoughts actually take on a psychotic (out of touch with reality) quality. At times, schizotypal personalities may have brief episodes of insanity in which they demonstrate full-blown delusional thoughts that they appear unable to distinguish from reality (e.g., "Gandalf is in trouble and he needs me to find him and free him no matter what," "a demon is trying to influence me at this very moment; only I can see him"). In these rare instances, your schizotypal partner may require medication and hospitalization.

What Makes a Schizotypal?

It is very unlikely that a person with this personality disorder had a "normal" or happy childhood. Although genes may factor in — especially if one's parents were schizotypal, or worse, schizophrenic — early experiences with parents probably had more to do with becoming odd. For one thing, parents of odd personalities may have been cold and indifferent to the child, causing him to withdraw into a world of disconnected fantasy. Alternatively, or in addition, parents may have been punitive, derogatory, or shaming of the child causing him to avoid contact with others for fear of more of this treatment. Later, as adults, these persons are apprehensive, anxious, and very slow to adapt to new situations.

One of the biggest contributors to Schizotypal Personality Disorder is a communication pattern on the part of parents that is bizarre or disturbed. These parents may do and say things that come across to the child as chaotic or fragmented. For example, parents may punish or ridicule children for doing or saying rather normal things — perhaps even before they do or say them. Naïve children may wonder how parents can predict what they were going to say or do next and thus may attribute magical powers to their parents — something that contributes to the later continuation of odd and bizarre thinking. They may both fear and develop a strong curiosity about what they perceive to be amazing and magical powers. Parents may also shame children for leaving the home; this may interfere with normal development of early peer social skills and cause the child to develop an early pattern of social withdrawal, idiosyncratic fantasies, and odd habits.

The Schizotypal as Partner

Here is a paradox: Many schizotypal persons end up remaining single much if not all of their lives because they are so sensitive to rejection or simply unable to connect successfully with someone else. And yet, you may have begun dating just such a person and may wonder what you can expect if this relationship continues. You should understand that his odd and eccentric traits will probably persist in some form over the course of your relationship; the reality is that his unusual personality characteristics are very resistant to long-term change. Here are some elements to life with an odd personality that you should consider carefully:

Your partner will be prone to giving voice to strange thoughts and demonstrating odd behavior at times. You may have been intrigued or beguiled by some of these idiosyncrasies early on, but you probably also now see that your parents, friends, and your partner's employers do not find them so sweet or cute; from the perspective of others, they are *weird!* This has many consequences for you. You might find your social circle progressively shrinking as family and friends begin to retreat from interaction with your partner. You might discover tension developing with loved ones where none existed before, or they may actually be afraid for you, wondering if your new partner is prone to dangerous acting out or psychosis. When a partner talks about being from another planet or recites from memory the lines from the fortieth episode of *Star Trek*, it is easy to see why loved ones might be concerned.

Beyond your own loneliness and social isolation, another consequence of loving a schizotypal person is financial stress. Unless your partner has discovered just the right niche, he may have difficulty holding down a job or may only have aspirations of low-level, low-paying jobs. You may need to assume primary financial responsibility in the relationship — especially if your partner has episodes in which he becomes briefly delusional.

In addition to social and financial problems, you will discover that your odd partner has genuine difficulty attending to your emotional needs. Remember that this person likely grew up in a perpetual state of social isolation and avoidance. It will be very difficult for your partner to successfully read your nonverbal cues and understand things you try to communicate about your wishes in the relationship. In many respects, you are speaking a language your partner does not speak. And although adults can learn the language of emotional expression, including subtle cues, it takes a very long time.

At the same time that your partner is proving that she can't easily understand you, she will be responding to you, at times, as though you are dangerous or malevolent. After a childhood and adolescence of social rejection and ridicule, your partner may be incapable of avoiding some measure of suspicion and distrust. Seemingly innocuous comments may be quickly interpreted as teasing or rejection, triggering a period of sullen withdrawal and avoidance. There may be a spike in bizarre thinking and behavior after such incidents.

This pattern of perceived rejections or ridicule may also predict periods of depression. Schizotypal persons are vulnerable to feeling quite depressed at times. Relating to other people has been the source of a great deal of pain over the course of their lives and so adult interactions and rejections may continue to trigger deeply ingrained feelings of worthlessness. When things go poorly in your relationship or when you attempt to benignly point out some behavior that you don't understand or wish her to curtail, do not be surprised if withdrawal and depression follow. This may begin to feel like a no-win situation for you. It may be quite difficult to successfully be honest with a schizotypal partner.

Although much of this news is sobering if not gloomy, there can be a silver lining for those in relationships with schizotypal partners. Quite often, these personalities are extremely creative and can be quite interesting for that reason. Your partner's eccentricity may be delightful to you in some ways and if not severe, can lead to success in certain occupations.

In an interview following the smashing success of her debut novel,

The Lovely Bones, Alice Sebold noted that she had always just been a bit "odd," and she encouraged fledgling writers to "inhabit your weirdness," in order to find success. Sebold's own life experiences do not include, to our knowledge, any personality disorder. She has, however, lived through more than her share of "odd" happenings, including parental alcoholism, rape, post-traumatic stress, heroin addiction, recovery, and a highly successful writing career (Sebold, 1999 & 2002). We think she would agree that her own comments about being "odd" and "weirdness" help to illustrate our point that notable differences ("oddness"), and unusual behaviors and preferences ("weirdness"), may contribute to creative success. After all, what does it mean to be "creative" if not to be on the cutting edge, finding new pathways for self-expression?

Nevertheless, while some schizotypal adults find true creative success by following their bizarre thinking to its conclusion, regrettably, in many other cases, an odd partner is likely to find only rejection, failure, and misunderstanding as a result of her "weirdness."

Why Am I Attracted to Odd Partners?

So what is it exactly about your schizotypal partner that drew you in? Let's review: If you find yourself attracted to a person with this syndrome, you are attracted to someone who has more than a few of these traits:

- He thinks that other people or events are referring to him when in fact they are not.
- He has whacky beliefs, magical thinking, or odd speech that can be embarrassing and make others think he is weird.
- He has bizarre feelings or experiences at times.
- He appears frequently suspicious and distrustful of others and has very few friends.
- He has emotions that are inappropriate or don't really fit what's happening or being discussed.
- He dresses in a strange way at times.
- He is extremely uncomfortable in social situations and expects other people to reject him.

It is quite easy to see how anyone reading this guide could end up in a relationship with an odd personality now and then. Depending on the severity of the syndrome, this partner's eccentricity can at first seem novel, intriguing, mysterious, or at least entertaining. Schizotypal personalities can be very attractive, accomplished in specific areas, and creative. Developing an infatuation with an odd partner or two may in fact be a normal experience. But what if you find yourself in numerous relationships with odd types or you find yourself in a relationship with someone who has a severe form of this disorder? Or what if you have gone so far as to marry someone with a fairly serious Schizotypal Personality Disorder?

First, you may simply be a person who finds herself enticed and deeply intrigued by characters who are "different" in some pronounced way. Perhaps you admire their willingness to go against the grain with respect to appearance or social behavior. Perhaps you become enamored with the odd partner's absolute focus on a specific hobby or unusual social cause. If you come from a home in which there was either profound pressure to conform or a home with at least one very eccentric parent, then this type might be further appealing to you. In the first instance, hooking up with an odd type can be a way to make a break with a restrictive past and try on a new identity vicariously through the eccentric partner. In the second instance, you may be drawn to something familiar and comfortable in your odd partner.

A second possibility to consider if you are frequently in relationships with schizotypal types is that you yourself have some odd characteristics. Please excuse us for suggesting this, but it is a possibility that you should not overlook. Old clichés such as *"It takes one to know one"* and *"Birds of a feather flock together"* may be especially apropos here. In our clinical experience, we find that partners tend to be attracted to the familiar — things in a lover that remind them of themselves. So, even if you do not feel that you are as overtly odd as your current partner, is it possible that you share many of his or her eccentric beliefs and habits? Have you too suffered from social isolation because of difficulty fitting in socially? Is struggling in social situations a familiar part of your story? We recommend that you at least consider the criteria at the beginning of this chapter in terms of your own experience; honestly consider if you have schizotypal traits.

Of course, no exploration of attraction to the odd type would be complete without consideration of your drive to caretake and protect. Is there something utterly compelling about the socially bumbling, relationally wounded, and insecure type? Why do you feel such a strong desire to protect this person from further pain and rejection? Perhaps you had a parent or family member with schizotypal traits, and now in an effort to do what you probably could not as a child — protect a much loved adult — you find yourself playing the parental role in romantic relationships. The schizotypal partner will be a never-ending "project" for those among us who desperately need to take care of somebody else. Of course, this is typically not a solid foundation for an adult love relationship. Because your odd partner will probably stay odd in most ways, you can bank on being a perpetual parent.

Living with a Schizotypal

After reading this chapter and perhaps after a relationship with one or more schizotypal types, you no doubt understand that life with this person can be "odd." We do not recommend it. Should you choose to stay in a relationship with a person with these traits for the long term, you will need to find a way to gracefully acclimate to your partner's tendency to withdraw, push you way, and expect humiliating rejection. You will also need to develop a reasonably thick skin — both for your partner's eccentricities and bizarre thinking and for the perplexed reactions and snide comments you will almost certainly get from friends and family members. At times you may feel protective, at other times confused, and frequently you will feel exasperated. But should you decide to stay attached to a schizotypal partner, here are some strategies and recommendations for relating to him more effectively.

Accept Your Partner Unconditionally

Human beings with schizotypal traits have nearly always had a rough go of it. Life has been a struggle and as the experiences of rejection and alienation have stacked up, this person has grown more and more insular and distrustful of others. Many therapists who work with odd personalities see themselves as providing a corrective emotional experience or reparenting a wounded child. The schizotypal partner will look at the world through a grid of abandonment, vulnerability, alienation, and distrust. A loving partner will need to work patiently at providing an environment in which the schizotypal partner can test the waters anew and experience a safe relationship — perhaps for the first time. What can you do? First, practice unconditional regard and acceptance — no matter what sort of odd thoughts or behaviors your partner expresses. Highly defensive and self-protected, this person will need a constant display of patience, kindness, positive regard, and acceptance without any evidence of ridicule or rejection. Over time, your partner may feel more comfortable, trusting, and willing to disclose in your relationship.

Don't Push Too Hard or Too Fast

Most of us hope for mutuality and reciprocity in our love relationships; we want to both give and receive emotionally. Even though we appreciate the schizotypal's deeply ingrained avoidance and distrust, it is all too easy to become frustrated and to begin to apply pressure on our partners to self-disclose, to become more socially engaged, or to decrease their odd thinking. This is a mistake and if you are going to remain in a relationship with the schizotypal type, it will behoove you to remain patient. Remember, these partners have accumulated years of bad social and relational experiences. Like the proverbial tortoise, they will simply retract behind a defensive shell when pushed beyond their relational tolerance. Pushing them to trust you, to tell you what they're feeling, or for details about their childhood may be enough to drive them to silence and even more odd behavior.

Help Your Partner Establish Consistent Social Relationships

If your partner is schizotypal, a long-term goal should be the development and maintenance of steady and meaningful relationships. We are not suggesting that you take all the responsibility for "brokering" your partner's friendships, but why not facilitate these connections whenever possible? Because this partner desires social relationships and often wishes to have more and closer relationships with people, motivation is often on your side. The hurdle, of course, will be your partner's ingrained anxiety about new social situations and strangers. Consider finding social networks that match your partner's interests (e.g., movies, fantasy games, or computers) and participate in these groups with your partner. Seek out a handful of individuals or couples who you are sure will be tolerant and accepting of your partner's nontraditional behavior and nurture frequent exposure with these potential friends; familiarity should reduce anxiety. Finally, reinforce your partner's fledgling efforts to be social.

Reinforce Appropriate Social Skills

Without infantilizing or condescending to your partner, there may be times when both modeling and reinforcing improved social skills may help her to feel more confident in social situations. As one who regards social situations as dangerous battlegrounds, your schizotypal partner has probably not developed very effective skills when it comes to simple things like knowing what to say and, more importantly, what not to say. Other social skills you may have to model and reinforce include knowing how close to stand to others, how much eye contact is comfortable for others, and how to use good nonverbal cues. While these skills may sound simplistic to you, they are quite mysterious to many odd types and difficult to master without modeling and practice. Actively reinforce gradual improvements in social interactions.

Help Your Partner Evaluate the Validity of Beliefs

One consistent problem for the schizotypal adult is the tendency to engage in bizarre thinking and to hold magical ideas about self, others, and the world. Once your partner begins to trust your benevolent intentions, you may have earned the right to also challenge your partner's irrational beliefs. So when a partner says, "You knew what I was going to say even before I said it! You can read my mind can't you?" respond gently but firmly with something like "We both know I can't actually read your mind, but I know you so well now, I can sometimes predict what you might say." If delivered kindly and consistently, such corrective statements can help a partner to recognize the boundaries between magical and rational thinking.

Remember, the Goal Is Not to Eliminate Oddness

If you dislike the odd attributes of your partner, find someone else. People diagnosed with Schizotypal Personality Disorder will be perpetually odd, eccentric, and weird. Perhaps some of these idiosyncrasies attracted you in the first place. If you embark on a crusade to change this fundamental truth about your partner, your time will be misspent and you will inevitably end up frustrated and disheartened. Instead, a reasonable goal is to bring your partner closer into the mainstream and away from the periphery when it comes to social interactions and self-confidence. He will nearly always maintain some oddities of speech and habit and will certainly never be comfortable as the center of attention at parties, but schizotypal persons can become significantly more comfortable — with you, with themselves, and with others.

When It's Time to Leave

At some point, you might discover that you can no longer continue in a relationship with an extremely eccentric and socially withdrawn partner.

What will happen when you leave? There is no evidence that schizotypal persons are prone to violence. Unless she has been threatening or extremely delusional in the past, there is no reason to expect that your leaving will push her in this direction.

It is true, however, that your schizotypal partner will be wounded and hurt by your departure. This personality type has a great deal of experience with rejection and will be quite sensitive to perceived disparagement. If there is a way to slow the process down and avoid an extremely abrupt departure, this may be helpful. Use the period of detaching to affirm and reinforce the things you like and find attractive about this person. Alert others in his support system so that they can be more attentive and involved with your odd partner during this period.

Summary

The schizotypal partner may seem novel, intriguing, and "unique" at first. But over time, you will probably come to see this person as just plain weird. Although all of us have quirks and odd habits, the odd partner suffers from weirdness that reaches disordered proportions. She has bizarre thinking and behavior, and she will be quite uncomfortable in new social situations and may say and do things that result in consistent social rejection. If you are drawn to extreme eccentricity in a partner, then a relationship with a schizotypal might work. If not, it is only a matter of time before you feel like asking Scotty to beam you up too!

DRAMATIC, ERRATIC, AND DANGEROUS PARTNERS

The Dangerous Partner
The Antisocial Personality

The Stormy Partner
The Borderline Personality

The Theatrical Partner
The Histrionic Personality

The Self-Absorbed Partner
The Narcissistic Personality

The Undermining Partner
The Passive-Aggressive Personality

CHAPTER 7

THE DANGEROUS PARTNER
The Antisocial Personality

Antisocial Personality Checklist

- ✔ He engages in unlawful behavior and may have been arrested or had legal problems.

- ✔ He has lied, been deceitful, or conned you in order to further personal pleasure or needs.

- ✔ He is impulsive, doesn't plan ahead, and fails to think about consequences.

- ✔ He has been physically aggressive, assaultive, or irritable toward you.

- ✔ He has exhibited a blatant disregard for your safety or welfare.

- ✔ He has failed to sustain consistent work or to honor financial responsibilities.

- ✔ He shows a lack of remorse, exhibits indifference, or rationalizes his behavior when he hurts, mistreats, or steals from you.

Do any of these warning signs sound familiar to you? Do you date people who manipulate, lie, and act irresponsibly? Do you feel like you are at the point where you question what your current partner says, what he is doing, and who he is with? Do your relationships begin to unravel before your very eyes because you find that people you become involved with end up taking advantage of you? Does the love you had for your partner now feel tainted by his exploitation and manipulation? Angie's story sheds more light on the traits of a particularly dangerous personality type and how evidence of this disorder often plays out in relationships.

Angie's story

Rich and I began dating shortly after graduation from high school. We were from the same town and had many mutual friends. Rich was very good looking, a good athlete, and had lots of friends. He was confident and self-assured and things just seemed to come easy to him. He was known for having a long line of girlfriends and for being a womanizer. Although I was aware of his history with women, he had a way of making me feel as if I was different than the rest, and somehow more special. I was instantly attracted to his easy style, his good sense of humor, and his romantic gestures. He would show up on my doorstep with flowers, and he remembered my favorite things. Our relationship seemed to take on a life of its own, and we quickly became close and intimate.

For some reason, I felt like I had known Rich forever. He confided in me and told me things that he said he had never told anyone else. He was tender, and when we were together I felt like the only person in his life. We were going to different colleges and both had part-time jobs. I was working in a record store and Rich was working at a hospital as a tech. We usually spent all our free time together at night and on weekends. With both of our school schedules and working, it was hard to see each other during the day, but I tried to stay connected with him through phone calls and emails. I definitely made more effort than he did, but I kept telling myself that that was what women did. He was more aloof than I but always seemed glad to hear from me. There were those times, though, when I couldn't reach him, when he wouldn't answer his phone, and when he refused to tell me what he was doing or who he was with; he was often evasive. When we were together again he went out of his way to make me feel special and there were so many times when I gave up my anger or frustration and went with the good feelings instead. The few times that I really pushed him to tell me what he was doing, he became defensive and his mood would turn dark. He always came up with what seemed like a good explanation at the time for why I couldn't reach him. He'd tell me that he was with his guy friends, had had a few too many drinks, and passed out at a friend's house. Or he would say that he couldn't get cell phone service and didn't get my messages until the next day. He was always so sweet afterward that for a long time I really believed him. He had an uncanny ability to convince me of anything.

I noticed that Rich drank more than others around him, and on weekends he was never too far from a beer. If I ever brought it up he would get really angry, and so I learned it wasn't worth the energy. I guess I focused on the positive things about Rich. One time I found a girl's phone number in his pocket and explained it away to myself. He loved to flirt with other women, even in front of me. If I mentioned that it bothered me, he would just tell me not to worry and that he was with me, or he would get defensive and angry and tell me I was insecure and jealous.

One day I decided to stop by the hospital for lunch and surprise him. I went in and asked for him at the front desk and after a long search through their computer system I was told he didn't work there. I insisted that there must be some mistake and so the nice man checked again for me. He told me that Rich had never worked there. I was shocked and angry. I called Rich and when I finally reached him I was yelling and crying at him on the phone. He got angry and explained it away so easily. He told me that I never listened to him and that I must have forgotten when he told me he had only applied for a job there but had never gotten it. He said that he told me that he had to take a job he didn't want, instead, cleaning swimming pools. I started doubting myself and wondered if I had forgotten this. I began to feel guilty for yelling and being so upset, so I eventually apologized for not listening to him more closely. Things got back to normal, but I couldn't hide from the seeds of doubt about him that had slowly begun to sprout. I fought back the worry, but there were too many times when I couldn't reach him, when he was evasive, and when I found other women's numbers.

One day I saw him having lunch with another woman after he told me he was going skiing with his friends. When I confronted him, the lies began again. It was the first time that Rich really became aggressive, and I remember feeling very scared and taken off guard. He began screaming and cussing at me — I had never seen him this way before. I tried to leave, but he grabbed me and threw me down. I began to cry but that seemed to infuriate him even further. I eventually became passive just to stop the situation, and of course, I ended up apologizing for upsetting him and causing a fight! I can't believe I let him control me so much. I remember waking up one morning and realizing I was very unhappy and that I had given up and changed a lot. I think I lost my sense of self in my relationship with Rich, and I realized that I had to build my self-esteem back up and get away from his abusive nature. I had finally had enough of the lies, deceit, and manipulation — I worked up the courage and ended the relationship. I felt like such a fool for believing the lies and stories he told me. I spent two years of my life being lied to, manipulated, and conned by him and I'm not sure whether he even cared or felt bad about it at the end. I'll bet anything he's doing the same thing to some other woman right now.

The Dangerous Personality

When first attracted to someone, it is natural to focus on the positive qualities and traits of this new love interest. Perhaps we are drawn in by the way the person looks, his sense of humor, his intellect, or his kind and generous behavior. We are naturally inclined to accentuate the positive. In the case of the dangerous personality type, this is especially easy to do. Dangerous personalities are notorious for initially appearing charming, kind, attentive, and caring. He can be vigilant about his appearance and have an uncanny awareness of how to maximize his appeal to others. Because he can also be intelligent, witty, and smooth, the dangerous type creates a knockout first impression. People with a dangerous personality have what psychologists call **Antisocial Personality Disorder**. They are so savvy about relationships and how to win potential partners over early on that their ability to draw people to them can seem unreal or supernatural. Sometimes, this talent for coming across as sincere and trustworthy — even though they are neither of these things — can be thoroughly frightening. The old saying *Looks can be deceiving* seems tailor made for the antisocial type because what you see isn't what you ultimately get.

The essential feature of the antisocial or dangerous personality type is a constant pattern of disregard for and violation of the rights of others. This pattern of behavior starts early in life — often in childhood — and continues into late adulthood. If your partner is the dangerous type, you will come to know him as defined by deceit, manipulation, and a false façade. Superficial charm, unreliability, poor judgment, and a lack of remorse for bad behavior are some of the hallmarks of the antisocial personality type. About the term *antisocial:* This person is against society and against social rules (laws), not asocial, as in the case of the withdrawn and reclusive detached type. You may, at this point, be wondering what we mean exactly by the label *"dangerous."* We selected the label dangerous carefully to describe the antisocial type. This partner can be destructive for you on many levels and in a countless number of ways. Read on to learn more about how this partner can wreak havoc on others.

It is quite common for someone with an antisocial personality to violate the law and to show little regard for the legal system; antisocials seem to truly believe that society's rules apply to everyone *except* them. They may shrug off laws and rules as idiotic, inconvenient, or simply made to be skirted. Your dangerous partner will probably feel that he is above the law and that laws were made to be broken. Consequently, these persons will break or evade laws whenever it suits them or helps them further their own agendas. For the antisocial type, here are two interpretations of the golden rule: Do unto others before they do unto me, and do unto others whatever I feel like doing! As you look back over an antisocial person's life, you will see a pattern of behavior defined by failure to conform to social norms and rule breaking often leading to arrests or other consequences. As children and adolescents, the antisocial may have stolen, lied, cheated, been aggressive to people and animals, set fires, destroyed property, started fights, abused substances, and had several run-ins with the authorities. Of course, when dating an antisocial type, he will probably lie to cover up these facts so it may only be after the fact that you learn the full extent of this person's criminal pattern.

As this dangerous personality type grows into adulthood, some of these antisocial acts may continue. There will often be a clear pattern of violating the rights of others in the service of asserting one's own will and agenda on others — even forcefully if necessary. Here is a warning: The intelligent antisocial is often very good at breaking laws and violating societal norms without ever being detected or getting caught. The dangerous type may fly just "under the radar" and avoid consequences for lengthy periods — particularly when the manipulative and antisocial behavior is less obvious or criminal. As you might have guessed, the higher an antisocial person's IQ, the more dangerous she will be. Many of the most notorious serial killers and rapists in history — those who were toughest to catch — were also the smartest. The less bright and astute antisocials often end up in jail early and stay there.

The antisocial type is also dangerous because of his uncanny ability to appear genuinely sorry when finally caught by the police (for criminal behavior) or by a partner (for manipulation, exploitation, cheating, or lying). When his lies and acting out are revealed, he does indeed feel bad — that he was caught. But he does not feel true remorse about the acts he committed or the pain he caused others. Antisocials are masters at rationalizing their behavior, making up excuses on the spur of the moment, and faking sorrow for their actions. Experts who work with antisocial types in prisons refer to this contrite manner as the *crocodile tears look;* sad only that he has been apprehended, this dangerous character is probably biding his time, waiting for you to draw close enough to be taken in — or devoured!

Another good reason for thinking of the antisocial type as dangerous is that they steadily and consistently corrode relationships — and the emotional health of their partners. It is hard to be in a relationship with a chronically deceitful, manipulative, and exploitive person without experiencing a painful degradation of one's own health and sanity. The damage to the partner of an antisocial may be emotional, financial, physical, or some combination of these. Dangerous personality types have an uncanny ability to utterly disregard the feelings, needs, and desires of others. They lie, deceive, and manipulate almost automatically and always to serve their own immediate aims. When you do finally catch and confront the antisocial partner, he will show a smooth knack for convincing you that you are all wrong or at least mistaken in your accusations. He may twist your words and facts around so that eventually you are convinced you yourself are wrong, insecure, paranoid, or ultimately to blame for the problem. And don't expect others to confirm your concerns about an antisocial's behavior — at least not at first. Because this person creates such a positive and sincere first impression, your friends and even your family may wonder what you're complaining about. The dangerous partner will be an expert at making you feel scared, vulnerable, and alone in the relationship.

Antisocials are also chronically sensation seeking. These people require more stimulation and a constant variety of thrills and sensations than others. This is one of the reasons members of certain military Special Forces and elite law enforcement units are selected based on some antisocial features (need for stimulation, not illegal behavior). It is common for the antisocial partner to abuse substances, drive recklessly, overspend, gamble, have illicit affairs, and have multiple sexual partners. Not only does the antisocial enjoy the thrill of such activities, he may also go out of his way to engage in them. Without a variety of thrill-seeking outlets and risky behaviors, the antisocial may complain of boredom. Of course, the antisocial partner's risk-taking behavior comes with consequences — both for the dangerous partner and for you. The fact that an antisocial person has tremendous difficulty anticipating and appreciating consequences for his actions will often place a partner in harm's way.

Think of the antisocial as constantly irresponsible — often across multiple domains. The antisocial is irresponsible with money, with legal requirements, with relationships, and with obligations to his offspring. Numerous job changes, job firings, and frequent or extended periods of unemployment are common. Expect the antisocial to have a poor record when it comes to accumulating and appropriately managing financial resources. His self-centeredness, impulsivity, and need for constant stimulation all bode ill for his ability to avoid financial scrapes. This may be evident in routine requests for "loans" and exploitation of those with whom he is close for frequent financial bailouts.

By way of summary, the antisocial person can be a dangerous partner. He will fail to conform to social norms regarding lawful behavior and can often come across as irritable and aggressive — especially when confronted or held accountable. Expect repeated failures to honor financial obligations and a record of exploiting others to meet personal needs. This person fails to plan ahead and acts on impulse — often part of a larger pattern of sensation seeking. The antisocial can be reckless and irresponsible with both his own and others' safety. Although this person will be beguiling and smooth at first, he will typically trail a long wake of brief superficial relationships. Finally, the antisocial person does not experience genuine remorse and instead feels justified in having harmed or manipulated others.

A Word of Warning

After reading the foregoing section, we hope you have a sober appreciation for the many different ways that antisocial people can be dangerous. But there is more: Antisocial personalities can, at times, become quite threatening — verbally and physically. Unlike the doubting partner who might act out of suspiciousness, the dangerous partner may act out violently simply to gratify himself or prevent you from taking away something he wants.

Although "antisocial" is the official diagnostic term for the dangerous type, other words often used interchangeably with antisocial include sociopath or psychopath. Lest you have any doubts about how dangerous the antisocial can be, consider the case of one of the most famous antisocials in American history, Theodore Bundy. A prolific serial rapist and serial killer, Bundy had raped and murdered approximately thirty-five women by the time he was finally caught and put to death. In contrast to a drooling madman, Bundy's demeanor was suave and polished. He was educated, charming, and handsome and appeared to have no problem convincing women he was not only good dating material, but also safe. Of course, most potential partners with antisocial traits will not be killers or rapists, but the fact that they share some of the same patterns of thinking and exploiting without regard for others should raise your anxiety level.

If there are children involved, you have more reason to be alarmed. People with antisocial personalities can be extremely irresponsible parents. As their needs usually come first, they may not be duly diligent with their children. For example, antisocials often fail to pay child support, fail to care for children's basic needs, and fail to get them necessary medical care. Their children may also not be adequately cared for nutritionally or hygienically. Antisocial people have a difficult time meeting others' needs emotionally as they are very focused on their own gratification. They may not be engaged with their children emotionally and may, at times, become emotionally or physically abusive. We have seen all of these scenarios occur in our professional experiences, and we ask you to be aware that the dangerous type may require careful supervision when around children.

What Makes a Dangerous Personality?

You may be wondering what on earth could have happened in the childhood of an antisocial person to make her so self-centered, cold, and dangerous. Keep in mind that, as in the case of all the personality disorders, the antisocial syndrome probably has some genetic predisposition. In fact, antisocial tendencies seem to run in families quite frequently. Criminal parents can both contribute genetic vulnerabilities to their offspring and serve as models for antisocial behavior. But dangerous personality styles require more than just genes to develop fully: Some complex interaction of predisposition and experiences with significant adults seems to be the key.

So what were the parents of antisocials like? People with this personality disorder often describe discipline in their home that was inconsistent and erratic — perhaps vacillating between passive and punitive. In many cases, parents were harsh, demanding, and abusive. Alternatively, parents may have been utterly neglectful and detached. Parents were deficient when it came to providing role modeling of socially appropriate and respectful behavior. Having learned that parents were utterly unreliable or essentially absent, the antisocial becomes fiercely independent, focused on meeting her own needs at the expense of everyone else. For this person, survival demands taking what she wants and needs and always looking out for number one. Other predisposing factors include parental neglect, having a caregiver model dangerous behavior or exploitation of others, or having a home defined by such chaos and neglect that "upping the ante" or acting out was the only way to get the attention she needed. Boys are significantly more likely to become antisocial adults than girls.

The Antisocial as Partner

Although your relationship with an antisocial type may begin rapidly and with some intensity, you will discover that life with an antisocial isn't easy. At different points in the relationship you may feel like a detective, police officer, judge, parent, boss, and child. Your roles will continue to change often in this relationship as your partner's erratic and irresponsible behavior fluctuates. You will notice that the antisocial partner pushes limits and patience — both yours and that of everyone he encounters. Just when you feel ready to throw in the towel, your dangerous partner will turn on the charm and minimize the issues that feel quite serious to you — all in the service of restoring just enough harmony in the relationship to keep you around. You will soon recognize this pattern: His trail of lies, deceit, and manipulation is quickly followed by brief exemplary behavior and promises of genuine change.

Sadly, if you love an antisocial, you will have to come to terms with the fact that your partner is not as distressed as you are about these antisocial behaviors. You must understand that your partner is not likely to feel bad about his behavior or about the way he treats you. He simply does not have the capacity to "feel your pain." Need proof?

Consider this: When antisocials are connected to brain imaging machines and shown emotionally laden scenes — scenes that make you and me experience anger, sadness, or euphoria — their brain scans reveal very little activity in the areas of the brain responsible for processing these emotional stimuli. In other words, their brains are simply not wired for empathy; they can't feel what you feel — even if they try (Hare, 1993).

Dangerous personalities are cunning in relationships and they can often read people quite well. This means that your partner will be aware of how far you can be pushed and how you are likely to respond to different violations of your expectations, rules, or values. It is in your partner's best interest to be able to "read" you to best get his needs met, while staying out of trouble. Your partner will also do this with others in his life, often including the authorities. Pushing the limits as far a possible is common and is also one way your partner will get sensation-seeking needs met. You, however, will be feeling like you are being played like a finely tuned fiddle. You actually may reach the point of engaging in detective work to see if what your partner is telling you is true.

The nagging feelings of suspicion about your partner will probably grow over time and you may eventually not know what to believe. If you love an antisocial you will become hyperalert to your partner's moves, motives, behaviors, and alibis. Furthermore, you will be tired of being the person who covers up for your partner's indiscretions — both personally and occupationally. You should be suspicious: Past behavior tends to be quite predictive of future behavior. You will also find it harder to accept or forgive your partner's behavior as you begin to realize that he actually feels very little, if any, remorse. If your partner's apologies ring false, it is because they are. He does feel bad, but it is because he has been busted, not because he has hurt, lied to, or manipulated you. The dangerous partner has a profound knack for turning the tables and convincing his partner that the problem is hers: She has "trust issues" or she is naive, insecure, unwilling to listen, or just too rigid.

If you have begun to question your own sanity, you may be in a relationship with an antisocial type. Remember, an antisocial can't really appreciate your distress or experience and doesn't really care. Controlling each exchange and achieving the upper hand is a well-learned survival mechanism — even when control requires subtle feigning of empathy and caring. Although all of us hope to enter into a partnership that is relatively equal and balanced, dangerous PDPs are not capable of such mutuality. Antisocials display characteristic indifference and sometimes even callousness toward the hardship and suffering of others. If you expect this person to be present for you, you are likely to be repeatedly let down. Keep in mind, this deficit may not signify a lack of desire to be empathetic but, as the brain scan research noted above suggests, a biological deficit in this area. It is unreasonable to expect the antisocial partner to "learn" empathy.

As a partner, you may find the dangerous personality to be shallow and artificial. What at first seemed charming and emotionally engaging now seems hollow and self-serving. Dangerous partners harbor high opinions of themselves and can be glib and overconfident about their skills. They don't hesitate to brag or to share their strong opinions. While they love to debate, they have little capacity or patience for others' opinions or thoughts. They can move easily into verbal sparring and become hostile and aggressive with little warning. As a partner you will feel like you can never win an argument.

Infidelity is another frequent problem with someone who has a dangerous personality. In fact, a trademark of the antisocial type is the failure to maintain monogamous relationships. Expect this person to have multiple sexual partners and numerous short-term relationships. Remember, the antisocial has terribly poor impulse control and a deficit when it comes to appreciating the consequences of his actions. As sensation seekers, partners with this personality type will act on their sexual urges in order to meet their immediate needs. And when you discover these indiscretions, the antisocial partner is likely to be indifferent, blow it off, or attempt to evade or lie to get out of the situation.

Finally, the antisocial's chronic irresponsibility can be death to a relationship. This partner never seems to hold up his end of the bargain financially or otherwise. Expect to be left with all the responsibility financially, occupationally, and for raising any children. When confronted with his failure to contribute or follow through, the antisocial may make sincere-sounding promises to reform and become more reliable, may blame you for being too demanding, or may simply ignore you. Life with an antisocial partner may soon begin to feel like life with an oppositional child.

Why Am I Attracted to Dangerous Partners?

Now that you have become informed about dangerous partners, it may be helpful to reflect on how you might fall for this type in the first place and whether you have a history of attraction to antisocial types. If you are involved with an antisocial, you were attracted to someone who

- violates the boundaries and rules of your relationship.
- lies to you and cons you.
- is impulsive in your relationship and won't plan ahead.
- is aggressive physically or verbally toward you.
- has a blatant disregard for your safety and that of your children.
- expects you to be solely responsible for your life together emotionally and financially.
- is indifferent to your feelings and needs.

We can imagine that reading this list is disheartening. Yet, if you are attracted to the dangerous type, you are not alone. There is something compelling about the charisma that antisocial personalities can exude; it may be enough to keep you coming back for more. And when things are going well in this relationship they are REALLY going well. In these moments, you may feel like you are part of a finely tuned, exciting, and mutual relationship. Your partner may, at times, come across as skillfully attentive and caring. During these periods, it is easy to delude yourself into believing that things will get better.

Dangerous personalities are quite shrewd at reading people; your antisocial partner is likely to know just how far he can push you and when he needs to rein his behavior in. There may be something that has bound you to this dance of distance and intimacy with an irresponsible partner. Perhaps there is something about your own psychology that makes this kind of relationship especially appealing.

It is easy to understand how one can fall head over heals for an antisocial partner. It is easy to be charmed and caught up in the excitement and confidence that this partner initially exudes. It naturally feels good to be wooed and cared for by an attractive person who seems to intuitively read you. The antisocial partner will initially display a convincing aura of smooth charm, good humor, and boundless confidence. Interesting, engaging, and maybe even a bit enticing precisely because he has a rough edge or a naughty boy persona (think James Dean), you will soon come to discover that the first impression is largely a false impression. We understand that this is often a difficult realization, but we would rather that you recognize now that your antisocial partner is probably lying, manipulating, and faking to get his way and to get in with you.

A defining feature of antisocial personality types is a basic lack of regard for the feelings and needs of others. Initially, she may have presented herself to you as having very clear boundaries; her independent toughness may have been alluring. But you have no doubt discovered over time that this person has essentially no empathy and no ability to connect with others' pain or deep feelings. Her connections to people are shallow and don't feel sincere. In addition to this emotional disconnect, you will find the antisocial partner turning her well-tuned manipulative skills to the task of twisting your words and concerns around so that soon you are questioning the validity of both your own feelings and whether or not the demands you are making of your partner are even reasonable. So what is it about dangerous partners that attracts you? Did you come from a home in which your job was to pursue and to try to connect with an antisocial or emotionally distant parent? Or have you taken on your antisocial partner as a challenge, believing you can change this partner because you are different from her past partners? Another possibility is that if antisocial relationships have become the norm for you, somewhere along the line your self-esteem has taken a hit and you are settling for less in a relationship than you deserve.

Person's with this personality style typically have histories of short-lived relationships, infidelity in relationships, and sometimes multiple short marriages. Needless to say, the ability to trust this person may be compromised from the start. Do you have a pattern of becoming involved with people who cannot be faithful to you, or do you too easily overlook these indiscretions? If you do, we encourage you to consider why. Was one of your parents chronically unfaithful? Are you too willing to chalk up affairs to his "just being a guy?" Now is the time to pause and ask yourself why you are putting yourself into relationships that are doomed to disappoint you from the start. It is especially difficult to move on from infidelity when you have reason not to trust your partner and when your needs are naturally overlooked in the relationship. If you find yourself staying in a relationship with a partner who is repeatedly unfaithful, you may be deluding yourself with a fantasy such as "he really intends to change this time." Alternatively, you may have become so dependent that you are willing to stay in an abusive relationship because it beats the alternative — being alone.

The catch-22 for people in relationships with dangerous personalities is that they can start to lose perspective of their own rights, needs, and wants. You will be repeatedly exploited, manipulated, and ultimately left to assume primary responsibility for income, the household, and, often, the children. You may become so used to being controlled and always "cleaning up" for your antisocial partner that you may find yourself waking up one day and wondering what happened to the strong, independent person you used to be. At some point, you will have to admit that you have become lover and parent to a difficult child — a big one at that.

If you find that becoming involved with antisocial partners is a pattern for you, it may help you to ask the question: Why do I end up in relationships where I ultimately feel victimized, used, and manipulated? Being in a relationship with an antisocial personality can be emotionally crushing. What is it about you and your life history that may lure you to these sorts of relationships? Were you treated this way as a child or were you somehow given the message that you deserved less than an honest relationship with someone of integrity? Do you constantly labor under the sad fantasy that if you try hard, it will be enough to finally "tame" your wild, out-of-control, charming partner? Do you find that over the course of these relationships you slowly start to lose sense of who you are and what is important to you? If you find that the answer to any of these questions is "yes," then we recommend you take some time out for self-examination with the help of a professional.

Finally, never forget that your charming and wily antisocial partner can be dangerous to you on multiple levels. It is easy to overlook the potential danger in this relationship when the abuse is limited to emotional or verbal mistreatment. But by continuing to place yourself in these relationships or by continuing to remain in one, you are giving yourself the subtle, or not so subtle, message that you are not worthy of more. Your partner is self-absorbed and motivated exclusively by his own desires. If you don't take care of your own needs, they will go unmet. And if you are not vigilant, you may become the victim of physical violence. This is a good time to carefully reflect on why you may not be keeping yourself safe.

Living with an Antisocial

If your current partner is the dangerous type, you must decide whether to stay in this unbalanced relationship or leave. We need to be very frank with you when we emphasize that continuing in a relationship with someone with antisocial personality traits can be dangerous (especially when the personality traits are severe). In our experience as clinicians, we have found that persons with dangerous personalities have traits that tend be deeply entrenched, chronic, and only rarely prone to change. You should not hold out high hope for lasting change in your antisocial partner's manipulation, exploitation, and disregard for your needs. We strongly recommend that you accept the fact that this relationship is not healthy for you and that you strongly consider getting out.

Having erred on the side of bluntness, we also recognize that you may ultimately, for a variety of reasons, decide to stay in this relationship. You may believe your partner's antisocial features are not as severe and therefore less likely to present risks for you. Or, you may have children together and you may feel that your partner's behavior has not (yet) had adverse outcomes for the children. Or, if married, you may be quite committed to honoring your marriage vows. Each of these rationales must be considered by the person living with an antisocial. If you decide to stay, we hope the following tips help your relationship run more smoothly.

Change Will Come in Tiny Increments

In order to meet the criteria of antisocial personality a person has a long history, dating back to at least adolescence, of deceitful, manipulative, disruptive behavior that violates boundaries and norms of relationships and society. Change, then, will not come easily or quickly. Person's with a dangerous personality typically do not see or understand their own dysfunctional thoughts and behaviors and they are certainly not bothered or upset by them. Antisocial partners try to convince you that your unhappiness with the relationship is your problem, not theirs. Expect small changes and don't get your hopes too high!

Take Necessary Precautions for Your Safety

Because person's with dangerous personalities may be irresponsible and reckless, you may find yourself in situations that are not safe for you or others. Remember that some persons with antisocial characteristics are abusive; therefore, please use all of your resources to ensure that you are safe. This may mean that you need to look for alternative living conditions until you and your partner are in therapy, or it may mean increasing your social support system so that you have other people to call on for assistance. This is truly a time to ensure that you (and your children, if you have them) have others whom you can count on for support and reality checks as needed. If you have children, be on guard for their emotional and physical safety. If your partner has become threatening or has a history of violence, be perfectly clear that you will call the police immediately if threatened or abused, and always follow through. And if there is any evidence of infidelity by your partner, for goodness sake, please avoid unprotected sex and the very real risk of exposing yourself to a sexually transmitted disease. Do not hesitate to secure the services of lawyers, financial advisors, private detectives, and physicians.

Kindly but Firmly Hold Your Partner Accountable

It is the M.O. of any antisocial partner to try to slip out of trouble and leave you holding the bag. While it is natural for most people to want to restore order in their lives when there are messes, this is one place where you need to hold your partner accountable for taking care of his own messes. Do not cover up for your partner; this would amount to enabling the behavior and ensuring that no change will occur. Why should he change when you're kind enough to clean up his messes? If you waffle on this point, your partner will definitely push your limits and ultimately exploit you to no end. By setting and enforcing limits, by calling the police, and by demanding separation when the time comes, you are creating the best possible scenario for change. And when you do confront, use positive self-assertion in the form of "I" statements that communicate assertiveness; let your partner know that you mean business.

Trust but Verify

When dealing with the Soviet Union, President Ronald Reagan coined the phrase *Trust but verify* to mean "Yes, we will trust the Soviets to abide by the nuclear treaties they have signed, but just to make sure, we will be engaging in intensive intelligence gathering to be certain our trust is founded!" It seems to us that this is also excellent advice when it comes to dealing with an antisocial partner. Antisocials lie compulsively; they often lie even when there is absolutely nothing to gain from doing so. For this reason, you should strongly consider requiring proof or evidence that your partner is where he says he is, that he is maintaining employment, that he is paying the bills, and that he is generally doing what he says he is. For example, when a partner has lied about other relationships, a condition for allowing him to have one more chance might be that he provide you funds for hiring a private detective whom you will employ randomly or whenever you feel the need to verify your partner's fidelity.

Therapy Is Not Likely to Be Helpful

Persons with this personality type do not feel any need or desire to enter into therapy; they simply don't believe they have a problem. It's everyone else and the world in general that has a problem! When you request counseling, expect heavy resistance from your partner about entering into any professional relationship. Don't be surprised if your partner tries to push the relational problems onto you as your own. Or you may find that your partner begins trying to convince you that he, or the two of you, can address your problems without outside interference. If your partner does agree to enter into therapy, it may be merely an attempt to appease you and keep you around. Research indicates that antisocial adults do not persist in treatment for long. They generally undermine the therapist, have a poor history of attendance, and learn the therapy lingo without making any genuine personal change.

When It's Time to Leave

If your partner truly meets criteria for a diagnosis of antisocial personality disorder, it is difficult to imagine that there will not come a time when you are unable or unwilling to continue in a relationship with him. This partner will be pervasively irresponsible, unreliable, impulsive, prone to vengeance and fighting, incapable of all but the most superficial attachments to others, insensitive to your needs, disloyal, and prone to manipulative and exploitive behavior. We will therefore not be surprised if you decide that you, and any children involved, will be considerably healthier without this person in your lives. Because the antisocial partner can be dangerous, please exercise caution and good judgment when leaving. First, protect yourself physically by calling the police, family members, and friends when you make the break. Get a restraining order if needed and have friends with you at all times when you move out. Second, protect your finances immediately by talking to your bank and protecting your personal assets. Third, have an attorney walk through the process of separation with you — especially if you are married and/or your assets are combined. An antisocial partner will seek to exploit you up until the bitter end — and often long afterward. Be firm, no-nonsense, and use trustworthy third parties to communicate with your ex-partner.

Summary

We refer to the **Antisocial Personality Disorder** as a potentially dangerous partner for several reasons. The antisocial will be self-centered, incapable of genuine empathy, and unlikely to care about you on more than a superficial level. This person will manipulate, exploit, and violate you whenever this serves his or her best interests. Although exciting at times, relationships with the dangerous type will inevitably be shallow and sometimes quite costly — emotionally, economically, and even physically. We caution you to be vigilant and cautious about getting involved with the dangerous type.

CHAPTER 8

THE STORMY PARTNER
The Borderline Personality

Borderline Personality Checklist

✔ She is intensely fearful of abandonment and frequently interprets your behavior as rejecting.

✔ She has a history of intense, unstable, and volatile relationships.

✔ She has a very fragile self-image.

✔ She has a history of impulsive behavior (e.g., impulsive spending, sex, substance abuse, reckless driving, binge eating).

✔ She has made suicidal gestures or has mutilated herself.

✔ She has intense mood fluctuations (e.g., between depression, anxiety, and anger).

✔ She chronically feels "empty" and bored.

✔ She becomes inappropriately angry and lashes out verbally or physically.

If you have ever dated or loved a stormy partner, a person psychologists might diagnose with **Borderline Personality Disorder**, then there is little chance that you will soon, if ever, forget the experience. Borderlines tend to make an impression. This is largely because they act out repeatedly — often pulling their partners into what can only be described as relational quicksand. Life with a borderline partner typically begins with compelling excitement but just as quickly ends with shock, anger, or confusion. If you have dated or fallen in love with a partner who is volatile, impulsive, and prone to self-harm as a way of punishing self or others, or worse, if you have a record of involvement with partners who sound all too much like Zoë in the case study below, then it will behoove you to read this chapter very carefully.

Patrick's Story

I met Zoë one evening when I was at a nightclub with a friend. I noticed Zoë right away. She was extremely attractive and was dressed pretty seductively that night. She was alone, having a drink at the bar, and not looking especially cheerful. I sat down next to her and tried to make some conversation. It was slow going. She seemed pretty distrustful, and at first, I wasn't getting anywhere. She slowly started to talk and even smiled and laughed a little. We danced a few times. I was really attracted to her, and when we danced she got pretty physical — it actually startled me a bit. Things seemed to be going well until I said I needed to go check on my friend. I remember she said, "Fine" but seemed pretty icy about it. When I came back five minutes later, she was dancing with another guy and getting pretty close to him on the dance floor, looking over at me now and then as if to see how I would respond. We spent the rest of the evening together, dancing and talking. I remember feeling a little freaked out when she told me she was seeing a shrink because of some kind of abuse as a child, but I didn't worry too much about it at the time.

When I finally told her I needed to get going and that I'd like to call her sometime, she seemed momentarily panicked but then quickly became really sexual, touching me under the bar and urging me to have my friend get a ride home with someone else. I remember the intense and demanding look in her eyes. I think I was partly afraid, but mostly really aroused. Well, I did take her home to my apartment and it was pretty shocking. She was very aggressive sexually and I remember being both turned on and overwhelmed by her. When morning came, she teasingly demanded sex a couple more times, and it was afternoon before I convinced her to let me take her home. She wanted to see me again that evening, and the day after that. We started seeing each other every day and she stayed at my place more and more at night. Our relationship was mostly sexual from the start, but as time passed, Zoë became more and more demanding that we spend all our time together. She hated it when I went to work and started calling me there several times a day to "check in" and tell me that she loved me and that she had never loved anyone the way she loved me. When I left in the morning, she would go through this weird ritual of pouting and trying to convince me to stay with her. Sometimes, she would even start shouting things like "I thought you cared about me!" These episodes of anger seemed out of the blue, but when I came home she'd always be eager to make up as though nothing had happened. It was sort of like I never knew which Zoë I was going to find each time I saw her.

This was all happening in the space of ten days, and I began to get a little freaked out. My best friends and guys at work started raising their eyebrows and asking what was going on. They seemed to envy the constant sex but sort of hinted that Zoë was a bit too intense. This was confirmed for them when one of the guys spotted her sitting outside our offices one afternoon. I was really shaken up by this. She had taken the bus there without telling me and was just sitting on a bench outside, staring directly at the building, waiting for me to come out.

When I went outside and told Zoë she shouldn't have come without telling me and that I had work to do, she just lost it. It was bad because lots of people from the office were watching out their windows. She started screaming things like "Well fuck you, Patrick! I guess you just wanted to screw me and then blow me off, is that it? Fine, I'll just be your garbage then and you can toss me out like all the others!" She stormed off. I was humiliated and upset.

That evening after I returned home, Zoë called right away. She sounded drunk and said she had just taken some pills. She apologized for that afternoon and said she didn't deserve me and that she'd make sure I never had to worry about her again. She wouldn't tell me what she had taken or how much. She hung up the phone. Well, just as she knew I would, I raced to her place and found her on the floor looking really out of it. I noticed she also had some blood on her wrists. I panicked and called 911.

At the hospital, an ER doc explained that Zoë had only taken a few aspirin and that the cuts were quite superficial. He then took me into his office, closed the door, and said Zoë had come into the ER several times for similar gestures and that she had been admitted to the psychiatric ward of the hospital once after a more serious attempt a few years before. Needless to say, I was stunned. He said she had depression and some kind of personality problem that made her want to hurt herself now and then. He was sympathetic but said bluntly that this would probably be a long-term thing and that I should expect more trips to the ER in the future.

I did my best to hang in there with Zoë for a while after that and things would get better for a little while, but no matter what I did, it seemed she'd find a reason to accuse me of not loving her or getting ready to "run out" on her. I also began to learn more about her history and realized I was just one in a long line of guys she had been involved with. When she got really angry and insisted that I was going to dump her, she'd occasionally throw something out like, "No big deal, I'll find someone else." I know this was designed just to hurt me, but it took a toll.

After three months, we had a particularly bad fight and I actually did tell her to get out of my apartment. She marched strait into the bathroom, returned with a small bottle of pills and swallowed them all right in front of me. Another trip to the hospital. Well, that was really it. I was too scared to continue in the relationship. When Zoë was discharged, I took her home but said I needed more space and that things had been moving too fast. She sobbed and yelled — accusing me of being like other guys and just using her. She told me not to call her and that she never wanted to see me again. I felt sorry for her and ashamed of myself too. She called numerous times the next week, but I refused to get back together with her. About a week later, she left a fifteen-page letter in my screen door that was really weird. It rambled on about her childhood and about how insensitive I was and how she needed me but couldn't trust me. I never spoke with Zoë again after that. It was probably the most exhausting and disturbing three months of my life. Since that time, I have been extremely cautious about getting to know women really well before becoming emotionally or physically intimate.

The Stormy Personality

Adults with Borderline Personality Disorder — stormy personality types — will be among the most volatile and difficult people you will ever know.

The borderline person is a real-life relational tornado — ripping through your life with an intensity and negativity that may astound you. Interesting and exciting on occasion, the borderline suddenly erupts, becoming enraged or self-destructive. The main feature of the borderline syndrome is chronic and serious instability in relationships, self-image, emotion, and behavior. The term *borderline* was originally used to describe people thought to occupy the border between regular neuroses (e.g., anxiety, depression) and psychosis (i.e., out of touch with reality or "crazy"). This is a very serious disorder. Becoming involved romantically with a borderline person may be the equivalent of hugging a porcupine or juggling hand grenades.

In the movie *Fatal Attraction*, Glenn Close plays the part of a seriously disturbed borderline woman. You may recall that she begins an intense affair with a married man played by Michael Douglas. After spending only one day with him, she begins demanding to see him constantly. When he becomes alarmed and attempts to limit contact with her, she becomes enraged and stalks him. At one point in the movie, she even slashes her wrists in order to make him stay and care for her. Although most borderline adults do not stalk or attempt to harm their lovers, they are volatile, unpredictable, emotionally unstable, prone to self-harm, and terrified of abandonment.

The defining characteristic of Borderline Personality Disorder is intense fear of abandonment by a caregiver or lover. Not only do they expect everyone they care for to abandon them, they help to arrange this by demanding excessive time and attention and responding with rage and rejection when they believe they are about to be abandoned (even though this is often not their partner's intent). A borderline person will interpret lateness, changes in plans, etc. as sure evidence that they are about to be rejected. The borderline's response to this may be anger or depression — often accompanied by impulsive self-harm or a suicidal gesture of some sort. Such behaviors are impulsive and desperate attempts to avoid the terror of being alone — something they have frantically tried to avoid since childhood.

Borderline partners have a history of intense but chaotic relationships. While they initially idealize new partners ("You are the best! You are the only one who can really understand me!"), they quickly become disillusioned and disappointed and respond by angrily devaluing their partner for failing them in some way. Borderline partners have no boundaries and will move the relationship from first gear to overdrive in the first few weeks or even days of courting. For example, it is not uncommon for a borderline person to sexualize the relationship early on and to demand nearly constant time with a new love interest. She will disclose excessively — perhaps sharing extremely personal material during the first few meetings. Many experts believe that when the borderline rejects a new friend, lover, or caregiver, she is often using this as a means of circumventing or preempting what she anticipates will be another painful abandonment.

The self-image of the borderline is ill formed and incomplete. Her sense of self is fragile and constantly shifting. Although they often see themselves as primarily bad or evil, they may also feel nonexistent or anonymous. They tend to feel best when intensely involved with another person whom they see as nurturing and reassuring. However, because all their relationships are volatile and short lived, they are destined to constantly return to a state of self-loathing and identity diffusion.

Borderlines are impulsive in ways that are usually self-destructive. It is common for such people to make sudden (and unwise) decisions about spending money, having sex, using substances, binge eating, or driving. Such impulsiveness nearly always follows problems in a relationship or at the end of a relationship — even if this is only a real threat in the fantasy of the borderline. In addition to impulsiveness, the borderline person may engage in self-mutilation. It is quite common for borderlines to have numerous lacerations or burn scars on their arms and wrists (we have even seen scars from battery acid). Although difficult to fully understand this behavior, it usually occurs when the person is feeling especially worthless or when he is feeling so numb and disconnected that it serves to assure him that he is indeed alive. Borderlines will also often report that they sometimes self-mutilate because it is easier to deal with physical pain than the psychological torment and distress that they are enduring.

Emotional instability is an essential component of the borderline syndrome. This instability may include rapid cycling among primarily negative emotions such as depression, anger, irritability, and anxiety — with short periods of relative calm or even positive emotionality in between. Mood will be highly connected to whether they feel secure and nurtured in a relationship or anticipate rejections and abandonment — which is quite often. Unfortunately, the emotional life of many borderlines can be characterized by everyday depression and despair punctuated by shorter periods of stability and apparent well-being. Because borderlines are constantly working to avoid feelings of emptiness and boredom, they will often "stir things up" emotionally in relationships merely to experience something other than isolation with themselves.

In some cases, a severely borderline person may actually dissociate or appear to lose contact with reality in the here and now; that is, he may appear "spacey" and unaware of his identity or immediate surroundings. Such dissociative episodes are likely to come on the heels of a relationship trauma such as perceived abandonment by a lover or friend.

What Makes a Borderline?

Stormy types have never developed a solid, well-integrated sense of identity; even as adults, they simply don't feel secure or comfortable in their own skin. Think of their identity as porous and fragile. Borderlines will use you for affirmation and confirmation that they do exist and perhaps that they do have some miniscule worth after all. So how did your borderline partner get that way?

Here is a near certainty: Things went very poorly in the early childhood experience of a borderline man or woman. In the vast majority of cases, their childhoods were defined by chaos, perceived abandonment, severe neglect, or traumatic emotional, sexual, or physical abuse. As children, borderline types probably lived in families that were chaotic (e.g., serious fights, overt affairs, violence, incest) and in which the stormy child had her emotional needs ignored or derided. These children may have been attacked or ridiculed when they attempted to separate or establish their own identity. Add to this picture the real likelihood that severe emotional, sexual, or physical abuse took place and it is easy to see why this child struggles to feel worthwhile (versus evil and worthless) in adulthood.

Some studies suggest that as many as 60 to 80 percent of borderline women were sexually abused as children or adolescents. This may be one of the reasons a full 75 percent of those diagnosed as borderline are women. This fact also helps explain why some borderline lovers will have periods of dissociation in which they appear to "space out" or go away from the present for short episodes. Dissociating may have been an adaptive strategy employed by the borderline as a child. While learning to dissociate during an overwhelming experience of suffering was a wise strategy for a child, it obviously becomes dysfunctional and disruptive when it lingers in adulthood.

Not all borderline adults were sexually or physically abused as children. Some experienced more subtle but persistent neglect or emotional harm. Over time, they began to internalize many of the messages conveyed by the environment — especially caregivers (e.g., "you are irrelevant, you are invisible, you are bad, you are the cause of all the chaos in this family"). Whatever the mix of childhood ingredients, it is clear that by the time this person arrives at adulthood, he is void of the mostly positive and stable identity that most of us take for granted.

The Borderline as Partner

If there is one personality disorder in this entire book that is *most* likely to cause you confusion and anguish, it is the borderline type. If you believe that you may be sailing into a relationship with a borderline person, you had better batten down the hatches and tie yourself to the mast; you are heading into a hurricane. If you have been in the relationship for some time now, you know what we are talking about. You may have become all too accustomed to walking on eggshells and anticipating the next big fluctuation in mood, the next impulsive act, or the accusation that you don't really care.

In all likelihood, your stormy partner's primary issue will be an almost morbid and pervasive fear of abandonment. In his view, *everyone* — including you — will ultimately leave him alone and no one can really be trusted. At the outset of your relationship, you will be idealized as "the one" the borderline has been searching for. He will quickly become dependent on you — pushing for near constant time together and close physical proximity. The borderline partner will need constant nurturing and attention and may make you uncomfortable right away; both the sticky neediness and the excessively intimate self-disclosure may make you uneasy.

Eventually — usually this does not take long — you will *fail* in the eyes of the borderline partner; that is, you will prove to be inadequate when it comes to meeting all of her needs for constant attention, nurturing, and proximity. The question is really not if you will fail but, simply, *when*. We suspect that if you are dating this person, you have already failed many times. Like everyone else the borderline has been involved with relationally, you will fail to deliver the emotional goods she demands. Please know that it is not possible to meet the numerous and ever-fluctuating demands of the borderline. It is at this point in your relationship that the real tempest will begin. The borderline may respond to your failure with hostile control — attempting to demand more of your time and resources. She will respond with rage when you try to set boundaries or insist on more time alone. Alternatively, the borderline lover may begin to angrily and sarcastically devalue you, indicating that you are "just like all the others," meaning all bad and abandoning. Through hostile rejection, the borderline will be protecting herself from the pain of another perceived ending.

During this storm of anger and hostility, you should not be surprised when your borderline lover becomes emotionally and behaviorally impulsive — even dangerous, though she usually directs the dangerous behavior at herself. This impulsivity is primarily verbal and emotional. So, when you are ten minutes late for a date or need to do something on your own for an evening, you may hear "Fine! Fuck you! Just leave then and don't come back!" Impulsivity can also be physical and take the form of suicidal gestures (wrist cutting or small overdoses of medication), stalking (she follows you around or waits outside your home without invitation), or in rare cases, physical threats directed at you. This may also be the time the borderline partner will engage in reckless driving, binge eating or drinking, or impulsive spending. And stormy partners have been known to impulsively seek out other sexual partners. After a fight or to get back at you for what she believes is your intent to leave her, this partner might engage in brief affairs. Of course, you will be blamed for this!

Perhaps the most troubling aspect of your relationship with a borderline person will be the way you feel when the relational walls are tumbling down. Although you don't deserve it, you will be the target of sometimes vicious verbal assaults. Your borderline partner will suddenly become hostile, sarcastic, and bitter, perhaps verbally attacking you in public. This behavior may be rapidly followed by shame, guilt, and a sense of unworthiness on his part — perhaps eliciting self-mutilating behavior. In any case, you will be constantly on the ropes, confused about your contribution to the borderline's shocking and unpredictable behavior. You will be exhausted.

Considering that borderline people have failed to consolidate a reasonably coherent sense of self, it is not surprising that she will constantly fail in romantic relationships. Without some sense of self-as-constant, or self as "OK" apart from others, it is nearly impossible to be in a healthy and well-boundaried relationship with another. The borderline partner will never understand the notion of a boundary signifying the place where she ends and you begin; rather, she will make efforts to merge or become enmeshed with you. If you are like most people, you will respond to this suffocation by seeking some space and distance, which will of course trigger a desperate rage and fear of abandonment in your partner.

A relationship with a partner suffering from Borderline Personality Disorder will be doomed from the outset. Even professional psychotherapists often work hard to avoid accepting borderline clients. They are extremely difficult to manage and setting reasonable interpersonal boundaries with them is a constant battle. They will rage, make suicide gestures, and disregard limits you attempt to set. When a relationship is beginning to go well, a borderline lover will sabotage and undermine his own happiness, finding greater familiarity and comfort in rage, depression, and abandonment. Although you must ultimately make the decision about staying or not staying with a borderline partner, you must make the decision fully informed that your relationship will be stormy from start to finish.

Why Am I So Attracted to Stormy Partners?

Consistent attraction to the stormy type means that you are attracted to someone who

- is intense, unstable, and volatile at times.
- fears abandonment and interprets much of your behavior as rejecting.
- has a very fragile sense of self-esteem.
- is prone to extreme rage, acting out, and sullen depression.
- occasionally threatens suicide, takes small overdoses, or self-mutilates.
- chronically feels empty and bored.
- may lash out at you emotionally and physically.

Reading this list, you may wonder if you are just plum crazy for loving a stormy personality type. But if you have managed to fall in love quickly with a borderline partner, or if you find that you are frequently attracted to the borderline type, you are not alone. Remember: A salient trait of this stormy personality type is a history of numerous short-term relationships. Obviously, many people experience the same initial attraction to the borderline type — probably even to your partner! There are several facets of this person's behavior that can easily reel us in. Beyond sheer physical attraction, certain elements of the borderline can intrigue, beguile, and snare many of us; it takes deliberate reflection and caution early on to avoid getting sucked in.

Perhaps the biggest draw for many is the fact that relationships with borderlines often begin with great intensity and excitement. This person has poor boundaries and seems unfamiliar with the concepts of caution and propriety. In terms of the sexual dimension, things may go from zero to a hundred miles an hour in a matter of days or even hours. Stormy partners are prone to reckless behavior in many areas and you may find this novel and exciting. It may be especially alluring to many men when someone they meet appears intensely interested in them and is sexually aggressive and willing to throw caution to the wind in most regards. If you are particularly attracted to excitement and intensity in a relationship or if your own self-esteem as a dating partner is poor, the borderline may be a breath of fresh air and a surprising change from the humdrum dating scene you are accustomed to.

It is also easy to see why you might be attracted to stormy partners when you remember that they often idealize partners at the outset of any relationship. As black-and-white thinkers, they tend to see any new romantic interest as all good, wonderful, perfect, and the answer to everything wrong in their lives. You will be idealized — even worshipped — at the start. For some of us, such intense and thorough adulation can be intoxicating, arousing, and gratifying. It will be easy to believe that this is what life with your borderline partner will always be like: You as the star of the show — with seemingly endless reservoirs of sexual and emotional intensity from your new costar. What could be wrong?

Even after the initial period of idealization runs its course — this typically happens quickly — and the roller coaster world of ups and downs sets in, some find this kind of intensity alluring as well. After the short honeymoon phase of this relationship, the soap opera commences and you can anticipate your new partner fluctuating between seething anger, sullen silence, bottomless depression, self-harming behavior, and euphoric happiness and sexual intensity. Although most will quickly be exhausted (and at times terrified) by this rapidly shifting behavior, some love it. If you are one of the latter, it may be a result of your own early experience in a family that was equally chaotic, or perhaps you lived with a parent who also had pathological mood states that you were left to manage. There may be something comfortable and familiar about this pattern to you — even if it is absurdly unhealthy. Also, at an unconscious level, your efforts to "cure" your new partner may actually be an effort to reconcile with your past — an opportunity for the child to cure the parent who never got better and never affirmed you. Whatever your specific attraction to the dangerous twister of life with a borderline, it may be worth exploring why you are routinely drawn to this type.

Some people are drawn to the sullen, quiet, mercurial mood states of stormy personalities. After the intensity of the initial reckless connection subsides and the first lows set in, we may find our partner's' angry, withdrawn, disengaged jags intriguing and mysterious. Those among us who have been trained to be healers and caretakers might also find this irresistible. We consistently rise to the challenge of making our partner feel better and take the bait every time she threatens suicide or leaves us guessing whether this will be the occasion on which another small overdose or wrist-cutting episode occurs. Although our healthier friends may ask why we stay and shake their heads each time we rush to the ER to rescue our borderline partner, we just can't seem to break free from our sense of obligation to her.

Finally, you may have fallen for a stormy partner initially precisely because borderlines, on first meeting, often appear much healthier than they actually are. Especially when symptoms are not as severe, a borderline's pathologic mood states, relational storms, and self-harming behavior may not emerge right away. By the time they do, you may be far enough along in the relationship that a genuine connection has developed; you may have begun to develop high hopes that this is "the one." When the bottom drops out and you are plunged into a soap opera that you never anticipated, you can feel disoriented and willing to attribute the strange behavior changes to circumstances or worse, blame yourself.

For a wide range of reasons, it is easy to be attracted to stormy partners. They can appear quite healthy at first. They are often intensely exciting and hypersexual at the start of a relationship. They may exude a magnetic attraction for people who need to rescue and caretake. And the good times — even though few and far between — can be very good, especially in contrast to the intensely bad times life with a borderline will certainly afford you.

A Word of Caution

As noted in the foregoing sections, stormy partners are prone to periods of dark moods and suicidal gestures. While this behavior is part of the borderline personality spectrum, it is also true that adults suffering with this syndrome are more prone to clinical depression. Your partner's suicidal thinking and depressed moods may actually signal a genuine mood disorder that may require medication and therapy from a professional. At times, antidepressant drugs can be quite useful in preventing severe depressive states in stormy partners. It would be unfair to assume that your partner's low moods are merely the result of his strange personality pattern, and it will often behoove you to encourage your partner to seek professional help.

How should you respond to your partner's suicidal threats or gestures? Be careful! It is nearly always the case that suicidal threatening and minor self-mutilation is done for the purpose of manipulation, attention, and punishing partners for perceived abandonment or simply to feel alive and connected to life. BUT, borderline partners are more likely to die of suicide than other personality types covered in this guide. Eventually, they may get so depressed or desperate that they will deliberately take their own lives. Or, they may inadvertently take too large an overdose or make lacerations that are lethal — even though it was not their intent to actually kill themselves; their desire to garner attention and punish themselves or others may simply go too far.

One of us once treated a borderline woman who made about twenty-five suicide threats during a period of six months. She would call the office and say something like "Thank you so much for trying to help me. I know you did everything you could. I'm on the roof of my apartment building. Goodbye." At other times, she would finish a counseling session with something such as "Thanks for everything. I need to go now. Good thing I've been saving a lot of pills in the glove box of my car. . . ." She would then stand up and bolt from the office. Each time, the therapist was forced to call the police and have her evaluated and admitted to the hospital involuntarily for being a suicidal risk. At times, she actually made lacerations on her wrists or took small quantities of pills, but most of the time she did not. It was simply impossible to "guess" whether she really meant it each time; each occurrence required a full response from the provider.

The point is, you must understand that suicidal threats and gestures are part of stormy partners' M.O. and respond with calm limit-setting each time. And yet you must also take each threat or gesture seriously and never assume that they "don't really mean it," or "could never actually do it." At times, they do.

Living with a Borderline Partner

After reading this chapter, it may be quite difficult for someone who has never been attracted to the stormy type to understand the allure of a borderline partner. In fact, the thought of engaging a borderline person in anything beyond a distant and curious wave may seem crazy. We understand. Among all the potential partners in this book on difficult partners, this may be the very toughest person to sustain a relationship with. The borderline adult is emotionally unstable, erratic, and sometimes even volcanic — eruptions in the form of angry tantrums or self-mutilation may take you entirely off guard. And to be honest, most of us, professional therapists included, will just get exhausted by and sometimes hopeless about the borderline person.

Yet some reading this guide will be so in love with or connected to a borderline partner that they are willing to hang in there and try. Although we can't recommend this course — it is doubtful that life with a stormy partner will ever offer much stability let alone peace — we understand and respect the decision to stay and try. If you are going to "give it a go" with a borderline partner or if you are married to someone you think suffers from this personality disorder, we offer a few tips and strategies for making the road a little less bumpy. But make no mistake about this: The road will be very long; there will probably be breakdowns along the way, and the trip will be fraught with forces and events that seem bent on keeping you from your destination. Only the most tenacious travelers will make it.

Professional Help Is Mandatory

Here is a paradox: Although treatment for Borderline Personality Disorder is very long and only marginally successful, it is an absolute necessity. Why? Even if you are the most patient and loving partner in the universe, it will not be enough to "cure" a person with such a fragmented and wounded sense of self. If you are a natural born rescuer and healer, you might not want to believe this. It is tempting to believe that love will be enough. It will not be enough. Take our advice and avail yourself of professional help. By this we mean leverage your borderline partner into therapy as soon as possible. Help her locate a mental health practitioner with expertise in the treatment of Borderline Personality Disorder — these therapists inevitably make up a fairly limited group — then, make full participation in therapy a condition of your continuation in the relationship. Your partner needs to understand that your insistence on professional help is one expression of your love and that you will not be willing to watch her continue in a spiral of self-destructive behavior. Quite often, the best treatment for this condition will involve a combination of psychotherapy with a stable, long-term therapist and medication for depression.

Expect Turmoil!

One of the biggest mistakes partners of stormy types make is to expect that their partners *not* act stormy! That is, far too many people who try to live with a borderline lover get themselves into psychological trouble by demanding that their very disturbed partner miraculously "get better" and stop acting like someone with a chronic personality disorder. This is just crazy. Your stormy partner will have a lifetime of practice when it comes to expecting abandonment, arranging it in each relationship, and then reacting with characteristic rage and self-harm. Your partner will be a master at sabotaging relationships and undermining his happiness. That is what borderlines do. Extensive and effective therapy may help reduce and even eliminate the worst of these patterns, but they will probably exist in some form for a long time. If you are really committed to living with a borderline partner, don't make things worse by disturbing yourself when your partner is unpredictable, volatile, or difficult to be with. Expect it. Then, if things do begin to improve, you will be pleasantly surprised.

Accept the Reparenting Role

Like it or not, you will occupy a parental role with your partner at times. The sooner you can accept this, the easier it will be to understand both your partner's behavior and the strange dynamic in your relationship. Your borderline partner has developed several calcified schemas or ways of seeing the world — typically generated in experiences with parents — that will lead him to expect and assume abandonment, neglect, disapproval, and his own defectiveness and worthlessness. Because parents probably did a bad job of parenting the borderline partner, he will approach your relationship with a sense of basic mistrust — assuming that any minute you too will become rejecting. Although knowing that your partner sees you through the eyes of a child at times may not be very appealing romantically, it will help you to understand your partner's odd and infantile behavior. This appreciation may help you to become less defensive and angry with your partner. This awareness might also help you to be more careful, calm, and thoughtful about how you choose to react to stormy behavior; if you can provide healthy (emotionally corrective) responses to your partner, his improvement will probably be hastened.

Do Not Reinforce Self-Destructive Behavior

It is easy to inadvertently perpetuate your stormy partner's suicidal threats and gestures by responding in ways that reinforce them. Here are some responses we recommend avoiding: (1) rushing to your partner's side, even though it means neglecting your other responsibilities, each time she suggests a suicidal thought or makes a suicidal gesture; (2) becoming frantic and pleading with your partner when suicidal talk or behavior occurs; (3) responding with hostility and rejection, thereby confirming that you will abandon her when the going gets rough; and (4) becoming provocative and accusing your partner of manipulation — perhaps even daring her to "do it."

Whatever you do, do not unwittingly reward your partner for threatening and manipulating. This will require profound patience, nerves of steel, and the ability to see your partner's behavior as equivalent to that of a child who is pushing the limits and testing a parent's resolve to be firm. Although you should never disregard or ignore suicidal talk or self-mutilating behavior in a partner, you should be just as careful not to respond in a way that gratifies and rewards her with attention, caretaking, or assumption of responsibility for her' decisions. Have a predetermined plan for responding to suicide threats or self-harm, share this with your partner in advance, and then follow through. This will probably mean calling your partner's mental health provider, calling the police (911), and alerting other family members or friends as needed. But this must be done in a calm, disengaged, contractual way so that your partner reaps no emotional gain. Here is what you will be communicating: I love you; I will not sit by and watch you speak or behave in a self-destructive way; I will not give you more attention when you act out; I will not drop what I am doing to take care of you; I will make sure you get the necessary assistance you need.

Challenge Black-and-White Thinking

One of the most troubling and aggravating aspects of life with a borderline partner will be his tendency to see and interpret everything through a black-and-white grid. Psychologists refer to this as *dichotomous thinking* and it can wreak havoc on a relationship. For instance, your partner will say (and believe), "You hate me," instead of "You are really mad about something I did." He will say, "I can't trust you at all; you're just like all the rest," instead of "I felt abandoned when you called the police after my overdose." Because your partner sees the world in stark right or wrong, black or white, and love or hate terms, it is very hard to occupy a reasonable middle in your relationship for very long. Your challenge then is to encourage your partner to accept shades of gray in perceptions and beliefs. So, when he says, "You hate me," you might try a response such as "I was unhappy about your threat to hurt yourself, but I don't hate you. Does it seem likely that I would be here right now if I hated you?" The idea is to create discomfort with a black-and-white view of the world so that your partner begins to accept that you and the relationship defy simple categorizations.

Reinforce Strengths

Because your stormy partner will be so conditioned to expect abandonment and so convinced of her utter worthlessness, it is imperative that you become the broken record of praise and reinforcement in her life. Work hard at identifying your partner's gifts and talents and frequently mention these. These may include intelligence, a sense of humor, exuberance, creativity, or kindness. But because these elements of your partner's personhood have never been endorsed or praised, it will take consistent work on your part before she begins to take them in and accept them as legitimate. By emphasizing your partner's assets and helping to solidify a more positive sense of self, you are increasing the probability that she can understand and accept your commitment as genuine and perhaps warranted.

When It's Time to Leave

Adults with Borderline Personality Disorders usually have a long history of brief, tumultuous, and superficial relationships. Their relationships end. Please keep this in mind if you are embarking on a dating or more serious relationship with a stormy partner. Reaching the end of a relationship with a partner of this type probably has relatively little to do with you — even if you are just shy of a saint when it comes to patience and commitment. Remember that the borderline personality is programmed to sabotage relationships, to drive partners away, and to paradoxically be most "at home" when suffering from yet another perceived abandonment — even when the borderline partner worked hard (often unconsciously) to arrange this outcome!

Sadly, we predict that there may well come a time when your partner storms out or when you finally say enough is enough; for your own mental health, it is time to say goodbye. When this day arrives, we recommend telling your partner clearly and with no false promises that the relationship is over — PERIOD. Although it may fall on deaf ears, be clear that you continue to value and care about your partner but that a continued romantic relationship will not occur. We encourage you to expect acting out in the form of self-mutilation and suicidal threats. Be prepared to call the police or medical personnel if this should occur under any circumstances. An inpatient hospitalization or a visit to the ER may ensue; don't get sucked up in this. Instead, let professionals take care of your ex-partner. Finally, be prepared to set firm limits and boundaries around phone calls, drop-in visits, and even stalking if this should become an issue. The sooner and more fully you can make the break, the better it will be for both of you.

Summary

If you are fan of relational bedlam, if you savor never knowing what to expect from a partner, and if you don't mind constant chaos, frequent breakups, and a full-time job managing a partner's emotional crises, then the stormy partner may be just right for you. Of course, if you are attracted to these traits in a lover, we worry about your own mental health! Dating a borderline person will be disorienting, and staying in a relationship with a borderline person can become deeply confusing and depressing. When a new love interest displays extreme intensity, volatility, mood swings, or desperate clingy behavior, watch out!

CHAPTER 9

THE THEATRICAL PARTNER
The Histrionic Personality

Histrionic Personality Checklist

- ✔ She is uncomfortable in situations in which she is not the center of attention.
- ✔ She is often sexually seductive or provocative with other people.
- ✔ She tends to have shallow behavior that quickly changes.
- ✔ She utilizes physical appearance to draw attention to herself.
- ✔ Her speech is impressionistic and doesn't have much detail.
- ✔ She often has overly dramatic, exaggerated, and theatrical behavior.
- ✔ She is highly suggestible.
- ✔ She thinks that her relationships are more intimate and intense than they really are.

Do these traits remind you of your current partner or someone you have dated? When you are with this person, do you get the feeling that there isn't much substance to her opinions, thoughts, and actions? Does your partner frequently feel the need to be the center of attention and the life of the party? Life with the theatrical type will be entertaining but exhausting, stimulating but shallow. Read on to find out more about the theatrical or **Histrionic Personality Disorder** and how your relationship is likely to evolve with this person.

Tom's Story

I should have listened to my friends when they told me that I shouldn't date Bella. I met her at a strip club after all and I'm not sure why I thought it was a good idea. I do know that when I saw her she took my breath away. She was tall with dark hair and an incredible body. I had had more than a few beers, and I was with all my buddies having a good time. Despite all the other men in the club, Bella really came on to me and spent most of the evening giving me lap dances. Before I left I gave her my phone number, and she gave me hers (like other girls in the past). I never, in my wildest thoughts, expected to hear from her and I wasn't planning on calling her. I had a job in the financial district and was making decent money. I had lots of friends and an active social life. I was dating a few different people, most of them with lives and values similar to mine. I hadn't felt that "right connection" with anyone yet, but I was happy just hanging with my buddies and having a good time. I knew it would happen eventually but I wasn't in a big hurry.

Bella called me a few days later and I agreed to meet her one evening that she was off from work. I met her at a restaurant and when I walked in she was as exotic and beautiful as I remembered. She was dressed in tight jeans and a low-cut shirt, and I have to say I was instantly sucked in. She wasn't shy at all and, in fact, helped to ease that first date awkwardness. She was quick to tell me all about her life and her family and her dreams and hopes for the future. She told me she really wanted to be married and have kids. If I wasn't so attracted to her, I think I would have been overwhelmed and scared at how quickly it all started. We had dinner and a few drinks and ended up back at her place. One thing led to another and we had sex that night. She was totally uninhibited and more open than the other girls I had been with. It was a fun night, but I didn't expect to have another. She wasn't the type of girl I usually go for.

I couldn't stop thinking of Bella and while I knew it wasn't a good idea, I called her and we soon hooked up again. The crazy thing is that I didn't tell any of my buddies at first. I knew they would just give me grief for dating a stripper, and I didn't want to deal with it. I was actually pretty twisted up inside about it because I knew she wasn't right for me. But she sure was fun and easy to be with. She really seemed to dig me and was into what I said and did. She bought new clothes and lingerie and loved to have fashion shows for me to show off her purchases. Our sex life was unbelievable and I started spending most of my time with her.

Bella started pressuring me to meet my friends. She wanted to get to know them and be included in their plans. One night I decided to take her to a party a friend was throwing. She wore a really skimpy outfit and too much makeup. I wanted to ask her to change but didn't have the heart. My friends were taken aback by her, and I could tell they were trying hard to be polite. At one point in the evening, after she had a couple of drinks, she started hugging everyone and dancing suggestively with some of my friends. It was a bad scene and it didn't go over well with me or my friends' girlfriends.

When we went to restaurants or out in public she spoke too loudly and liked to draw attention to herself. One time she ran into her dentist at a concert and started hanging on him and introduced him to me as her "dear friend." Oh man! I was so embarrassed but not really surprised. She overemphasized her closeness to everyone, especially if she thought they were influential. She loved to drop names and it didn't take long for that to become old hat. I can't believe I glossed over it for so long.

I hated that she was a stripper, but she kept reassuring me that it was just a job and it was good money. But, I mean, she was out taking her clothes off for other guys, and she would get mad at me if I ever went out with my friends without her. She'd pout for days after that and I'd have to kiss her ass and tell her how great she was until she was over it. When I suggested she go out with her friends, she told me she didn't get along well with other girls. I wonder why! I'm still mad at myself for giving up six months of my life to hang out with her. I liked the way she initially loved to talk and just hang out and chat. But when I started getting at issues that I felt were important or if I wanted to have an in-depth conversation about politics or world issues, she couldn't go there with me. She had no opinions about anything meaningful at all. Ask her about fashion or makeup though, and she could go on forever. Sometimes, she'd try to take a stand on an issue like politics or religion but when I tried to have a debate with her or even a discussion, she had nothing to back up her initial thought. She was really beautiful, but there wasn't anything behind it.

My friends started really giving me a hard time about Bella. They stopped inviting me to parties because of her and I felt like I was leading a double life. I'd lie to cover up when I was out with her, and I was making up excuses to her about why I wasn't taking her out with my friends. It all became too much and, to be honest, Bella was exhausting. Life was all about her and I totally couldn't meet her high maintenance demands. It got to the point where it was too much being with her, and I couldn't do it anymore. I just got fed up one day and broke it off. Of course, her histrionics over the breakup were out of control and she begged me to make it work. Thankfully, I stuck to my guns and walked away. I couldn't be happier to have Bella out of my life. All the daily drama and high emotions are gone, and I find myself happier and more emotionally stable. I'm into dating boring girls now, with normal jobs and normal lives.

The Theatrical Personality

Have you ever heard the saying *It is the empty can that makes the most noise?* This nicely sums up the theatrical personality! This personality style essentially means lots of noise but very little substance. What you will notice with theatrical personality types is that they are very loud emotionally and love to be the center of attention. They go out of their way to ensure that they are noticed by others and, quite frankly, it makes them angry to not get the attention they feel they deserve. Emotions run high with this partner and when things are good, they are great; but when histrionic types don't get the attention they want, they can become quite volatile and demanding.

Theatrical partners share the common trait of being really "out there" with their appearance and behavior. What exactly do we mean by this? Typically, persons with this histrionic style wear suggestive or provocative clothes and are meticulous with their appearance. There is little that gives them more satisfaction than to be noticed by others. Therefore, a great deal of time is spent staying up on the latest trends, shopping, dressing, and grooming. They are keenly aware of others' appearance and want to ensure that they look better than those around them — and that everyone knows it!

Histrionic partners crave attention and compliments. If compliments are not forthcoming, they will fish for them until they feel sufficiently noticed. They love to be the "life of the party," and if they aren't they will engage in some sort of extreme behavior or create some sort of scene to make sure they are noticed. Theatrical partners have a flare for the dramatic. Their behavior is exaggerated, their opinions are overstated, and their appearance flamboyant. You don't miss this person in a crowd!

What becomes apparent, however, is that this style and the appearance of the person with a theatrical personality are really over the top. What at first appears to be careful attention to grooming and outlandish behavior is quickly revealed as a cry for attention. The problem lies in the fact that these partners' provocative dress and behavior is not just directed toward their partners, but toward everyone. It isn't uncommon for this partner to be flirtatious and overly friendly with just about anyone. Remember, it's all about attention and recognition. Sexually provocative behavior and in-your-face flirtation is a tried and true way to keep others riveted (at least for a while).

Romance is the name of the game for the theatrical partner. They love to wine and dine and flaunt themselves in an effort to create passion and intrigue. They deeply value closeness to others — although their relationships are usually very superficial — and they tend to look at relationships through rose-colored glasses. They fall head over heels quickly and become deeply passionate about partners. They have a fairy tale notion of relationships that can seem naïve and silly to other adults.

They quickly cross the line of familiarity with people and push for more intimacy than is appropriate to most people early in any relationship. For example, histrionic types are notorious for insisting on being on a first name basis with their physicians and other professionals. They love to drop names and to let others know how well connected they are. Of course, this behavior is merely one more way to bring attention to themselves. Histrionics exploit connections to others for the gratification and attention they reap.

Theatrical personalities are perfect for the stage. They are good actors in life and easily take on whatever role is best for them at the moment. This is reflected in their speech and their behavior. They are natural chameleons without realizing that they change colors on a whim to secure attention. Their speech is often shallow and dramatic, and their emotions also fluctuate with the demands of the situation. When we think of the histrionic person, the term *drama queen* comes to mind. Think of all the actors who sound like this, and then think about how difficult it seems to be for them to maintain long-term relationships. Many actors in Hollywood are theatrical personalities and it is mind boggling to think about how few of them stay married to anyone. These days, it seems as if their relationships change with each new movie and costar. Because theatrical types so desperately need the excitement and stimulation that accompany attention from new admirers, it is easy to see how they may grow bored with the same old partner.

Finally, the person with a histrionic, or theatrical, personality style rarely has her own deep thoughts or personal opinions. This partner's M.O. throughout life has been about impression management. Imagine being so concerned about the impression you create and the approval of others that you couldn't develop your own thoughts or convictions. The theatrical partner is very suggestible. Histrionics tend to be very trusting and to believe, even with little evidence, what others tell them. They incorporate others' opinions and thoughts as their own, and therefore they have a difficult time supporting these ideas. Deep, meaningful discussions about firmly held beliefs are unlikely, and if challenged she is likely to back down and adopt the opinions of her partner.

What Makes a Theatrical Personality?

How does one grow up to become a theatrical and attention-seeking adult? This is one of the least studied personality disorders. We know that histrionic personality disorder tends to be much more frequently diagnosed in women than men. There are some hypotheses as to the origins of this personality style. Clinical experience with histrionic adults indicates that as children they grew up in homes with an inconsistent parenting approach; they experienced insensitive noninvolvement alternating with periodic rewards for exhibitionist behavior. They were likely to have had a lack of adequate maternal attention and nurturance and consequently had to perform to get their needs met. Histrionics often got a lot of reinforcement and attention as children from being flamboyant and theatrical. At an early age, theatrical personalities learned how to manipulate others to get attention and nurturance. Finally, many histrionic adults report having a histrionic role model in the house; one of their parents was equally flighty and attention seeking.

The Histrionic as Partner

You may be wondering whether you are in a relationship with a partner who is an emotional bottomless pit, or you may be frequently attracted to the theatrical type. Being connected with a histrionic partner can be a dichotomy. On the one hand you likely have a partner who is really into you and the idea of being in a relationship. Yet, you also have a partner who craves unlimited amounts of praise and affection from you and everyone else he comes across. The big question is whether you have enough energy to keep up with your partner's shifting moods and a thick enough skin to weather the embarrassing social situations your partner is likely to create.

The initial attraction to your histrionic partner probably hit like a brick. It was sudden, out of the blue, and deeply intense. The histrionic, as a partner, can go after a mate with the tenacity of a bulldog and not stop until she has conquered her prey. When you take time to reflect back on this relationship later on, you will probably say that it became serious very quickly. Initially, the histrionic as a partner was likely to be fully available and really fun. They are high sensation seekers — game for anything. They are fun to hang out with and are keen to be open and to self-disclose. Theatrical personalities help new acquaintances feel comfortable, and people will report that, from the beginning, they felt like they had known the histrionic forever.

The histrionic partner believes he has a closer and more intimate relationship with others than is actually the case. He plunges into new relationships and quickly discloses intimate and very personal information. The theatrical person is intense in new relationships and seems deeply passionate about his new partner. Remember that the theatrical partner has intense and idealized romantic fantasies. It is easy to get sucked into this level of intensity and passion, yet it is also easy to become overwhelmed by it.

Entering into a relationship with a histrionic partner also means that you must be prepared to exert a lot of energy to meet this person's emotional needs. The histrionic partner is very emotional and sometimes quite volatile. He gets emotional and psychological needs met through praise and attention, yet he can become so needy that he alienates friends and lovers. His feelings are easily hurt. The theatrical partner can interpret even the smallest slight as deliberately hurtful. When his feelings are hurt he may lash out at you loudly and, sometimes, publicly.

There is a manipulative flavor to this cycle of behavior. Histrionics have learned from an early age how to get the attention they crave. Not only do they desire your attention and accolades, they desire everyone's. Frankly, this can be difficult for you to manage in your relationship. Over time, you will (if you haven't yet) become increasingly aware that your partner's emotional needs are insatiable. At parties, your partner is flamboyant, dramatic, and flirtatious. She is "on stage" and willing to go to great lengths to not only steal center stage but also maintain a tight grip on it. This can be embarrassing and also leave you feeling ignored and insecure.

There are quite a few facets of histrionic personalities that will feel inauthentic or contrived. One of them is the nature of their relationships. On the one hand they can be needy and demanding, and on the other they often have profound difficulty sustaining deep, ongoing, meaningful, emotional relationships. The theatrical personality has been known to be fickle in love, and when you are in a relationship with someone with these traits you may notice a shallow quality to her behavior. This is because the histrionic doesn't really have the capacity for deep, ongoing commitment. Further, no one person can adequately satisfy her insatiable appetite for affection and stimulation. A histrionic partner may drive you away with her never-ending dramatic and flirtatious behavior.

There is a sense of self-indulgence in the theatrical spectacle of the histrionic. When someone is so self-focused and directed exclusively toward getting her own needs met, partners are naturally left to fend for themselves. One of the things that may have initially attracted you to your partner was the openness and candor in the relationship. But think back to the beginning — were those deep meaningful discussions really about you? Did the discussion ultimately weave its way back to your partner? And did these moments of sharing really have more to do with your partner regaling you with stories and flirting? Do you notice that when you bring up something important to you it gets shoved aside and your partner's needs or feelings quickly come to the fore? Have you noticed that over time the relationship is mostly about your partner occupying center stage? These questions are designed to help you recognize the selfishness and self-indulgence that characterize histrionic personalities.

Another facet of this personality style worth noting is the histrionic's lack of, or limited, relationships with those of the same sex. People of the same sex tend to avoid this personality. They report feeling threatened in their own relationships by the histrionic person's flirtatious behavior and provocative dress. Consequently, the people whom theatrical personalities are closest to are nearly all members of the opposite sex, and given the histrionic's insatiable needs, there will usually be many of these acquaintances. If you are the partner of a theatrical personality, you may naturally find this person's numerous opposite sex relationships to be threatening.

As a partner of a theatrical personality you may find yourself making up excuses and explanations for your partner to other people in your life. The behavior and dress of your partner is not likely to go unnoticed by others. If it does, then your theatrical partner isn't going to be happy about it! Your partner's shallowness, dramatic behavior, and demands for attention can alienate others and be quite embarrassing to you.

Why Am I So Attracted to Theatrical Partners?

About now you may be wondering how you were ever attracted to such a high-maintenance partner. You may be asking yourself, What does this say about me? How could I have fallen for someone who is so profoundly superficial? These are good questions to be asking yourself as you determine the next step in your relationship. If you have begun dating or are deeply mired in a relationship with a theatrical partner then by now you know that

- Your needs will go unmet in order for your partner to be the center of attention.
- Your partner's interactions with others, usually the opposite sex, are sexually seductive and provocative.
- Your partner will not be able to have deep, enduring emotions for you.
- Your partner will use appearance to elicit attention from everyone.
- Your partner has a dramatic, theatrical, inauthentic style of communicating.
- You can easily influence your partner's thoughts, emotions, and opinions.
- Your partner considers her other relationships to also be deeply intimate.

To be in a relationship with a theatrical person means that you are essentially willing to share your partner — emotionally at least — with everyone else who comes along, be it a good friend, an acquaintance, or a stranger. What does being drawn to someone so needy and self-absorbed say about you? Maybe it says that you are secure in your relationships regardless of your partner's behavior. Or perhaps it says that you, like your partner, have a difficult time with deep, committed relationships. Some exploration of whether you are truly ready to enter into an enduring, mutually satisfying relationship may be warranted at this point.

To be quite frank, some of us are satisfied to be in relationships in which physical needs are met, even if emotional and intellectual needs are not. If having a passionate physical relationship is enough for you at this time in your life, you may find yourself deeply attracted to a histrionic partner. The reality is, however, that this is a relationship that will probably never carry you far beyond the fascination of erotic novelty and sexual excitement. If you find that you yourself lack emotional or intellectual needs or capacities, you may be quite content. If, however, you desire a reciprocal relationship in which both partners share needs, desires, and emotions and in which the attention is evenly distributed (and we imagine you do, or you wouldn't be reading this book), then it is important to examine why you have chosen someone who cannot ever offer that. Those who have a pattern of denying their own needs can find themselves attracted to those who are exceedingly demanding; high maintenance partners such as the histrionic tend to seek out and find those among us who are willing to play second fiddle and put our own needs on the back burner.

Of course, it could also be that you yourself are high maintenance and are attracted to others who value appearance and attention as much as you do. You may both appreciate and seek out this dramatic lifestyle and crave being the center of attention. You have likely heard the saying *Birds of a feather, flock together*. Actors are frequently attracted to each other because they understand theatrical impulses and needs. This may also be true for you, especially if you notice a tendency toward dating histrionic partners.

A final explanation for your attraction to a theatrical personality is that although you are not typically a sensation seeker, you are attracted to people who are. You may find yourself challenged and excited by your partner's passion and flamboyance for life. Living vicariously through your partner may stimulate and entice you. Could this be due to your own rigid style of suppressing internal needs for thrill seeking? Some people can go on indefinitely in a relationship with a histrionic, while others may find that over time this relationship is progressively less enchanting.

Living with a Theatrical Partner

Remember the classic song by the The Clash "Should I Stay or Should I Go?" It is always disheartening and sometimes frightening to make drastic decisions about intimate relationships. Yet, this time may come soon with a histrionic partner. Questions flashing though your head may include Is my partner likely to change? Does my partner have the capacity to be calm and mature? Am I likely to get my needs met in this relationship? It is a healthy sign if you are tired of competing with your partner for attention or if you find your friends and family are concerned about this relationship — and specifically, your partner's over-the-top behavior. Unless your energy level and reservoirs of praise and attention are limitless, it may be wise to seriously rethink staying in this relationship.

If, however, you are deeply committed, or even married, to a theatrical personality you may decide that leaving, at this time at least, is not the right alternative for you. After grappling with the above questions you may have decided that, for the moment, you are content to try to work on your relationship with your partner. If that is the case, we can provide some tips that you may find helpful in your relationship.

Set Firm Boundaries and Limits

As with anything in life, it is important to know our own limits. This is especially true when in a relationship with a theatrical personality. Persons with theatrical personalities push limits and boundaries — sometimes without realizing it. This is likely to occur as they try to get their needs met by grabbing the attention of others. They will demand a lot from you and they can be relentless and even infantile about being your sole focus. It is important for you to be aware of what your boundaries are physically and emotionally. How much embarrassment and damage control can you tolerate? Even more, you must be able to positively assert your boundaries when these limits are reached so that you can maintain integrity and avoid exploitation.

Be ready for backlash when you do set limits. Considering what you do know about the histrionic's behavior, you can anticipate that your partner will not be happy when you curtail the amount of time and attention you offer or when you decide to separate following an affair or constant inappropriate flirtation. Be ready for your partner's anger, volatile emotions and even an escalation in attention seeking. Continue to hold steady to your requirements — particularly that you be treated with respect, loyalty, and reciprocal care.

Provide Your Partner with Consistent Feedback

Over time, in relationships, we can become so accustomed to our partner's behavior that we stop providing each other positive feedback. Additionally, your partner may not be aware that his behavior is causing you concern or distress. This is a good time to be candid about the behaviors that you value as well as the ones that are causing you angst. Your partner is hypersensitive to criticism and therefore may not fully really hear you; if you just approach him with criticism, he is likely to become unreasonably angry. Your chances of being heard increase dramatically if you approach your partner from an emotionally neutral position. Yet, it is paramount that you give your partner consistent feedback about how his behavior affects you. And don't forget to positively reinforce the behavior that is working in the relationship. The key here is to provide feedback in a kind, loving way so that it is heard and, hopefully, incorporated.

Encourage Warmth and Empathy

Genuine warmth and empathy are difficult skills for theatrical partners to master. If your partner is histrionic, she is often so self-absorbed and needy for the spotlight that anything beyond cursory attention to your needs and concerns will be difficult to sustain. By accepting the fact that a theatrical partner has limited capacity for authentic and deep connection in a relationship and by acknowledging that her expressions of intense intimacy hover mostly at the superficial level, you will be well on your way to accepting this slice of your partner's personality. But is there anything you can do to encourage mutuality and empathy?

There are two keys in this regard. First, be an excellent model of empathy and unconditional positive regard for your partner. That is, in all circumstances, work at taking time to really listen to your partner: Reflect back not only what your partner is saying but also what his behavior reveals about his feelings. In so doing, you are communicating a genuine desire to understand and "be with" your partner. Often, such thorough and thoughtful empathy will help the histrionic person slow down, reflect, and perhaps develop some insight about the need for attention. Moreover, your empathy will serve as a model for your partner. The second key is to reinforce any improvement in your partner's own empathetic expressions. That is, the moment he demonstrates real interest in you or works to understand what you are feeling, praise him. Articulate how this regard for your welfare makes you feel — especially about your partner!

As Always, Realistic Expectations Are Warranted

If you love a theatrical personality type, then by all means, be realistic about how much your partner can actually change. Remember: These histrionic behaviors were learned early on and they are now thoroughly calcified. Just as your partner's histrionic behavior causes you embarrassment, frustration, and distress, it is also likely to cause your partner repeated failures and distress as well. Your partner may be vaguely aware that her excessive neediness and insatiable desire for attention point to a thinly disguised insecurity. Your histrionic partner may become depressed at times. But even though you feel sorry for your partner's predicament, you need to see her with eyes wide open. Yes, your histrionic partner can become less needy and demanding over time, and yes, this will be slow going. It is unlikely that your partner will ever reach a point at which others no longer find her theatrical. You will need to find a way to accept a certain degree of emotional chaos and entertainment or make a decision to move on.

When It's Time to Leave

You may have already tried some of our tips above or you may be at the point where you feel there is little that may salvage your relationship. A relationship with a histrionic partner can be exhausting and even overwhelming. Earlier we encouraged you to set clear limits. Sadly, good boundary setting can sometimes take the form of deciding to leave a relationship with a partner who is perpetually flirtatious, attention seeking, and superficial.

If you decide to leave the relationship you should be mindful that your partner may become very emotional and angry. It may be your partner's tendency to resort to extreme behavior to try to keep you in the relationship or to seek revenge. Your partner's history probably suggests a pattern of emotional manipulation that may get turned up a notch if he begins to feel desperate and scared that you may leave. Again, we suggest that you stick to your guns and take good care of yourself. Surround yourself with a strong support network and engage in good self-care. Although it is difficult to end any relationship, it is more difficult and painful to stay in an extremely bad one.

Summary

Something about the theatrical personality type might be quite alluring to you. Perhaps it is the seductive come-on, the entertaining emotional shifts, or the way this person basks in the limelight. Whatever the initial tug, life with a histrionic partner will eventually be plagued by unending attention seeking, unpredictable emotional outbursts, socially and sometimes sexually inappropriate behavior, and an emotional shallowness that may leave you feeling lonely. In a real way, you will be the full-time "handler" for this partner — always trying to keep her contained, appropriate, and gratified by your full attention. This can be an exhausting job. Most of us need more reciprocity and genuine emotional connection in a long-term love relationship.

CHAPTER 10

THE SELF-ABSORBED PARTNER
The Narcissistic Personality

Narcissistic Personality Checklist

✔ He has an inflated sense of self-importance and often exaggerates his talents and achievements.

✔ He is preoccupied with fantasies of success, power, beauty, or ideal love.

✔ He believes that he is "special" and can only be understood by or should only associate with other special, talented, or famous people.

✔ He requires you to offer excessive and constant admiration.

✔ He shows a strong sense of entitlement; he expects others to give him special treatment or automatically comply with his wishes.

✔ He exploits other people, often taking advantage of you and others to meet his own ends.

✔ He seems to lack empathy and fails to recognize or respond to the feelings and needs of others.

✔ He is often envious of others or believes others are envious of him.

✔ He is frequently arrogant in attitude and behavior.

If you find yourself ignoring your own needs, desires, and interests while focusing exclusively on a partner with an insatiable appetite for undeserved admiration and praise, then perhaps you have a penchant for self-absorbed partners. What does it mean if you are always living in the shadow of someone with a super-sized ego? Why do you always seem to attract partners who have little room in their lives for anyone but themselves? If your current or recent partner is self-absorbed or if you always seem to end up with the egomaniacs, it is important for you to read this chapter with care.

Anne's Story

My relationship with Rick might best be described as a slow escalator ride down to the depths of self-doubt and despair. At thirty-five, and free of the guy for the last two years, I still don't feel as good about myself as I did at thirty-one, before ever meeting Rick. At that time I was fresh from law school and working as an associate in a prestigious law firm. I was doing well and fully expected to make partner within a few years. I felt good about my looks then too and enjoyed dating without letting things get too serious.

I can trace the start of my downward spiral to the year I met Rick. I actually met him at a big party our firm threw for its high-profile clients and constituents. It was strictly an invitation only event, but Rick managed to weasel his way in. He convinced the judge he was clerking for that summer to take him along. At that time he was a second-year law school student at one of the worst law schools in the state. He just sort of walked into this exclusive party and started shaking hands and introducing himself as though he really belonged and as though everyone was glad to see him.

I still remember being impressed by the way he just walked right up to me and introduced himself as the state's future attorney general. I didn't know whether to laugh or be disgusted at his arrogance. He was nice looking — really muscular and tall — and he was so self-assured and smooth, I half believed he just might become the next attorney general. Replaying that first meeting now, I realize he asked almost nothing about me, just went on about his great achievements in law school and how the judge he was working for was going to "fast-track" him to the top. After about half an hour, he asked me out, saying something like "I think it's safe to say you won't be disappointed counselor." Although thinking about him now makes me want to puke, at the time I was bored, fatigued from work, and in between relationships. I was vulnerable and he took advantage of it.

For our first date, he invited me to his place for dinner. He had prepared a really nice meal and his place was immaculate. I should have been worried from the start though when I noticed a huge framed photograph of Rick in the hallway of his apartment. It was nearly life-sized and showed him doing a bodybuilder's pose in some kind of G-string. Believe me, he had a great body, and he was obviously proud of it, but it just struck me as unusual. I later discovered that he spent about three hours a day at the gym lifting weights (and flexing in front of the large mirrors there). During dinner that night he constantly used French terms for things he had prepared and hinted that he had some training from a French cooking school (I later learned he had none and had just read a book). He fished for lots of compliments about the food and said very demeaning things about various chefs at different restaurants in town — suggesting they "had no clue" what they were doing. Again, I remember that most of the dinner conversation focused on Rick. Even when he asked about me, he would use whatever I said as an entrée to tell me more about himself — especially why he was uniquely suited to the law profession.

At that time, I figured the poor guy was just working hard to impress me. I put up with it and regret it now. We continued dating. The funny thing is that the more time we spent together, the more lonely and fatigued I began to feel. If we spent five hours together, four and a half would be spent processing why Rick's law professors didn't fully appreciate his genius (he got average grades) and how unfair it was that they refused to give him special accommodations if he missed class or was late to an exam. If I had trouble at the firm or wanted to talk about a case, he would listen briefly then sort of brush it off and start talking about something it reminded him of at school. I never got the sense Rick really "heard" anything I said. I certainly never felt that he really cared a lot about how I felt or what I was going through. I soon found that if I didn't constantly tell Rick he was wonderful (as a cook, a student, a physical specimen, or a lover) he would get impatient and more demanding. It was like he was a dry sponge — constantly soaking up any attention or praise in a room.

In the bedroom, Rick insisted on a lengthy sexual warm-up that always began with him doing a slow striptease routine. Sometimes this would go on for fifteen or twenty minutes and mostly involved him flexing muscles in some wild G-string. At first, I found this really sexy and appreciated the time he took to arouse me. At some point, though, I realized the whole thing was mostly for him. He really just wanted to hear me "oh" and "ah" about his great body and to watch himself in the mirror while he performed. I began to see that I was really just a prop for his show. If I ever became impatient or stopped coaxing him on verbally, he would get angry and say things like "Babe, if this isn't getting to you, you must be dead." When it came to lovemaking itself, Rick was fast, rough, and focused mostly on what he wanted. The few times I tried to tell him what I desired sexually, he got really offended and sort of indicated he knew a heck of a lot more about what pleased a woman than I did. In fact, I don't ever recall him asking me if something felt good or how I wanted to be loved physically. To top it off, after we made love, he would seek lots of compliments about his performance — things like "Now, tell me the truth, have you EVER had you mind blown like that before!?"

I think the worst thing about dating Rick was the way I ended up feeling about myself. During the months we dated, I can see now that I started feeling less and less attractive and less and less competent as a lawyer. It was hard for me to understand exactly why this was happening then, but now I do see it. Rick was a master at making himself feel good by making me feel awful. It was really quite subtle most of the time. For example, he would say things like "If you could find a little more time to work out with me, we could tone up those thighs and get them sculpted like mine," and "I read your brief. It looks OK, but I'm pretty sure I could really sharpen it up for you." Before long, I was pretty doubtful about my own attractiveness and I wondered if I was functioning competently at work. I began getting depressed.

The end of our relationship came when one of my girlfriends from law school, Jill, came to visit. She stayed with Rick and me for a week. Jill seemed to see right away how I had changed and how Rick was entirely unable to really hear me or see what I needed. One afternoon, hearing Rick go on about how brilliant he was in one of his classes and how I could learn a thing or two from him, Jill just exploded. She confronted Rick's arrogance and self-absorbed way of seeing the world. She pointed out that he was actually a mediocre student at a lousy law school and that I had graduated from a top-ten Ivy League program. Rick had a meltdown. He demanded that she leave at once (it was my apartment) and insisted that I choose between him and my friend. I seemed to see him completely for the first time then and told him to leave. He did, and I never heard another word from him. I mark that day as the first day of my recovery from a strange sort of fog, a fog that so diminished my self-esteem that I nearly lost my mind and my career. I am forever grateful to Jill for rescuing me that day.

The Self-Absorbed Personality

The self-absorbed partner is high maintenance in the sense of requiring constant admiration and praise. Mental health diagnosticians refer to seriously self-absorbed adults as having **Narcissistic Personality Disorders**. You will know the narcissist by three primary characteristics: (1) an exaggerated sense of self-importance, (2) a preoccupation with being admired by others, and (3) an inability to empathize with or even understand the perspective of others. You may recall that the original Narcissus was a character from Greek mythology — a young man who fell deeply in love with himself and ultimately met his end by drowning in a pool in which he was admiring his own reflection. This is a fitting image of the narcissist — excessive love of self that makes truly loving others nearly impossible.

A narcissistic partner will have what psychologists describe as a "grandiose sense of self-importance." This means she is the human equivalent of the animal kingdom's peacock; constantly overestimating her abilities and accomplishments and never missing an opportunity to draw attention to her inherent greatness. If your partner is a narcissist, you will often feel that your own traits and accomplishments are deflated or diminished — sometimes subtly — by your partner (e.g., "Let's just say the men can't keep their eyes off me! Oh, and you don't look bad either, dear"). Keep in mind that narcissists are not consciously faking or exaggerating; rather, they truly believe they are superior, special, and uniquely talented. Narcissists will often be preoccupied with fantasies of unlimited success, power, and brilliance. These fantasies may be secret, but more often than not you will hear samples or catch glimpses of these fantasies. If your response is not affirming, the narcissistic lover will appear wounded and may become angry.

This partner constantly boasts and brags and will likely be experienced by others as arrogant and obnoxious. Also, because he believes himself to be so special and unique, he may be willing to affiliate only with others he views as special, "perfect," or famous in some way. This of course means that the narcissist may only be dating you because he sees you as uniquely attractive, wealthy, or successful — thereby making a reasonably suitable (though probably not fully adequate) match for his own greatness. In a real sense, you are merely the frame for the masterpiece or window dressing for the real view. The narcissist may only go to the "finest" or "top" physician, accountant, or hair stylist because such affiliations boost his own sense of idealized value.

The narcissistic lover will be tremendously high maintenance and perhaps exhausting to care for simply because she will demand constant and unfaltering attention, praise, and admiration. In this way, the narcissist is actually quite like a child: Her self-esteem is so fragile, her need for constant positive appraisals is nearly insatiable. Should you refrain, even briefly, from admiring and praising the narcissist, the relational price may be substantial and may take the form of anger, sullen pouting, or even caustic and dismissive comments about you.

Entitlement, or an expectation that one is deserving of special consideration and treatment, is a hallmark of the narcissistic partner. No matter the context or circumstance, the narcissist will simply assume that others will make special accommodations for him and that rules apply to other (common) people. If a restaurant or new acquaintance does not so accommodate him, he will be astonished and may become infuriated. For example, your narcissistic partner will expect that it is perfectly fine if he is late to a gathering (others should wait for him) or if he interrupts a conversation (obviously what he has to say is more important). Failure to accommodate the narcissist's entitlement will certainly result in some form of relational punishment or conflict.

In addition to being generally arrogant, haughty, snobbish, and patronizing, the narcissist has a severe relational deficit that no amount of kindness or patience will help her to overcome. This deficit is empathy. The self-absorbed partner will be truly unable to take your perspective or really understand or appreciate your feelings, experiences, and desires. In other words, the narcissist is incapable of emotional reciprocity — there is an inability to see the world through the eyes of another, yet even if this were possible, her own needs and experiences would quickly claim center stage again. The narcissist is forever envious of others (although she works hard to cover this up) and may assume that others are also envious of her. Narcissists believe they are more deserving of the riches or successes of others and will frequently feel compelled to point out the weaknesses or shortcomings of those around them as a way of highlighting their comparative superiority.

Finally, the narcissistic person is extremely vulnerable to what has been termed narcissistic injury. A *narcissistic injury* occurs when the fragile self-esteem of the narcissist is threatened or exposed. This may result from any perceived challenge to his grandiose self-portrait. Thus when a lover fails to offer praise, does not accommodate entitled behavior, or questions an excessively grandiose self-appraisal, the conditions are ripe for the narcissist to feel attacked and slighted. He may respond with sullen withdrawal, rage, humiliation, or a vengeful verbal (and in some cases physical) counterattack.

What Makes a Narcissist?

How does a child grow up to become a narcissistic adult? There are two well-worn routes to a final diagnosis of Narcissistic Personality Disorder. The first route is primary narcissism. Here, parents of narcissists worship their child; they offer exaggerated and distorted assessments of the child that are repeated often and with great sincerity (e.g., he is "brilliant," "perfect," the "best"). Of course all parents believe their child is wonderful and special, but the parents of narcissists fail to teach their child that everyone has vulnerabilities, relative weaknesses, and imperfections. Also, these parents may fail to communicate their own needs and separate interests, thus allowing the budding narcissist to believe that others exist only for the purpose of basking in his greatness. The child becomes dependent on constant praise and admiration and internalizes the parents' unrealistic appraisals. Of course, when the child reaches adulthood, he will expect, others — including you, the romantic partner — to continue this tradition of admiration and unconditional praise.

The second route to adult narcissism is compensatory narcissism. In this (quite common) form, the narcissist develops her disorder in compensation for severe abuse or neglect in childhood. In such cases, the child feels so desperately awful about herself that the only options are despair (clinical depression) or a flight into grandiose fantasy. As a child experiencing abuse, emotionally degrading treatment, or utter neglect, narcissistic compensation is actually quite adaptive. By engaging in this strategy of denial and grandiose fantasy, the maltreated youth can stave off the grim reality of how she actually feels inside. Of course, by the time this self-protective and compensating child reaches adulthood, the compensatory narcissism has become a calcified and unconscious facet of the self. In 50 to 75 percent of cases, the narcissist is male.

The Narcissist as Partner

By now you will have gathered that the idea of the narcissistic person as a "partner" in the sense of mutuality, reciprocity, and sharing is a misnomer. A relationship with a narcissist will be lopsided from the outset, and unless you are willing to offer nearly constant affirmation and admiration, the relationship will be doomed. There are many reasons you should avoid romantic relationships with narcissists; if you are already connected romantically to a narcissist, then much of what follows will be sadly familiar.

First, narcissists will only enter a love relationship if it appears likely to advance their purposes or enhance their self-esteem. That is, by dating you, the narcissist stands to "look good" or get something he wants by way of admiration or enhanced status. If you are successful, wealthy, or physically attractive, it is quite probable that the narcissist is primarily attracted to these attributes — viewing himself as deserving of someone like you. In this way, the narcissist will be like a sponge, eagerly soaking up all the attention and resources you have to offer.

As a lover, your narcissistic partner feels entitled to all of your attention and will be easily wounded, angry, and shocked when this is not available. She assumes that you will always alter your schedule and change your plans to accommodate her preferences and whims. In this way, the narcissistic partner is like a perpetual adolescent — self-absorbed and unable to comprehend that her needs are not paramount in the lives of others. And like a child, the narcissist who does not get her way will be given to tantrums or sullen withdrawal anytime you dare to place her needs and desires anywhere but first.

If you wish to remain largely anonymous and unknown in a love relationship, then the narcissist may be right for you. Try to bring up your own needs, desires, experiences, or feelings, and your narcissistic partner will either ignore them — quickly shifting attention back to himself — or will become impatient or demeaning — perhaps viewing your feelings and experiences as signs of weakness. A more sophisticated and socially intelligent narcissist will pay attention to you just long enough to give the illusion of authentic concern and empathy. However, once this is accomplished, the focus will quickly be diverted back to where it belongs — on the narcissist! In this way, the narcissistic lover will actually be quite emotionally detached and truly incapable of understanding how his actions and comments impact you. For example, when describing a former girlfriend, a narcissistic man may say, "She was the most intelligent woman I ever knew," without considering how this comment may make you feel.

Finally, your relationship probably becomes severely strained anytime you dare to confront, criticize, or correct the narcissist. Thus, as is true with the paranoid and borderline partner, your relational life will be characterized by eggshell walking. For example, any attempt to temper the narcissist's grandiose sense of his performance as a lover, will be met with shock, anger, and, most likely, some counterattack regarding your own lovemaking prowess. Also, you must anticipate relational upset if ever you outperform or become more successful than the narcissist. Increasing evidence of your superiority in any area will be met with dismissal (e.g., "You were lucky") or disparagement (e.g., "It can't be that hard").

Why Am I So Attracted to Self-Absorbed Partners?

So what does it mean if I'm drawn to self-absorbed people? How did I get into a relationship with a narcissist in the first place? What did I ever see in her? Here is a sobering reality check: If you are attracted to narcissists, you are attracted to a romantic partner who

- has a totally inflated ego.
- is preoccupied with fantasies of unlimited power, brilliance, or beauty.
- actually believes only elite or special people can possibly understand her.
- demands constant admiration.
- assumes she is entitled to special favors and treatment.
- exploits others to feel good and get her needs met.
- can't really understand, appreciate, or even care about your feelings or needs.
- is terribly envious of others but claims others envy her.
- is seen by others as arrogant, stuck-up, and totally full of herself.

Not a very savory picture is it? Read this list through a few times. Is there any room in the narcissist's world for a genuine partner? No, probably not. So how come you ended up with a self-absorbed type, or worse, why do you always seem to end up with partners like this? Actually, there are lots of reasons to fall for a narcissist.

First, self-absorbed personalities can initially come across as larger than life. Particularly when they are smart, narcissists make a big first impression. They seem accomplished, confident, self-assured, and experienced, and they present an amazing resume of achievements and life adventures. In fact, on meeting a genuine narcissist for the first time (especially if he packs intelligence and social charm), it is very hard not to be impressed! What will later be understood as exaggeration, fantasy, and even out-and-out lying may at first seem amazing. What will later reek of arrogance can initially be credible and astounding. The fact that the narcissist often caries himself with an air of importance and sophistication can make it quite hard to detect the fabrication at first. Later, the things we initially admired may come to little more than a lot of puffery. Any of us could be duped when regaled by a charismatic narcissist with stories of exploits and one of a kind experiences.

There are those among us who must admit being drawn to a partner who will take control, be in charge, and establish a firm place for us in a relationship. If you are one of these people, it may not be easy to admit that you were drawn to a narcissistic partner precisely because she seemed strong, capable, all-together, and just the sort of take-charge relationship leader you were looking for. There is something safe for you in a relationship with one who appears to have not even a flicker of normal self-doubt and who is willing (and even demands) to take the lead in all important decision making in the relationship. Sadly, the narcissist takes control not to afford you security but because only her feelings and concerns really matter.

Some adults are drawn to Narcissistic Personality Disorders precisely because they see through the narcissistic veneer to an insecure little child. Enter the rescuer and healer. Those who fit this description are effectively trying to reparent the narcissist — perhaps believing at an unconscious level that they can prop up their partner's fragile ego long enough for a more mature relationship to develop. Here is the problem: Reparenting a narcissistic client takes years of psychotherapy. In general, it is unwise to enter into a relationship based on your attraction to the role of therapist or parent. And if these roles sound familiar to you, it is time to explore your own childhood experiences with self-absorbed adults. What narcissistically self-absorbed adult were you always working to manage and take care of? How did you develop an affinity for the egotistical type? What needs is the narcissist meeting for you?

Some otherwise healthy adults are drawn to partners who have no capacity for empathy. This person may be most comfortable when living in the shadow of her partner. Is it the case that you are the classic shrinking violet or second fiddle who is happiest in the background? Ironically, this person is most comfortable or "at home" when her needs are ignored and desires discounted. Again, we must ask what relationship you are recreating in your partnership with a narcissist. At some point in life, you must have learned to be content stroking another's ego, deflating your own needs, and working around the clock to keep someone else together.

Here is the final — and by far the saddest — reason you may find yourself hooked up with self-absorbed partners: You may actually begin to see the world from the narcissistic partner's perspective. That is, you accept and adopt the egotistical partner's view of himself, of you, and of others. Through this lens you can only be grateful for the crumbs your brilliant and beautiful partner allows to fall your way. Through this lens you are comparatively worthless, you have little in the way of redeeming qualities, and your partner's dismissal of your wishes and desires makes perfect sense — he really can't be bothered. Tragically, you may find yourself defending your partner's arrogance and abrasiveness in public and agreeing that only truly special people can possibly understand him.

There are many reasons you may be engaged in a relationship with a narcissist. She can be alluring and larger than life. She often takes control and captivates others with tales of exploits and unusual capacities. Or, you may be drawn to caretaking roles with fragile personalities. Worse, your self-esteem may become so diminished in the course of a relationship with a narcissist that you soon come to believe you have little value apart from her.

Living with a Narcissistic Partner

What should you do if you are involved with a self-absorbed partner? Is there any hope? Can the relationship be made more livable for you? Let's be clear, living with a narcissist will never be a rose garden. Your narcissistic partner is experienced by others as obnoxious, egotistical, and lacking all empathy. Your partner is profoundly arrogant and actually believes in her unsurpassed brilliance, talent, or fame. Putting up with you and your imperfection is a painful burden the narcissistic partner must bear, and your partner probably lets you know this time and time again. Your partner is probably insufferable in most social situations, and your friends and family members wonder why you can't see it.

Still, some reading this chapter are already committed to a narcissistic partner; perhaps you have children together and are reluctant to leave — at least now. As with all the personality disorders, narcissism exists on a continuum of severity and some self-absorbed partners will be more flexible than others. We now offer several recommendations for weathering and perhaps even improving a relationship with a narcissist. But remember, someone with a severe Narcissistic Personality Disorder will be extremely hard to live with regardless of your own patience and strength of character.

First, Take Care of Yourself

Among the PDPs covered in this guide, the narcissist is near the top of the list when it comes to high maintenance. Living with a self-absorbed partner often seems to require herculean levels of patience and attention. In a real sense, you are always on duty — around the clock, the narcissistic partner will have unremitting need for your admiration, attention, and affirmation. And no amount of validation of his unique talent and "special" qualities will ever be enough. The narcissist's craving and appetite for your affirmation and time will feel ravenous, and the satisfaction he gleans from an episode of ego stroking will be short lived. Much like the parent of a newborn infant, you can begin to feel fatigued by your partner's demands. What's more, you will also feel personally diminished. Narcissists wreak havoc on the self-esteem of all but the most self-assured partners. Remember, narcissists can only feel adequate by disparaging the talents and attributes of those around them — maybe especially those they love. In order to stay sane and psychologically healthy, it is imperative that you carve out time for yourself. Set firm boundaries around time for self-care (e.g., exercise, solitude, reflection, and rest), socializing with friends and family, and perhaps even personal counseling to keep your own self-esteem up even when your partner sometimes seems determined to run you down at every turn. In essence, you must stay rejuvenated and buoyed in your own emotional health if you are going to try to help your narcissistic lover get his needs met.

Provide Narcissistic Mirroring

Keeping in mind that your narcissistic partner is actually a fragile child on an emotional level, it makes sense that one of the key things you can offer on a routine basis is simple unconditional positive regard. When working with narcissistic patients, psychotherapists refer to this as *narcissistic mirroring:* Your partner needs constant reflection of pleasure and satisfaction from you. In essence, you are conveying that the little child is good, adequate, worthy, and just fine the way he is. Narcissistic mirroring is most easily conveyed through a patient demeanor, positive appraisals of your partner, smiling nods, and understanding reflections of his experiences. Gentle, consistent, and accurate expressions of empathy for the things your partner experiences each day are likely to help him avoid the dramatic episodes of rage or depression that can sometimes plague this personality type. Interestingly, some bodybuilders who develop an extreme preoccupation with the activity actually harbor strong narcissistic needs. To their credit, they have arranged to spend many hours every day in an environment that provides just this sort of reflective feedback — a large room covered on every wall with mirrors! Be advised that constant unconditional mirroring is hard work though and can be taxing on you. You may feel exhausted by the task at times — especially when your partner's need for it does not seem to diminish noticeably. This tactic may not ultimately change your partner, but it may make your relationship easier and less conflictual for you.

See through Your Partner's Jealousy

Here is a consistent principle with self-absorbed partners: They tend to interpret any displeasure or complaint about their behavior as jealousy. They just assume that everyone can immediately detect their unusual brilliance and perfection, and they therefore understand any disdain or disgust from others as a sign of jealous desire. So, if and when you gently question your partner's grandiose claim of special prowess in some area, don't be surprised by an angry retort about you being jealous of her. And when your family members roll their eyes at the dinner table as your partner dominates the conversation with talk about herself, expect to get an angry earful later on about how your family is deeply envious of her. Rather than joining in the argument, remember that this is a primitive defense mechanism — projection. The fact is that your partner is envious of you and others and this feeling is unacceptable. Her envy and jealousy must therefore be projected onto others. Recognizing this tendency in your partner may make it easier for you to deal with and understand this behavior as a form of self-protection she utilizes to protect her fragile ego.

Set Limits on Demeaning Behavior and Narcissistic Rage

Narcissistic lovers are prone to fits of rage — nearly always the result of a perceived slight that threatens their fragile sense of self. If your partner is prone to rage episodes, be certain that you and any children are physically safe and set firm limits on the behavior you are willing to tolerate should your partner resort to physical violence or emotionally degrading comments. As a child with a broken self-esteem at heart, your partner is especially vulnerable to perceived assaults on his fragile ego. Like a two-year-old, rage may immediately follow a challenging comment or even an inattentive response on your part. And like the parent of a two-year-old, you must be crystal clear about what is appropriate and what is not when your partner becomes enraged. You must also be emotionally armored against your partner's caustic comments and devaluing behavior. Remember, his adequacy can only be established in comparison to yours — thus it will be a constant challenge to disregard your partner's mean-spirited criticisms and spiteful comments — as you shrink, he is inflated. Again, set firm limits on such verbal abuse and then follow through if needed by leaving for a period of time or even moving out if necessary.

At Times, Use Narcissism to Your Advantage

When the authors were psychologists in the Navy, it was not uncommon to consult with commanding officers who were "stuck" with a narcissistic sailor. If a narcissist emerged in the middle of a ship's deployment, we would sometimes counsel the captain to "go with" the narcissism. So, rather than get into a major conflict with the narcissist, we would suggest trying something like "You know, I have a special assignment and I need someone very bright and independent for it . . . hmmm . . . I thought that of all the sailors in this division, you might be most up to it. What do you say?" Of course, no self-respecting narcissist could easily refuse such a grandiose invitation, and he would often happily comply. The captain would then assign him to some solitary duty on the ship where the sailor's arrogance would cause little problem for the duration of the underway period. In your relationship, there may be times when you can try the same technique: "Honey, it's a good thing I have you because a lot of guys wouldn't be able to really hear and understand what I'm about to say. . ." While not entirely accurate, such an invitation appeals to the narcissist's grandiosity and he may then strive to validate your description of him as especially sensitive.

Reinforce Even Small Gains in Empathy

Perhaps the biggest challenge for any narcissistic partner will be the capacity for empathy. The narcissist has a terrible time genuinely understanding how you feel and what you experience in the relationship. Because grandiose fantasies preoccupy much of the narcissist's time, it is hard for your partner to really hear or even to really want to hear what you or others have to say. Thus it is very helpful to reinforce with copious praise any movement in the direction of accurate empathy. Sometimes, you will need to carefully explain how you felt when your partner said or did something or narrate what someone else (probably someone whom she offended) might have felt when your partner said or did something that smacked of arrogance: "When you said . . . , I wonder if . . . could have felt diminished or slighted?" If your partner seems to show some insight about this interpretation, comment on her insight and reinforce it.

Psychotherapy Is a Long-Term Endeavor

As with many others with personality disorders, narcissists resist entering treatment, and when they do, they will be especially caustic and sabotage the therapeutic relationship. Feeling threatened, narcissistic patients work hard to debunk the therapist's credentials, engage in competitive struggles for control of the sessions, and even engage in a war of interpretation with the provider — trying to out-therapy the therapist! Of course, this is all in the service of defending a brittle ego. At other times, therapists — maybe sensing how fragile the patient is — can be too reinforcing and supportive of narcissists so that they never want to leave treatment but also benefit little from the experience. Like most with personality disorders, narcissists don't believe that they actually NEED therapy. As you may have already experienced, your partner attributes any problems in your relationship to you. One strategy for getting your partner into therapy is to enter into therapy yourself and ask your partner to help you work on yourself by joining you for some sessions to meet your therapist and to give his opinions on the relationship and on you. This tactic also gives your partner the opportunity to be the "expert" on your relationship without feeling like the "patient." This is a backdoor technique to get a self-absorbed partner involved in the therapeutic experience without feeling threatened.

When It's Time to Leave

In spite of these strategies for enduring with a narcissist, and perhaps even improving things for a time, it is hard for us to imagine that if your partner is seriously self-absorbed you will find the relationship especially workable or healthy in the long run. At some point, you may be too exhausted, your self-esteem may be too diminished, or your level of disgust at your partner's constant demand for admiration may be too high for you to continue in the relationship.

When it is time to move on, be cautious regarding narcissistic rage and expect narcissistic injury. If your partner has a history of rage at being discounted or questioned and if there is any history of physical violence, then please take steps to ensure you are safe in the process of leaving. This may entail getting support from friends and family or even the police *before* giving any overt indication that you are leaving. We cannot imagine a case in which a narcissistic partner would not experience some ego injury at the prospect of a partner leaving. The injury may cause rage or an episode of depression, but in most cases a narcissistic partner will quickly reframe your decision to leave as evidence that you were never worthy of him in the first place. Your partner will rationalize your leaving: "If she'd had the insight to understand what a gem she had in me, she would never even have conceived of leaving." And do not be surprised when the narcissist tells others that it was he who dumped you! For the narcissist, reality must always be tailored to protect his ego.

Summary

A real narcissist is so "full" of himself or herself that there can hardly be any room left for another person. Staying in a relationship with a self-absorbed partner will require you to pay constant homage to your partner's absurdly grandiose sense of importance, talent, and achievement. It will ALWAYS be about the narcissist and rarely about you or even "us." If you frequently end up with self-absorbed characters, we highly recommend that you start exploring why. Life is too short to spend it hiding in the shadow of a partner's permanently inflated ego.

CHAPTER 11

THE UNDERMINING PARTNER
The Passive-Aggressive Personality

Passive-Aggressive Personality Checklist

- ✔ He passively refuses to fulfill routine job and social tasks.
- ✔ He complains of being misunderstood and unappreciated by others.
- ✔ He is often sullen and argumentative.
- ✔ He seems unreasonably angry and critical of authority figures.
- ✔ He is often envious and resentful toward those more fortunate or successful.
- ✔ He exaggerates and complains about his own misfortune.
- ✔ He alternates between passive compliance and hostile defiance.
- ✔ His behavior begins to undermine your happiness and success.

If you find yourself getting more and more angry at someone you are dating even though she doesn't ever do anything really aggressive or awful, or if you find your own previously good self-esteem starting to decline as a result of a partner's negative comments and subtle criticism, you may be involved with an underminer. Undermining types often have a **Passive-Aggressive Personality Disorder**. The underminer is a quietly toxic person who can slowly erode both your confidence and your happiness. Worst of all, you may end up feeling that the problems with the relationship are all yours. If any of the foregoing sounds familiar, read this chapter with special care.

Lynda's Story

I can't believe I ever saw anything attractive about Nick. Thinking about the guy now still makes me cringe. Being with him will forever be one of those terrible relationship mistakes; I still wonder how I ever let things get so far with a guy who was so obnoxious and screwed up! Still, at first, there were no obvious warning signs.

Nick and I met at a small career conference for junior professionals working in the publishing industry. Both of us were junior editors at small publishing houses and were just getting our careers off the ground. I remember that Nick sat next to me during several of the presentations and workshops. He was handsome, but what I really liked about him was his sense of humor. He would whisper sarcastic comments to me about the speakers or something they had said. He was hilarious — even though he said some pretty mean things about the speakers. It's hard to explain now but somehow the combination of Nick's nice looks and his sarcastic take on life — especially his ability to make me laugh through a boring conference — was very appealing.

Our publishers were located near one another in Manhattan, and we began having lunch together quite often. Because we were both at the same level career-wise, we shared a lot of experiences and used a lot of our time to vent to one another about people we disliked at work, office politics, and the crappy parts of the editing life. It was nice to have a confidant outside of work to share with. And Nick did keep me laughing — mostly because he would say the most outrageously caustic and negative things about other editors or even his own senior editor at work. These comments took me off guard and made me burst out laughing. Looking back now, I should have seen that Nick was constantly negative and fault finding. Even though he covered it with a veneer of humor, there was something genuinely mean just under the surface. Over a period of about six months, things really moved fast for the two of us. Although we never exactly moved in together, we dated seriously enough that most of our free time was spent together and I had a strong sense, at least at first, that he might be "the one."

The first red flags began to really wave after a few months. I began to see that Nick was constantly resentful and angry —

not just toward his boss but toward almost everyone above him in the publishing house and even toward his co-workers. He had started getting some bad feedback for what his editor called "shoddy" work, for failing to acquire new titles, and for letting his editor down more than once by missing key delivery deadlines for edited manuscripts. At first, I assumed that Nick's editor really was a jerk and that Nick was probably right — he was being singled out for criticism. But two things began to alarm me. First, it wasn't just this editor but several people at work who seemed to be abusing Nick. I began to wonder if there was actually something wrong with Nick's performance after all. Second, Nick was totally preoccupied with the bad treatment he got at work and with the unfair advantages and opportunities all the other junior editors seemed to be getting. I noticed that we rarely enjoyed a dinner or an evening together without the conversation sliding in the direction of how Nick was a victim and how nobody at work appreciated him. I began to find this exhausting.

Once I started taking an honest look at Nick's behavior, I had to admit that things weren't so great in our relationship either. I had begun to feel edgy and, frankly, angry around Nick much of the time. We were frequently fighting and when I tried to trace these episodes back to the start, I would usually see that Nick had made some comment about me that seemed innocent enough on the surface but that carried some real barbs and ended up making me feel terrible about myself or incredibly pissed off at Nick, or both. As one example, Nick would say or do things that indicated I needed to lose some weight. He never came right out and said this of course; that's not Nick. In fact, he said I looked "fine," but you could tell by the way he said it that he didn't believe it. For my birthday, Nick gave me a two-month membership at the local gym. He said something like "Hey, don't take it the wrong way; you look great. I just thought that if you could work out more often you might really get in shape." Of course, I did start working out more, but I also began to worry more about how I looked. Something similar happened when I asked him to let me practice a big work presentation on him. I had spent a lot of time preparing my talk and after giving it in front of Nick the night before, he smiled and said, "That was pretty good, and I have just the thing for you." He then went out and returned with a book on tips for effective public speaking. He circled about half the tips and recommended I really work on them. Needless to say, this made me tons more anxious for my speech the following day and I didn't have time to actually read the book, but I really questioned my own competence as a speaker and hardly slept at all that night. Ironically, my co-workers said it was the best presentation they'd ever heard.

I think things really hit the fan in our relationship on the day I got promoted. In contrast to all of Nick's problems at work and his very poor evaluations, I was doing well. I was delighted to be one of the youngest people in the publishing house ever promoted to senior editor. I knew right away that Nick wasn't going to be able to handle it. He offered praise and congrats of course, but they had a faint and insincere tone. I could tell he was upset. Over the next days and weeks, there were more and more brief comments about my "luck," about how the publisher must want to get me to bed, and about how it would be a different story if I had had to make it at his office. These comments ticked me off big time but I hoped things would blow over. They didn't. Things got worse in our relationship, and Nick seemed constantly sullen and resentful of my success. Our sex life also went downhill about that time. I should have realized how bizarre this was then, but Nick began having trouble with premature ejaculation. He'd climax right away and then apologize and say he just didn't understand it. But on more than one occasion, there was a subtle comment about me "taking too long" and once he even suggested that if I were in better shape "I'd be more responsive sexually."

Our relationship ended abruptly. I was facing my first major crisis at work. We were late meeting a crucial deadline. I was going to be awake around the clock for an entire weekend to get things done on time. Nick volunteered to help and I really appreciated it — I needed his experience and expertise in a big way. Given that the task I assigned him was very straightforward, I made the mistake of assuming he'd come through for me. I was wrong. On Monday morning, I discovered he had edited the entire manuscript using the wrong style. I was dumfounded and the manuscript ended up being delayed. When I called Nick and asked what he could possibly have been thinking, he said something like "Really good senior editors I know make these things clear at the beginning so that there are no mistakes. I had no idea what style you wanted so I just used the one I liked. Maybe you need to work on communication." I couldn't even respond. I just slowly hung up the phone. That was also the moment I hung up on my relationship with Nick. At that moment it all became clear to me. I was through with being undermined and sabotaged and then feeling like it was all my fault.

The Undermining Personality

The undermining or passive-aggressive partner tends to hold strong negativistic attitudes about many things, especially authority figures. From an early age, this person has passively resisted requests and demands for performance in a variety of areas (e.g., academic, occupational, social, relational) but is rarely directly aggressive or hostile to authority figures. The thing is, the underminer is quite ambivalent about authority: On one hand, he feels dependent and needy for approval and attention, while on the other hand he desperately wants to be independent and self-assertive. The result of this ambivalence is a simmering anger that gets directed in passive ways at anyone in the underminer's path. If you are in a relationship with this type — especially if you are at all assertive, successful, and confident — you will very likely become a target of your partner's undermining and negative behavior.

In work settings, the passive-aggressive can be a nightmare — which is why she often advances only so far before having run-ins with bosses and supervisors. This person seems to habitually resent, resist, and reject demands by authority figures to perform reasonable work-related tasks. On the surface, the underminer seems deferent and obedient, but her behavior shows a clear pattern of procrastination, forgetfulness, stubbornness, and intentionally "forgetting" to do things she promised to complete. In a phrase, this person "says yes, but acts no." The passive-aggressive takes on tasks with apparent eagerness or at least willingness but then fails to ever get started, or fails to produce anything useful, or may take so long that the ultimate product is no longer timely or helpful. And you may get much of the same behavior in a relationship with this type. Although the passive-aggressive seems agreeable on the surface, she obstructs success and constantly seems to "forget" or make "mistakes" that she claims are "accidents" but that begin to clearly come across as deliberate. In this way, the underminer is a genuine saboteur at work and in relationships.

Even though the passive-aggressive may smile at you or at bosses and others he presumes have some authority, he will often be sullen, angry, and argumentative just under the surface and frequent caustic and negative comments about authority figures will be expressed to colleagues or loved ones. This sullen anger will really kick into high gear if you try to make suggestions for improving performance or resolving conflicts. This will lead the underminer to feel wrongly accused, misunderstood, and unappreciated. Feeling that his work or relationships are just fine the way they are, this person will bristle and become bitter and even emotionally vindictive if you attempt to point out his poor performance, his passive-aggressive nature, or the incongruence between what he says and does. Expect the passive-aggressive personality type to come across as a wrongly accused victim whenever you confront him.

Undermining adults are ceaselessly complaining about bosses, parents, other loved ones, and virtually anyone else they perceive as holding power over them or wanting anything from them. To these people's faces, the underminer is contrite and compliant, but behind their backs, the underminer is bitter and accusatory; they thrive on seeing others as incompetent, cruel, unfair, and unwilling to recognize the underminer's fine performance and features. They feel that no one truly appreciates and understands them, they complain chronically, and they blame any failures at work and in relationships on others. Think of this partner as a cauldron of seething hostility and resentment disguised by a façade of innocence and apparent good intentions.

A particularly unsavory aspect of the passive-aggressive personality type is the chronic tendency to devalue and disparage the success and achievements of everyone around her. This person is perpetually competitive and antagonistic toward anyone who seems to do well or have more than the underminer. For example, co-workers who get promotions when the underminer does not will be privately accused of having more opportunities, special privilege, or even of cheating. In contrast, the underminer will believe she was unfairly expected to do more with less, was ignored, or was personally disliked by those untrustworthy and incompetent authority figures who made the promotion decisions.

One of the most difficult things about dealing with the passive-aggressive personality type is his tendency to constantly sabotage work and relationships by faking genuine effort and hard work while intentionally foiling the supervisor's or partner's plans. From your passive-aggressive employee or partner, you can expect forgetting key assignments, poor work quality, being late when punctuality is important, and doing things incorrectly specifically so that you will not ask him to do it again. At first, it may be difficult to become angry at the underminer because these behaviors seem honestly innocent and inadvertent. But as time goes by, the pattern of behavior becomes difficult to ignore. More and more of your interactions with this personality type will be negative and characterized by you yourself becoming quite angry. Here is a secret: If each (or most) interaction with someone leave you feeling personally diminished or somehow undermined and sabotaged, think passive-aggressive until proven otherwise!

What Makes a Passive-Aggressive?

You may be wondering what leads to the development of an undermining personality style. Although there are certainly a mix of contributors — some genetic and biologic and others environmental — experiences of the child with important caregivers seem to play the biggest role in passive-aggressive behavior.

As a child, the underminer probably got adequate care, attention, and nurturing. There may have been nothing especially remarkable about the parent-child relationship early on. At some point, however, the child experienced an interruption in nurturance and care and probably experienced this withdrawal of care as unfair and unjust. This change often happens around the time that a younger sibling is born and parents' attention shifts naturally away from full-time focus on the older sibling. The older sibling may feel outraged and abandoned by her parents. It is also likely that parents' expectations for greater independence and perhaps assistance with more responsibilities around the home felt unreasonable or too difficult. The child began to see authority figures as cruel, withholding, unjust, unreasonable, and perhaps incompetent as well.

But rather than vent anger or express any of these thoughts and feelings directly to parents, the passive-aggressive learns to show dissatisfaction and disagreement indirectly. This may be because the passive-aggressive saw parents as dangerous, violent, or vindictive. For some reason, he got this message: Don't be overtly disgruntled and don't express direct disagreement; either keep it bottled up or conceal it in hidden comments and resistant behaviors. So, when a parent gives the child a directive, he learns to go along and act as though fully willing to comply. But the child does the job wrong, does it poorly, does it after it is required, and makes numerous snide and negativistic comments to siblings about how "unreasonable or stupid" the directive was in the first place.

In some cases, passive-aggressive adults had parents who were quite emotionally abusive in the sense of squashing the child's early dreams and efforts at independence — perhaps shaming the child and suggesting that independence or direct expression of personal views or preferences was somehow defiant or unacceptable. As adults, these undermining personalities have discovered that the only way to express all of their bottled up resentment and anger is to sabotage others — especially those with even a modicum of perceived authority (e.g., parents, bosses, and public figures).

The Passive-Aggressive as Partner

If you are in a relationship with a passive-aggressive partner, you probably vacillate between confusion, anger, and self-doubt. Interactions with a passive-aggressive partner often leave you feeling bewildered and enraged. But wait, he never really said or did anything egregious or deliberately mean-spirited right? Your partner really tried to help out or really meant well when he made that critical comment delivered with a sincere smile, right? You see the problem: It's very difficult to discern exactly what it is about the passive-aggressive that is so enraging and undermining. He seems to mean well. The passive-aggressive partner's subtlety and stealth as a critical, undermining, malevolent force are what make him so dangerous to you emotionally, so entirely toxic in a relationship, and so unlikely to be the person you would ever want to spend your life with.

Loving an undermining adult will very often feel like loving an oppositional-defiant child. You are likely to grow weary of your partner's constant negativity and sarcasm — especially as it is directed to authority figures, bosses, and even you if you try to lay down the law, set limits, or make demands or requests of your partner of any kind. For instance, insisting that your partner help around the house or balance the checkbook may be greeted by a cheerful "sure" only to be followed by a sullen, negative silent period and lousy, mistake-riddled work. Or you may find that even asking your partner to help with a basic household chore turns into a silent battlefield of wills and sarcasm. The net effect is that you end up feeling punished for even asking for help and convinced that you'd be better off just doing it yourself next time. You will probably also hear comments from your partner about your lack of clarity in giving directions and the impossibility of getting the tasks assigned completed in a timely way.

Perhaps the hardest part of all this is the fact that your undermining partner is rarely direct with you about how she feels. The passive-aggressive smiles, nods, agrees, and seems willing to go along on the surface. But inside, she is angry and sees you as an unreasonable parent or other authority figure who must be resisted. This partner will take secret delight in your failure and be happy on some level when your plans are foiled.

If you stay in a relationship with the undermining type, expect your self-esteem to take a hit. As in the case of Lynda at the start of this chapter, your partner might make comments or give gifts that are given with a seemingly genuine caring smile but that are clearly designed to point out your weaknesses. So when your partner leaves ads for diet plans or articles on how to please a partner sexually taped to the refrigerator for you or when she mentions your exact age, weight, or education level in public — knowing full well you are quite sensitive about it — you are correct to see these as passive-aggressive behaviors. Of course, when you confront your partner about how these behaviors made you feel, expect to get a look of shock and feigned remorse: "Oh my, I had no idea you'd take it that way. I forgot how sensitive you were about that. I didn't mean anything negative at all, just thought I could help." Although you will eventually see this for what it is — bullshit — you may initially struggle with your own sanity and wonder if you are just too sensitive or too hard on your partner's sincere efforts to help.

Passive-aggressive adults can also be very difficult sexual partners. First, they may use access to sex as a weapon; their sullen negativity and sarcasm left over from earlier in the day may linger into the bedroom and either repel you or make you feel guilty for confronting them or making demands earlier. Second, and more important, the undermining partner will undermine your sexual pleasure as a means of getting back at you. For example, he may consistently ejaculate prematurely or, more likely, fail to achieve or maintain an erection on certain occasions. The comments that follow may indicate you are too slow or perhaps fail to arouse him adequately. Or, she may fail to have an orgasm and may instead dutifully comply while showing little or no genuine arousal or even interest; you may feel like you are making love to a mannequin. Of course, lack of arousal or failure to achieve orgasm themselves are not indicative of passive-aggressive behavior, but rather it is the inconsistency in sexual response, the tendency to perform poorly as a sexual partner or even to intentionally withhold sex when one is angry or determined to exact revenge for a perceived wrong.

In a nutshell, your undermining partner is ambivalent about you and your relationship. On one hand, he is attracted to you and probably committed on some level. At the same time, he feels put upon, unfairly treated, and unappreciated. These feelings probably have nothing to do with you; they are leftover reactions to relationships or to parents from earlier in life. Because your partner cannot express these feelings directly, he will constantly resist, sabotage, and undermine. In a relationship with a passive-aggressive partner, you will be consistently bewildered and angry.

Why Am I Attracted to Undermining Partners?

So what does it mean about me that I was drawn in by someone who is fundamentally undermining by nature? How did I get into a relationship with this person in the first place? Did I ever see something attractive about this pattern of behavior? Here is a sobering reality check: If you are attracted to the passive-aggressive type, you are attracted to a romantic partner who

- passively refuses to comply with your requests.
- complains that neither you nor anyone else really understands or appreciates her.
- is frequently sullen and argumentative.
- is frequently angry and critical of anyone in authority.
- is envious and resentful of your good fortune and success.
- exaggerates or complains about her own misfortune.
- alternates between appearing to comply passively and becoming defiant and angry.
- frequently leaves you feeling belittled and diminished but denies any intent to do so.

This discussion of how and why one might be attracted to passive-aggressive partners will be brief. Why? Because passive-aggressives are not easy to love and, usually, evidence of their pathology will turn us off and drive us away long before the relationship gets out of first gear. These adults are negative, caustic, sarcastic, and "prickly" in the sense of being difficult to please. Very soon, we end up feeling slighted and criticized around them; our defenses go up and our attraction drops off.

In most cases, you may be initially attracted to the undermining type because this person is physically attractive, smart, or funny. In Lynda's case, she found Nick's acid wit to be novel and entertaining. When coupled with their shared interests and her physical attraction to Nick, this was enough to get things started. Remember, like other personality disorders, unless the traits are extremely severe they are often initially difficult to pick up on. Passive-aggressive personalities are often subtle and savvy in the way they interact with others. These personality types are used to passively manipulating people and situations to get their own needs met. So what may have seemed like humor and sarcasm at first turns out to be cunning passive-aggressive behavior over time.

In some cases, those among us with a need to help, caretake, and rescue may be drawn in by the passive-aggressive's stories of maltreatment and woe at work or in other relationships. We are initially inclined to believe that this person has had a remarkable string of bad luck with tyrannical and unappreciative bosses and colleagues. Previous partners will be made to sound mean spirited, cruel, and hypersensitive. We want to believe that all this person needs is a lover who will really listen and care. We are gratified at the thought of being the good enough and reasonable partner this poor guy or gal has been searching for. Unfortunately, we too will soon be a footnote in the underminer's tale of misfortune.

It is also quite possible that there is something familiar and comfortable in the passive-aggressive's negativity and sullen anger. If you grew up in a home characterized by a parent with these traits, you may be used to walking on eggshells and to the strange rhythm of vindictive anger followed by apologies and claims that your loved one was simply misunderstood. Of course, the challenge of placating or curing a passive-aggressive person is doomed from the start. Remember: This person needs to see others as unfair and unappreciative; he needs to sabotage and undermine as a way of expressing himself. This style is habitual by the time your partner reaches adulthood.

It is difficult to imagine other reasons any reasonably healthy person might be attracted to the sullen mood and undermining behavior of the passive-aggressive. Although this behavior can be comical and entertaining when watched from a distance, it will feel entirely different when experienced firsthand within the boundary of a love relationship. We have encountered few adults — certainly none who want a healthy relationship — who savor being the recipient of passive-aggressive resistance and criticism.

Living with a Passive-Aggressive Partner

What should you do if you are involved with a passive-aggressive partner? Is there any hope? Is it reasonable to expect that your partner might change and become less sabotaging of your relationship and happiness? As psychologists who have worked with a number of couples containing an undermining member, we can tell you that the going will be hard. If your partner's symptoms are comparatively mild (e.g., occasional snide comments, taking excessive amounts of time to complete tasks, sometimes being negativistic and sullen) then you may already have made some adjustments in your own behavior and in your expectations. But, if the symptoms are more pervasive and severe (e.g., is constantly critical and sarcastic about you, nearly always fails to fulfill basic obligations in the relationship but always has a good excuse, punishes you frequently by withholding affection), you should run like the wind. Severe passive-aggressives will be miserable to live with. If you are actually contemplating a commitment to such a corrosive long-term relationship, please consider getting some professional couples consultation before you do.

If you are already in a relationship with an underminer and you are thick skinned or so independent that your partner's behavior takes little emotional toll on you, or if your partner's undermining behavior is only episodic and not noxious enough to deter you from hanging in there, here are a few ideas for making life more palatable.

See Your Partner's Behavior for What It Is

When living with an undermining partner, it is quite easy to be sucked into your partner's perspective and to begin to see yourself as incompetent, demanding, arbitrary, and inadequate as a partner or spouse. In order to have any shot at happiness in this context, you must become skilled at detecting your partner's passive-aggressive maneuvers immediately while recognizing that they have nothing to do with you. Instead, they reflect your partner's strong ambivalence about his own parents and unresolved anxiety about expressing negative feelings directly. So, when your partner becomes sullen or resists your requests through passive avoidance or intentional failure, it would help to see him as a little boy — stomping his feet, pouting, and otherwise discharging his anger in silly passive ways. Like the tantrums of a two-year-old, the behavior of the passive-aggressive works by controlling others in order to get his needs met. This quietly controlling behavior ultimately gets perpetuated because by and large, it works. By using such a lens to view your partner's shenanigans, they might appear ridiculous and sadly pathetic versus enraging or somehow designed just to make your life miserable. This perspective will help you to maintain emotional distance and avoid putting yourself down and blaming yourself all the time.

Set Firm Limits and Stick to Them

When dating or living with a passive-aggressive partner, there will be some things you might be willing to tolerate and other things you will not. Make your rock-bottom, nonnegotiable list of expectations crystal clear, and then hold your partner accountable to honor them. For instance, you may be unwilling to continue in the relationship if your partner's passive-aggressive behaviors at work result in her getting fired. You may have a clear-cut expectation that your partner never use children or family members to passive-aggressively get back at you (e.g., "forgetting" to pick up the kids, "accidentally" mentioning to your mother that you hate it when she comes to visit). You may even decide that you will not allow your partner to make demeaning or abusive comments to or about you — even if your partner later complains that you misunderstood her intended meaning; the mere fact that you interpreted it as derogatory may be enough. Whatever your ironclad expectations about what you will tolerate and what you will not tolerate from a lover, make these unambiguous from the start. If your partner's passive-aggressive behavior is so severe that she cannot refrain from any of the above, then unfortunately you may feel backed into a corner and must then decide whether to continue in this difficult relationship.

Recognize That Therapy Is Rarely a Solution

When you refer your passive-aggressive spouse to psychotherapy, expect to get some passive-aggressive responses. For instance, don't be surprised when your partner just can't seem to get around to scheduling the appointment; and when he does, expect that none of the therapists who are available will have adequate credentials or openings in their schedules. And anticipate some sarcastic comments (e.g., "Yeah, I'm sure sending me to see Dr. Phil will be just the thing to help you feel better about yourself," or "You seem to be the one who takes everything personally, shouldn't you be going to therapy?").

When undermining partners actually do begin treatment, it is quite common for them to be some of the most unpleasant patients with whom mental health professionals work. In the same way that they undermine you at ever turn, they will undermine treatment by placing responsibility for their improvement fully on the therapist while working overtime to disparage the therapist's credentials and techniques. The passive-aggressive partner is not an easy or pleasant customer and change is often difficult to achieve. Let us caution you to not be surprised if your partner consistently holds you primarily responsible for the problems you are encountering in your relationship all the while abdicating himself of responsibility for these issues. Your partner is likely to lash back at you and punish you passively to get you to back off on your requests or demands for change and to bring status quo back into your relationship. Your partner is not likely to feel comfortable being in therapy and having to address your mutual issues in a forthright manner. By holding firm to your expectations for a healthy relationship and by continuing to request dialogue with a third party, you are setting reasonable and healthy limits for yourself and your relationship.

Refuse to Validate Anger and Resentment at Authority Figures

A passive-aggressive partner would like nothing better than to co-opt you into his world of dangerous and unfair authority figures. Be careful not to validate your partner's complaints that bosses and supervisors are all unreasonable and untrustworthy. And don't concur that colleagues who are more fortunate or successful must have had special assistance or privilege. Keep in mind that your partner will see others' intentions through the jaundiced lens of a child still seething at adults for squelching autonomy or making unreasonable demands. At the same time, and through an objective lens, be aware that your partner is likely to do this to you as well. By firmly, yet kindly, not feeding into your partner's accusations and anger you will be modeling and setting appropriate and healthy limits. However, by refusing to engage your partner in his dialogue of anger and bitterness, you should know that you may face an increase in passive-aggressive behavior as a way of bringing you back in or punishing you. As difficult as it is, restrain yourself from feeding into these games with your partner and focus instead on working on and maintaining your integrity and sense of self.

When It's Time to Leave

Unlike some of the other personality types covered in this guide, the passive-aggressive is unlikely to become violent or otherwise dangerous to you should the time arrive when you are no longer willing to keep walking on eggshells and tolerating your partner's undermining behavior. Awareness that the time has come may arrive gradually, with increasing loneliness and declining self-esteem, or it may appear suddenly — such as when a partner says or does something especially demeaning or humiliating to you in public. It may be that simply reading this chapter and finally grasping the severity of your partner's condition has been enough to make staying in the relationship a psychological impossibility for you.

Whatever the reason for leaving, when the time comes, it is most helpful to be straightforward and clear about why you can no longer tolerate her undermining behavior. Be sure to place yourself in a position in which you are not dependent on your partner to leave. If you do, you may experience a lengthy period of resistance and sabotage (e.g., won't sign the papers, can't seem to get organized enough to move out). Take initiative to find alternative housing before you break the news or have friends standing by to ensure that your partner complies with your request.

Finally, you will need a thick skin during the detachment process as your partner cannot help but unleash a barrage of negativity and caustic blame about your rejection of her. Expect to be disparaged and put down, and if you are involved in a community, don't be surprised when you hear that your ex-partner is offering a malicious and unbalanced view of the circumstances of your breakup.

Summary

If dating or living with a sullen, complaining, and oppositional child sounds good to you, then a passive-aggressive partner is just the ticket. Quietly and subtly undermining, this person will suck the happiness out of your relationship by sabotaging you at every turn and then adopting a wide-eyed victim stance any time you try to confront the undermining behavior. Take our word for it, living with a passive-aggressive person can wreak havoc on your self-esteem; you can do better — much better.

ANXIOUS, WITHDRAWN, AND NEEDY PARTNERS

The Scared Partner

The Avoidant Personality

The Sticky Partner

The Dependent Personality

The Rigid Partner

The Obsessive-Compulsive Personality

The Glum Partner

The Depressive Personality

CHAPTER 12

THE SCARED PARTNER
The Avoidant Personality

Avoidant Personality Checklist

- ✔ He avoids occupational activities that involve a large amount of contact with others because of fear of criticism, disapproval, or rejection.
- ✔ He is not willing to get involved with other people unless certain of being liked.
- ✔ He doesn't share easily in close or intimate relationships for fear of being shamed or ridiculed.
- ✔ He is preoccupied with being criticized or rejected when in social situations.
- ✔ He is inhibited or uncomfortable in new social situations because of feelings of inadequacy.
- ✔ He views himself as lacking social skills, as personally unappealing and unlikable, and as socially inferior to others.
- ✔ He is often reluctant to take personal risks or to get involved in new activities because they may end up being too embarrassing.

If your current love interest has some of these symptoms, you may be involved with someone who is fundamentally scared of relationships. You may notice that your partner is deeply afraid of rejection or criticism or you may be having a difficult time getting close to your partner because he seems to be standoffish and distant. If you think that your partner may be genuinely scared of relationships, he may have what psychologists call **Avoidant Personality Disorder**. Read on to hear Jessica's story and learn more about the scared personality type and what you can do if your partner fits this mold.

Jessica's Story

I was working as a computer programmer when I met Gerry. He was sweet and quiet and he sat in the cubicle next to me. I wasn't instantly attracted to Gerry and it took some time to get to know him. Gerry was quiet and didn't talk to me much. If I didn't sit next to him day in and day out, I'm sure we never would have spoken. Now that I think about it, I didn't really see him talk to anybody. He kept to himself and seemed to be really focused on his work. We had the kind of job where it was easy to be solitary and not socialize. You could literally sit at your desk, in your own little cubicle all day, every day and not come into contact with anyone. I started saying hello to him and just engaging in some small talk. At first, he seemed pretty uncomfortable and wouldn't even really look at me.

As time went by, he would talk with me much more, and eventually he even started conversations with me. We started to have a nice, easy friendship that was based on work and talking about movies, which we both loved. At the time, I didn't have many friends as I had only been in St. Louis for about six months. I moved there during the winter for my job and enjoyed it, but to be honest, I hadn't really gotten out much. I had met a few nice people at work and at the gym but I was looking to expand my social circle and even to finding a relationship. Gerry was not the kind of guy I usually hung out with and I never thought of him as dating material. One day, though, he asked if I wanted to go see a movie we had both been wanting to see. I thought of him as a friend and didn't hesitate to say yes. He seemed pretty uncomfortable throughout the evening; he was very quiet and shy. I tried hard to help him feel comfortable so I spent most of the evening initiating small talk and asking lots of questions. It definitely wasn't an easy evening, and I came home tired from trying so hard to help us both have a good time. On the other hand, I felt I could really be myself with Gerry and he seemed kind. In some ways, I came to feel quite protective of Gerry and often defended him at work against other co-workers who thought he was a little aloof and weird.

We started hanging out more and more. We fell into a comfort zone with each other that was easy. I still thought of him as a friend and didn't have any romantic notions toward him. We'd go to the movies, go to dinner, go on bike rides, and just hang out. We talked a lot, but it is interesting that Gerry never shared many intimate or personal details of his life with me. He was reserved that way and he seemed to have a wall up around him that wouldn't let me get too close.

I remember the night he first kissed me. He walked me home from the movies, and when we got to my front door he clumsily pulled me to him and quickly kissed my mouth. He was clearly nervous and I wasn't expecting it. He had never even held my hand before. He blushed after the kiss and started apologizing. I kept reassuring him that it was OK and that I hadn't minded. He hurried off and I didn't hear from him for the rest of the weekend. I left messages and eventually when I saw him at work Monday morning we talked. I think he was relieved that I wasn't angry or upset with him. From there we started becoming more physically intimate. I never felt that spark with Gerry though. The sex was comfortable but not passionate. We continued to move into a closer relationship although in the back of my mind I knew that I wasn't going to stay with him forever and I began to feel guilty. I wanted more from a relationship than just comfort and convenience. Gerry was a great friend but he wasn't what I wanted or needed in a boyfriend. While I felt guilty that I wasn't really as into him as he was into me, I was also becoming increasingly frustrated with Gerry's constant anxiety about doing things with other people in groups. Although he was becoming a lot more comfortable around me, I could see that he hated meetings at work and social activities outside of work.

In my prior relationships we had other friends we hung out with and I was used to being more active socially. Gerry didn't really desire to have other close friends or to go out to parties and socialize. As I got to know him better he started talking about how others weren't really trustworthy and that most people would eventually turn against you. If I went out with other friends, he would sometimes get angry and think I didn't want to be with him anymore. He would sulk and become very sensitive. I would spend the next few days offering reassurance that I still wanted to be with him. Being with Gerry took a lot of energy and I seemed to be doing most of the work. He rarely put himself out there like that for me. I can't remember him telling me I was pretty or paying me other compliments.

The biggest mistake I made was moving in with Gerry. My lease was up and it seemed the easy, logical thing to do. Our relationship started feeling platonic to me, even though we were still having sex. Our sex wasn't exciting and I didn't look forward to it; it was routine and boring, just like our relationship. I knew that although I loved Gerry I definitely wasn't "in love" with him. He seemed content with our relationship and didn't seem to desire more. He was happy staying home and watching movies every Friday and Saturday night. He didn't seem to get excited about too much and he never seemed to change. He had the same haircut, wore the same clothes, and drove the same old car, and he seemed fine with it all. He didn't enjoy hanging out with my other friends because he said he had nothing in common with them and that they didn't really like him anyway. It is true that my friends thought he was a little strange, but it was because he never talked to them and acted really strange and uncomfortable. Sometimes, if he had to speak in front of a group, he'd get terribly nervous and could hardly make eye contact. He wouldn't put himself out there to change anything and would get upset and angry if I suggested that he should try or be anything different. He would retreat and almost punish me with his silence until I bent over backward with apologies.

One night I went out with my friends and I met Eric. He was easy to talk to, seemed interested in me, and was fun. I started seeing him when I could and we started talking. I got to know Eric slowly over the next few months and realized what I was missing in my relationship with Gerry. Gerry wasn't willing to take any risks; he was constantly worried people wouldn't like him. He didn't have a desire to grow, and he definitely wasn't passionate about anything. He was cynical of almost everything and particularly of other people. With Gerry, I wasn't going to have excitement or someone I could share the details of life with.

It took me time to work up the courage to tell Gerry because I knew he would be devastated. I told him one night after a movie and he just sat there and stared at me. He told me that I was just like everyone else who didn't value who he was and that he knew eventually I would reject him. He acted like he had been just waiting for me to tell him the news. I will never know whether he noticed that I had started to distance myself or whether it was his natural tendency to be so distrustful. He asked to change cubicles at work, and he went back to being isolated and to overworking. He hardly ever spoke to me again. I couldn't take the tension at work and eventually changed jobs. I'm still in a relationship with Eric and am so much happier.

The Scared Personality

As we move through life, we learn how to navigate relationships and we test the waters socially to meet new people and enjoy new life experiences. We learn to communicate, to assert ourselves, and to get our needs met, simultaneously appreciating that others are also testing the waters and seeking connection. Over time, we come to appreciate ourselves in relation to others and develop a measure of comfort with our own niche in the social world. Some people, however, never seem to learn to negotiate these delicate social maneuvers; they always seem a little lost in the relational world. It appears that they are truly scared that others will not like them for who they are nor value what they have to offer. As a result, they tend to instantly question the motives of those who interact with them. Of course, this fear is more reflective of their own lack of self-esteem than any truth about other people. Nonetheless, scared personality types project these feelings of unworthiness onto the world and consequently are very timid and fearful of disapproval and rejection from others. In a real way, their expectation of rejection sensitizes them to any microscopic thread of possible dislike or rejection in the reactions of those they meet. Unlike the detached partner, the scared partner actually desires connection, but fear demands that others be avoided.

People with scared personalities often have a difficult time feeling comfortable in occupational settings. Even though most jobs entail some form of contact with others, this personality type is fearful of being evaluated and critiqued; therefore, they are likely to try flying "below the radar" at work and may avoid social gatherings at all costs. For the avoidant, work can be dangerous indeed; avoidants may feel helplessly locked into situations that require them to be involved in group meetings or group projects. The avoidant does not like the limelight in any form and dreads the prospect of leadership roles — those most likely to require up-front exposure and potential evaluation by others. They will often not accept increasing levels of responsibility or job promotions that may put them in positions where others are evaluating or judging them and/or their performance. The avoidant is most content doing a job in solitude where she can skirt the likelihood of appraisal from others. Others will notice this, not just in her demeanor or interactions but also in her dress and mannerisms. Like chameleons, avoidants are skilled at blending into the environment to reduce the risk of detection and attention.

So far, you can see that the avoidant personality struggles with a great deal of internal conflict. On one hand, she wants and needs relationships that offer security and trust, yet she is afraid to put herself out there in order to initiate these relationships for fear of being rejected, criticized, and judged. Most of us discover early on that in order to be in relationships with others — whether intimate romantic relationships or friendships — we must be vulnerable and open enough to trust and let others into our lives. We expect, in turn, that others are going to be open enough and trust us enough to let us into their lives. Being relational entails trust and a certain amount of faith in others; we must be accessible and accessibility will always require a leap of faith that others are generally of good will.

Scared personality types are certainly not the only people who struggle with distrust and anxiety. As psychologists, we find trust issues to be among the most prevalent issues in therapy clients of all sorts. Most of us enter into relationships with the hope that they will be mutual, reciprocal, and safe. But in life we get hurt and we get let down. In order to move on from old relationships and try again in new ones, we learn to cope with these disappointments and make meaning from them without retreating for fear of future pain. In contrast, the avoidant person has developed a perpetual problem with trust. Avoidants will only enter relationships if given a guarantee that they will be loved and accepted. Of course, such relationship guarantees do not exist. Avoidants don't easily form relationships, and when they do, it is common for them to put partners through repeated "tests" of loyalty and sincerity. They tend not to learn from previous disappointments and cannot accept the fact that there is nothing especially unlovable or awful about them. Consequently, trust, or the lack of it, follows them into each new relationship and the anxiety it produces can undermine connections from the start.

Avoidants are scared, intimidated, and fearful of relationships. They have perfected the art of flying below the radar in both appearance and in behavior. You will not find any avoidants singing karaoke or volunteering to chair committees! They are hesitant to get close to others and are slow to establish new relationships or to reveal anything personal about themselves. They are much more content to have a few close friends than to have a large social network. Saturday nights are much more enjoyable at home in front of the television than out on the town or at a party. They aren't looking for job promotions or to become involved in group projects or social clubs. Again, the pattern for the avoidant is to depend on himself and to get the job done quietly, away from all evaluating eyes. Although many of us are shy to varying degrees, the avoidant's extreme shyness and anxious distrust leads to both career and relationship distress and impairment.

What Makes an Avoidant?

As a child, the avoidant person was typically very shy and quiet. Even as children, people with this personality style appeared to be socially inhibited and uncomfortable in groups of people or in social activities. The child may have refused to attend school because she felt uncomfortable with the demands from others at school and from being placed into new educational situations without guarantee of acceptance. Avoidant personality, like other forms of shyness, has a genetic link and these childhood behaviors tend to be carried over into adulthood.

However, environment may play an even more significant role in one's tendency to avoid. Persons who are avoidant often report a family and parental history of anxiety and fear. These parents tended to have a parenting style that was overprotective and fear based. They may have reacted to everyday situations with phobic avoidance or intense fear, thereby sensitizing their own child to overreaction and overevaluation of threat in social situations. When coupled with the child's natural tendency to be shy and withdrawn, these parental modeling effects can leave a powerful and enduring imprint. There have also been some retrospective studies with adults who meet the criteria for avoidant personality who report high levels of childhood emotional abuse. This evidence would further explain the lack of trust the avoidant person feels toward others and the need for constantly assessing loyalty and seeking unconditional acceptance.

The Avoidant as Partner

Sounds exhausting to be the person trying to have a relationship with an avoidant doesn't it? To be quite frank, it is. The tests and hoops that the avoidant puts romantic partners through are often relentless. The avoidant needs constant reassurance and uncritical acceptance. Your partner will want and demand unconditional love and affirmation from you but drive you crazy in the process by not reciprocating. And no amount of reassurance and kid-glove kindness on your part will ever really be enough. If you are in a relationship with an avoidant you may be feeling annoyed and resentful at the constant emotional demands your partner is placing on you. It isn't uncommon to feel burned out in these relationships; you are likely not getting your own social and emotional needs met, while trying hard to constantly convince your avoidant partner that your attraction, loyalty, and acceptance are the real thing.

Even the early phase of the relationship can be a challenge. The avoidant person is initially aloof and distant and your early courtship may feel like a cat-and-mouse game that may keep you challenged and stimulated. You may find yourself working very hard to entice your partner into dating or showing interest in you. You may look back now and recognize that without your herculean effort, the relationship would never have gotten off the ground. You may also recognize that your partner's anxiety and reluctance to trust tugged at your heartstrings and kept you engaged.

Even after you began dating, your partner was probably not very forthcoming with private and intimate information and may have actually become scared when you shared your feelings and desires with him. Although he may have welcomed your attention on some level, there will always be some lingering hesitancy to trust you entirely. Avoidants are terrified of revealing themselves due to an internal conviction that others won't like what they see.

You may also have noticed that over the course of your relationship, life with your partner has become more restricted. Avoidants play it safe socially and you may now see that their approach to life in general is mundane and unexciting. What at first felt cautious and responsible to you, may now feel somewhat boring. The person with an avoidant personality is likely to highly regulate her life and those in it in order to cope with fear and anxiety over being hurt and rejected by others. An avoidant partner owns a measure of suspicious doubt and expects to be let down and hurt by others. Therefore, any innocent quip or humorous comment is seen as evidence that others can't be trusted or that others are going to be critical or rejecting. If you, or someone else, are even minimally disapproving the avoidant person may feel extremely rejected or hurt. Consequently, you may feel as if you can't speak your mind in your relationship.

Over time, you may also notice that your partner has other anxieties and may also harbor intense sadness. In contrast to some of the other personality disorders, the person who meets the criteria for Avoidant Personality Disorder has a considerable level of internal distress. Freud may have called this person "neurotic." A life rooted in pervasive fear and worry can be exhausting and sometimes makes scared types depressed. You may have experienced your partner reacting with a lot of anxiety about having to be in social situations where he feels people are looking at him and then becoming depressed before or after these experiences. Such perpetual anxiety can lead to chronic emotional exhaustion and low-level depression. Ironically, these mood problems can cause actual rejection in relationships.

Why Am I Attracted to Scared Partners?

What if I am currently in a relationship with a scared partner or if I have a history of having relationships with scared partners? What if I keep getting drawn in by the scared and needy ways of the avoidant type? Essentially, it means that you are drawn to someone who

- believes you are naturally critical and disapproving.
- is scared to get or stay involved with you unless you are unconditionally accepting and constantly reassuring.
- withholds personal disclosures from you for fear you will be rejecting.
- feels inadequate and refuses to try new things for fear you will ridicule or criticize.
- is preoccupied with the idea that you will ultimately be rejecting and disloyal.
- actually thinks that you are malevolent in your thoughts and intentions.
- always avoids social situations because they may prove to be embarrassing.

So, what does this say about you and your own attraction triggers? It may be that the challenge of the cat-and-mouse game sucks you in. The avoidant person is initially difficult to get close to, and this challenge can be enticing to some. It is part of human nature to desire what we can't have and to be especially intrigued by things we must work hard for. This is especially true when romancing an avoidant person. Here is the classic scared rabbit character and it may seem that a good hug and lots of affection will do just the trick. This person seems so pathetically self-deprecating and skeptical that she could possibly have anything to offer that your heartstrings may be tugged furiously. Initially distant, avoidants are not forthcoming with emotions or self-disclosure.

You may also find that the more you work for the avoidant's trust and attention, the more you are rewarded. Such positive changes in trust and apparent interest can keep you wanting more. Substantial psychological research shows that intermittent or occasional rewards are the most powerful and effective when it comes to solidifying new behavior patterns (Beck, Freeman & Associates, 1990). Like a lab rat, you may be willing to press the bar constantly in hopes of a small reward — perhaps a small sign of affection, trust, or social risk taking. This is all fine, but the problem is that you are doing all the work while the avoidant partner cautiously waits for you to prove yourself perfectly reliable — an impossible task.

An important question to ask yourself is whether this pattern appeals to you on some level. Do you notice that in new relationships you seem to be attracted to the distant, aloof, uninterested type? Do you do most of the hard work to get your relationships off the ground? What is it about the need to win over a reluctant partner that so entices you? These are difficult yet necessary questions to grapple with. We all tend to re-create relationship patterns — including those that may not be healthy. This pattern probably has roots in childhood and has been reinforced along the way. Does this pattern continue for you in adulthood? Is this pattern of constantly seeking to woo the reluctant mate working for you? If not, it may be a good time to talk with someone who can help you make some change in this cycle.

Many of us enter the dating world programmed to take care of others. But at what point do you give too much of yourself? If you are attracted to an avoidant personality precisely because of her profound need to be taken care of and protected from humiliation and rejection, we would suggest that this may be a no-win relationship. Because the avoidant has an ardent and insatiable need to be reassured and reaffirmed, you will be perpetually providing these things. Your work will never be done. You may be discovering that what once felt sweet and endearing now feels like an onerous demand.

People often stay in relationships with the avoidant longer than may be healthy because they feel bad about leaving. As you have probably noticed, the avoidant person can easily become dependent for several reasons. First, their support system is fairly limited, causing them to become more dependent on the few souls they do have connections to. Second, because avoidant's social skills are often underdeveloped, they rely heavily on their few close confidants for advice and support. Third, an avoidant may become comfortable with your caretaking over time and therefore more complacent about the relationship. They are content to have only a few friends, and they don't feel the need to venture out as long as these relationships are reliable.

Living with an Avoidant Partner

If you are dating or living with an avoidant personality type, you appreciate the fact that your partner's personality traits are deeply entrenched and pervasive; scared partners have a lifelong history of social unease, fear, and withdrawal. Containing a scared partner's anxiety is a full-time job and you may be on your own when it comes to addressing your own needs. Like many of the personality disorders covered in this guide, the avoidant type is high maintenance — most of your emotional resources will get tied up in constant reassurance. If, in spite of this sober assessment, you plan to stay in a relationship with an avoidant partner, we offer you a few ideas for reducing the worst conflicts associated with loving an avoidant person.

Be Realistic about Your Expectations

Once again, we must underscore that the deeply entrenched and pervasive behavioral and emotional patterns of any PDP are not easily changed. Keep in mind that your partner's anxious avoidance and difficulty with trust is now a part of his very being. At least take this into consideration when you think about asking your partner to change. Asking your partner to trust you to be reliable, venture into new social territory, or take more initiative for helping to nurture and grow your relationship can feel quite daunting or overwhelming for your partner.

If you can manage to keep your expectations small and reasonable, you are more likely to celebrate small successes.

Gently but Honestly Tell Your Partner What You Need

You are in a precarious position when trying to work on issues with your partner. The very act of voicing concerns may inadvertently reinforce your partner's fear of critique and abandonment. Your partner may react with anger or sadness or may withdraw from you when you attempt such discussion. Be mindful that this is your partner's effort to protect himself from intense fear of rejection. Concern about your partner's fragile ego may keep you from moving forward with your wish to work on the relationship or asking to get some of your own needs met. Real change cannot occur if you join with your partner in avoiding conflicts and your own dissatisfaction. We suggest that you kindly and gently — but assertively — address your needs and concerns while continuing to show commitment and care. If your partner can come to accept that your desire is not to exit the relationship but to strengthen it, he may, over time, be better prepared to hear you and respond constructively.

Try to Open New Doors for Yourself and Your Partner

Growth and change are essential ingredients in any healthy relationship, yet it is not uncommon for the avoidant person to be "stuck" in a safe and isolated routine. Trying new activities and experiencing new social adventures is terrifying for the scared type. She is much more comfortable with the same routines and the predictable stability you have helped her to create. Your relationship may feel like a cocoon while everything else outside is potentially embarrassing or anxiety provoking. Nonetheless, remaining stagnant in order to appease an avoidant partner can be stunting for you and can cause deep resentment in your relationship.

Consider ways to gently push your partner's comfort envelop and meet some of your own needs in the process. For example, talk to your partner about setting up a date night. Pick the activity together and by all means go through with the date. At first, you may want to pick something that is less adventuresome (go for a long walk and then grab a bite to eat at your favorite low-key restaurant). Over time, add some new activities to your date night (a new restaurant, an art opening, a concert). The key is to continue to spend quality time together outside of your usual routine. Over time, try to integrate new people or other couples into your time together. If your partner refuses to participate, set up some time with your friends or even alone to go out and have some fun. Of course, you shouldn't expect your partner to celebrate your independence; be ready for some possible emotional backlash. But all things considered, you will be a healthier partner and person if you refuse to allow your partner's avoidant anxiety to restrict your own social life.

Urge Your Partner to Seek out Professional Help

Although you now understand the resistance of personality disorders to change, we always remain hopeful that some movement along the continuum from rigidity to flexibility can occur. Some personality traits — with time, patience, and hard work — can be attenuated. But rather than try to achieve this on your own, we strongly urge you to seek the help of a professional who has advanced skills with personality-disordered adults. The avoidant personality is unique among personality-impaired partners in that he is often in psychological distress. It is difficult and exhausting to live with high levels of anxiety and fear, and your avoidant partner may be quite motivated to reduce his own suffering. Because the avoidant person often feels unhappy and distressed, your partner may seek out help and change.

When It's Time to Leave

After much soul searching and attempts at promoting change, you may come to the realization that this relationship isn't working for you. For your sake and for that of your partner, it is helpful to leave the relationship peacefully and to be sure that you handle the ending with integrity. We recommend honestly, yet gently, letting your partner know the reasons you are ending the relationship. It would be especially useful to remind your partner that there is nothing inherently "wrong" or "bad" about her but rather that you need more from a relationship. Honestly, the avoidant may be one of the most difficult partners in this guide to leave. The reason is she is so profoundly sensitized to rejection. You may feel a little like you are crushing a child's hopes and dreams, you may feel guilty and ashamed, and you may worry whether your partner will ever recover from the blow. Although none of these trepidations should be enough to keep you locked in an unhappy relationship with an impaired partner, be prepared for them. Seek support from friends and family, eat well, exercise, and be socially engaged. You may also be willing to maintain some friendly contact with this partner as a way of helping her transition out of the relationship. But this will depend on your own tolerance for your partner as well as her ability to have appropriate boundaries and to acknowledge the reality of the breakup.

Summary

Although avoidant personality disorders are rarely malignant or dangerous, an avoidant partner can be quite exhausting. Deeply reticent, terrified of disapproval, and preoccupied with his or her own inadequacy or unworthiness, this partner will be too scared to fully enter into a relationship with you without your constant reassurance and approval. Even then, the connection will be tenuous and you may feel more like a therapist or a parent than a lover engaged in a mutual relationship. It is difficult to imagine that this partner will ever feel like a genuine peer. Think twice before taking on the full-time job of loving a scared partner.

CHAPTER 13

THE STICKY PARTNER
The Dependent Personality

Dependent Partner Checklist

✔ She has difficulty making everyday decisions without a lot of advice and reassurance from you and from others.

✔ She needs you, or others, to assume responsibility for most major areas of her life.

✔ She has difficulty disagreeing or taking a stand against others for fear of disapproval or loss of support.

✔ She has a hard time starting projects or doing things herself because of a lack of confidence in her abilities or judgments.

✔ She goes to great lengths for nurturance and support from others and will sometimes even volunteer to do things that are unpleasant to feed this need.

✔ She often feels uncomfortable and helpless when alone because of intense fears of being unable to take care of herself.

✔ She quickly and urgently seeks new relationships for care and support when a close relationship ends.

✔ She is unrealistically preoccupied with fears of having to take care of herself.

A re some or all of these symptoms all too familiar to you? Are you currently trapped in a relationship with someone who clings to you like a barnacle? Do you feel cornered because your partner seems unable to get by without your constant presence? Or maybe you have a pattern of relationships with sticky and clingy partners? Sticky partners — those a psychologist might label **Dependent Personality Disorders** — can be profoundly difficult to manage and quite hard to separate from should this become necessary. If you find yourself taking care of dependent partners, pay special attention to this chapter.

Peter's Story

I grew up in a pretty traditional home. My father worked as an accountant and had his own business. My mom was a teacher at the elementary school down the street from our house but decided to stay home to raise my brother and me after we were born. We lived in a small town where you knew everybody and my parents were very involved in my life with friends and school. I remember coming home from school every day to a house that was happy. My mom took care of everything and really made our lives quite easy. My dad was the breadwinner and he and my mom seemed happy. She volunteered in the community and had lunches with her friends, and it seemed that that was how life worked.

I finished high school, moved to the big city, and met Chrissy. She was a little shy at first but seemed really caring and nice. It took me a while to feel like I really knew her, but she had a way of making me feel special, like she would do anything for me. When we met she had a job working at a library, her own apartment, and a few friends. She seemed independent but had a side to her that was endearing and naïve. I liked the complexity of her personality; she seemed capable but also really needed me. I was far from home and liked having someone around who was supportive; she was always there for me. She was also a great cook and seemed to love waiting on me!

As soon as Chrissy and I became exclusive, I noticed that things had changed — or maybe I was just more aware that she was dependent on me for everything. It wasn't long before I began to feel really smothered. It was more subtle at first — lots of phone calls to check in with me, to find out what I was doing, to ask questions about my opinion on things. The more I got to know her the more I noticed that her "friends" took advantage of her. She was one of those people who were "always there," and people sort of treated her like a doormat. Even though I knew she didn't like it, she let it happen over and over again.

There were times when I even did it, and I always felt bad about it afterward because she was so nice about it.

Making a decision — about anything — was hard for Chrissy, and she asked for my thoughts and advice on everything. It was almost like when she had to make a decision she would become paralyzed. If she couldn't reach me, she would call her mother or anyone so that she could run the idea by them. Also, when she couldn't reach me, she would call me over and over again: There were days when I checked my phone and she had called over twenty times. When I got angry at and frustrated with her, she would cry and be apologetic and sweet. She would go out of her way to make everything OK with us. She would fall apart if I stayed angry at her; she just couldn't handle it.

As our relationship progressed, her passivity became worse. I knew that we had different political and religious views. She wouldn't have a conversation about it with me I think because she was afraid to disagree with me or that I would be angry that she didn't believe the way I did. I used to push her to talk to me about hot topics and we would either have a fight because I would become angry at her for not standing up for what she believed in or she would become tearful and walk out of the room. She would call her mother or a girlfriend and cry on the phone for hours about the situation. Eventually, she would come back to me and smooth things over. I loved Chrissy but I wanted her to be stronger and more independent.

I began wondering if this was the type of relationship I really wanted. Did I want to take care of someone the way Chrissy needed to be taken care of? Did I want to be in a relationship with someone who needed me for everything? Did I want to make all her decisions? Chrissy couldn't even pick out a restaurant when we went out. I picked literally every movie, restaurant, and event we went to. I initiated sex every time and I even had to help her pick out which clothes to wear sometimes! In some weird way I think that she was so afraid I'd leave that she would do anything I asked her to do, even if it was degrading.

I finally couldn't do it anymore. I felt drained and I dreaded her phone calls. I was starting to be really cold to her and I could tell my responses to her were hurtful and mean. She tried really hard to keep us together, but I knew it wasn't healthy. It took a lot to walk away from her because I knew she was a kind, warm person. But, I knew that I wasn't the right person for her and that I needed someone who was more of a partner to me; I just wasn't attracted to someone I had to look out for and take care of all the time. I felt really smothered and responsible for her happiness. Although when I look back I am thankful I walked away, I felt guilty about it for a long time.

The Sticky Personality

The defining feature of the sticky person is the need to be taken care of. This person seeks excessive reassurance and guidance from others and has a profound lack of self-assurance. Dependents work so desperately hard at pleasing that they are often quite easy to get along with. In fact, dependents are often described as nice, caring, and accommodating to a fault. But they require such copious quantities of reassurance and connection that they become a burden to anyone but another dependent type.

Because they fear being alone and not having someone to help them through life, sticky types typically assume a passive role vis-à-vis others as a way of arranging to have others take initiative and in the process take care of them. They lack the ability to be truly independent and often feel a sense of desperation when someone is not there to help them navigate life. In order to achieve and maintain the level of emotional intimacy and caretaking they require, they are often willing to go to great lengths to maintain harmony in their relationships. The person who was initially so pleasing and easy to be with may evolve into a person who is highly clingy or "sticky" emotionally. Of course, the dependent partner has not actually changed, you have simply become more aware of the extent of her neediness. It may dawn on you at some point that your dependent partner feels like the psychological equivalent of a child.

This tendency to need others perpetuates a cycle of diminishing confidence in the dependent person's self-esteem. In other words, the more he need someone else, the less he believes in himself, which in turn, causes him to have less self-efficacy — ultimately leading him to depend on others more for a sense of adequacy. This negative cycle can, in turn, cause the dependent person to become depressed, sometimes quite significantly so. When dependents are asked how they would define or describe themselves, they often have a difficult time finding the right descriptive words. When one never looks inside for approval and acceptance, it is hard to know oneself independent of the views of others; the dependent is truly defined by connections to others.

It is also difficult always trying to live up to other people's expectations or desires, yet the dependent person strives for this kind of constant support and guaranteed acceptance. Of course most of us are simply unable to offer this amount of constant assurance and unwavering caretaking, especially in a romantic relationship that ideally feels more like a partnership than parenthood. Efforts to encourage more independence may leave the dependent person feeling anxious and sad. When a romantic partner demands greater autonomy, the dependent person can easily become clingier, more "gluey," and more emotionally demanding. Insecurity and anxiety are the primary emotions motivating the dependent. In terms of thought processes, expect the dependent partner to be both naïve and suggestible — often denying real problems in life and in relationships — and prone to catastrophic thinking about how awful, terrible, and unlivable it would be if you were to leave.

For all of these reasons, one label often attached to the dependent is doormat. Fear of being alone and helpless drives the dependent person to great lengths. She forgives what others frequently will not, and she will engage in behaviors that are demeaning and cling to unfulfilling or even abusive relationships in order to keep peace.

The dependent person also has longstanding conflicts surrounding trust. He has unjustified fears of abandonment and seeks considerable reassurance from others of loyalty and affection; he is needy and demands time and attention. In our own practices, we think of dependent persons as black holes of need: No amount of attention or empathy is enough to genuinely satisfy him or encourage thoroughgoing independence.

Dependents' lack of self-esteem and efficacy contribute to their fear that they cannot function in society without the help of others. They rarely engage in projects or tasks by themselves, and if they do, will seek out reassurance from others. They work best in an environment where they are assigned tasks and will function optimally when given constant praise and encouragement along the way. Without this guidance, they are not likely to complete a task or to be successful. At her core, the dependent person has a deep feeling of ineptness and inadequacy that leads to feeling profoundly incompetent.

The underlying preoccupation of dependents is the horrifying prospect that they will be left alone in the world to fend for themselves.

This unrealistic fear frequently drives their flight into relationships in the first place, and it may keep them mired in relationships that have long since stopped working. The dependent, by definition, "needs" others and so will seek to surround himself with people who can meet this demand. If, for some reason a relationship ends, the dependent person will quickly find a new relationship in order to get the support and care he requires. Many counselors and family members can testify to the fact that dependent adults seem to constantly "jump" from one bad relationship into one that is equally bad — often with a similarly incompatible partner.

In summary, the sticky person is largely driven by fear — fear of being alone. People with Dependent Personality Disorders are more likely to define themselves by what they lack than by what they have. They are happy when others are present and when they have created an environment in which they believe they have secured guaranteed companionship. They crave encouragement and the counsel of others. They are at their best when they have others to initiate projects on their behalf and when they are then showered with advice and praise. Consequently, their sense of self is poorly defined and they continually reinforce the notion that they are not capable or competent.

What Makes a Dependent?

How does someone become so dependent? What happened in this person's childhood or later development that contributes to this dependent style? There is likely to have been a confluence of events that molded this personality style. Beyond certain hardwired personality traits and styles, dependent personalities are likely to have grown up in a home characterized by significant parental control, overprotection, and excessive nurturance. It may have been the case that one or both of her parents took care of the child's every need and not only failed to encourage independence, but undermined it at every turn. Therefore, the child did not learn how to make decisions and meet her own needs. This child may also have been teased or mocked by peers as a "sissy," "baby," or "wimp." All of these experiences, together with an innate predisposition to fear being alone, shaped the dependence that you are witnessing in your partner and experiencing in your relationship today. While this personality style may have worked at one point as your partner adapted to the bumps along the road of life by clinging to others, it is no longer productive.

Considerably more of those diagnosed with Dependent Personality Disorder each year are women. There are several reasons for this gender difference in the prevalence of dependence. First, girls are more likely than boys to be reinforced for showing dependent features early in life; girls are rewarded for nurturing, caring for others, and placing the needs of others — especially males — first. Second, some cultures prize dependent behavior in women; subservience, passivity, and selfless service may be admired in specific cultures or geographic contexts. Finally, in circumstances of stress, men and women may react differently; men may resort to violence or other active strategies, while women may turn to protective and nurturing roles — both of these strategies probably have evolutionary value. But don't forget, dependence does occur in men. The following example illustrates this fact.

One of the authors had a male client who returned unexpectedly from an extended business trip to find his wife in bed with another man. Rather than confront the situation head-on — so afraid was he of losing his wife and being alone — he began living in his car, parked a few blocks away from his own house. While his cheating spouse insisted she simply needed "time to sort things out," he continued to give her his paychecks and did not tell anyone what was going on. He was so worried about alienating his spouse that he did not argue when she told him he could not see his own two-year-old daughter. Eventually, this man became so depressed and dysfunctional at work that his supervisor learned the truth and took charge of the situation — leading this now-depressed man through the steps of a separation, child custody, and financial reorganization. Of course, he then became quite dependent on his psychologist and required considerable reassurance and encouragement in the process of finding appropriate support groups.

The Dependent as Partner

If you are or have been in a relationship with a dependent person, you have probably felt smothered and overwhelmed. A relationship that at first seemed sweet and alluring has probably become restrictive and oppressive. If your current partner is dependent, the relational demands you bear likely crept up over time and now consume much of your life. Consequently, finding time alone and enjoying independence has taken second fiddle to the emotional requirements of your partner. The more you try to assert your independence and push your partner to do the same, the more insecure she becomes. Your partner does not have the emotional strength to allow you your own time and space. This may ultimately cause you to feel resentful and angry. Setting firm boundaries or backing away is likely to cause your partner to become clingier and needier. This negative cycle is relentless and exhausting. What's the fundamental problem? Your partner does not have the skills or the sense of self to be an equal partner in your relationship.

Here is the dilemma: Can you maintain the demands of this relationship over time? This is a relationship that is not likely to be emotionally balanced. Your role in this relationship is emotionally parental, and it is not unusual for the dependent person to become more demanding over time. The needier the dependent person becomes, the more her self-esteem and self-efficacy suffer. Burnout in this type of relationship is high, and ultimately both partners face crisis. Ultimately, it is likely that neither you nor your dependent partner will feel satisfied and fulfilled in this relationship.

In summary, the dependent person has unrelenting emotional needs and places overwhelming demands on both the relationship and his partner. This person goes to extraordinary lengths for attention, caring, and support that may prove exhausting to any partner. Both partners ultimately feel as if their needs go unmet, which causes unhappiness and distress. The prognosis for an increasingly and mutually interdependent relationship is modest at best. Staying with a sticky partner means a commitment to tolerating at least some dependence in the relationship for the long term.

Why Am I Attracted to Sticky Partners?

So what does it mean that you were drawn to a dependent partner? What if you have a track record of relationships with the sticky type? For starters, it means you are drawn — at least on some level — to someone who

- has difficulty making everyday decisions without reassurance from others.
- needs others to assume responsibility for all aspects of life.
- rarely disagrees with others for fear of loss of support or approval.
- has difficulty initiating projects.

- goes to excessive lengths to obtain nurturance and support.
- feels uncomfortable and helpless when alone.
- quickly seeks new relationships when old ones end.
- is fearful of being left alone to care for self.

Why might you be drawn to dependent types? If your current relationship is an anomaly and most of your love relationships have not been with dependent persons, then it may simply be that the person you are currently with was physically appealing or otherwise interesting. Perhaps his quiet approach and desire to be quite close most of the time were endearing. Yet, you do not generally find dependent features to be attractive in partners.

But others reading this chapter, when honest with themselves, admit that they have a long history of love connections to sticky partners. In this case, it is essential to honestly explore the dynamics of relationships with dependents that might lure you in time and time again.

Far and away the biggest contributor to repeated relationships with sticky types is the need to caretake. Some of us are natural nurturers and find the needy behaviors of a dependent personality too much to ignore. It is as though we are wired to respond with attraction and even arousal to the person who clings to us for security, comfort, and reassurance. Perhaps you came from a family in which you learned early on to take care of one or both parents, your siblings, or others in your environment. Something about this was gratifying and rewarding, and your parenting behavior continued through early adulthood. You may have been the same person who couldn't say no to adopting a new puppy or kitten. In some ways, you may be at your best when taking care of someone who needs you. What's the problem then? The problem is that you are reading this book and wondering what went wrong in your love relationship. This tells us that taking care of a dependent partner is no longer gratifying or has somehow ceased to work for you. To be honest, this may signal that you are getting healthy and relinquishing the childhood pattern of focusing all your energy on the needs of others.

Beyond a simple need to caretake, some people find the deferring, needy conduct of a dependent adult to be arousing or romantically attractive. Perhaps your opposite sex parent had these traits, or maybe you have just always been attracted to the endearing element of a person who seems to lack self-esteem. Rushing in to comfort or rescue feels familiar and meaningful to you on some level. You repeat this pattern in different relationships, and each partner ends up being chronically and seriously sticky.

At times, those among us with strong needs for affirmation and ego stroking may continually choose dependent partners because they are usually happy to focus all of their attention and energy on whomever they are currently attached to. You may realize that you like being in relationships where you have more control and power. Having little self-esteem or ego separate from her partners, the dependent person will continually defer her own needs in the interest of serving you. However, what may at first have felt flattering and gratifying may now feel restrictive and smothering.

And there is another powerful reason some people with dependent partners end up staying in these relationships long after they have ceased to be mutual or satisfying in any way: Fear. Some of us are just too afraid of hurting or wounding a partner who already seems fragile and profoundly needy. Each time you come close to leaving, your partner's desperation and panic may be so upsetting or hard to watch that you back down and convince yourself that things really aren't that bad or perhaps that you couldn't live with yourself if you crushed your partner emotionally by abandoning him. Of course, fear of dealing with a partner's emotional reaction to your leaving is a lousy reason for staying in any relationship; it is a powerful motivator nonetheless.

Living with a Dependent Partner

As you can see, life with a dependent partner can be emotionally smothering and relationally claustrophobic. Here is the question: Can you live with a dependent partner indefinitely? One thing to consider is whether your partner seems distressed about the nature of your relationship. The prognosis or likelihood of change for people with a personality disorder is usually based on whether they are motivated to change and whether they have insight into their behavior. People with personality disorders have notoriously limited insight regarding their problem, and they also have a tendency to blame others when things aren't going well. Your partner may accept little responsibility for your relationship predicament. Dependent PDPs are worried their lovers will not accept them, and they are worried about abandonment. When your partner discovers that you are unhappy, her worst fear may be confirmed — that you may not be able or willing to continue to make unconditional reassurances or that you may want to leave. This may cause your partner to go into crisis, or even trigger flight into another relationship where she hopes to get dependent needs met. If you decide to commit to a dependent person, here are some strategies that might help you and your partner.

As Always, Be Cautiously Optimistic

True change takes time and dedication; it takes a lot of practice and perseverance. The old adage A leopard can't change its spots certainly holds true here; however, the dependent person may, in fact, be able to lighten them a little! It is our experience that when a couple containing a dependent partner comes to therapy, they are in quite a bit of distress and turmoil. The dependent person is often terrified of losing the relationship and is also tired of feeling so desperate and needy. It is not uncommon for this person to be clinically depressed and anxious. The upside here is that distress often comes before important change. After all, growth rarely occurs when times are good. Here is a caution, however: Your partner may go through the motions of seeking change merely to please you. Passive approaches to change are seldom fruitful.

Help Your Partner Enjoy Small Successes

Your partner has long been dependent on others to initiate activities and to make decisions. Help your partner slowly begin to make his own decisions. Don't fall into the daily trap of keeping your partner dependent. Think about baby steps here! Popular parenting magazines often suggest that parents help their children learn to make decisions by presenting them with choices and letting them decide. This helps build self-efficacy and self-esteem. If your partner can't decide what shirt to wear, mention that you like both the red one AND the green one and he should choose the one he feels like wearing.

We are also taught to positively reinforce behaviors in others that we want them to repeat in the future. In relationships we sometimes inadvertently reinforce behaviors in others that we don't like. Think of this as unintentional reinforcement. When a child has a tantrum we give in to stop the yelling and screaming that drives us crazy. Of course, the child learns that yelling and screaming get him what he wants. Paradoxically, giving in to stop the loud, obnoxious noise actually increases the likelihood that the child will repeat the pattern. If you want the screaming to continue, then by all means, give in and reinforce it with attention! Now, think about your dependent partner. Do you feel guilty when your partner is upset, sad, and clingy, and do you give in and offer the nurturance and excessive contact your partner is angling for? Here is the question: If you reinforced that clingy/sticky behavior, why are you surprised when it continues? Stop and look at your role in the relationship. Is there a way to change the cycle by setting firmer boundaries and reinforcing your partner for making her own decisions?

Open up Your Partner's World

In dependent relationships social circles become fairly limited. The dependent person often has a few close friends or relationships that provide the level of intimacy and caretaking desired. Research continues to show that the larger one's social circle and support network, the healthier and happier people tend to be (Myers, 2000). If your partner has a wider support system, he may start to get his needs met in multiple places, thereby lessening the demands on you. Help your partner to meet some new friends and to get involved in some new activities as a way of widening his social sphere. In doing so, you may find that you meet some new people and create more social outlets as well.

Reinforce Acquisition of Competencies

Because the fundamental stance of the dependent partner is self-protection against the dire prospect of abandonment, this partner has spent a lifetime avoiding the appropriate acquisition of competencies. This is a sure-fire way to ensure that others must take care of the dependent. It is not unusual, for example, to find that a dependent person has never gotten a driver's license, has never lived fully independently, or has never prepared a resume or gone to a job interview alone. In a long-term relationship, you will need to take every opportunity to shape and reinforce small steps toward many of the adult competencies you take for granted. And remember, reinforcement will always work better than shame, humiliation, or threats of abandonment. If you can find ways to celebrate your partner's steps toward independence while allowing her to feel simultaneously secure and confident about your commitment, the soil will be fertile for growth — even if the plant you are growing seems reluctant to bloom sometimes!

Allow Your Partner to Be the Expert and Call the Shots

Dependent people usually don't allow themselves to be the expert on anything, so why not try something new with your partner and enact a role reversal? Ask your partner's advice on where to go for dinner or on what shirt you should wear one morning. Dependent people often don't spontaneously voice their opinions on matters for fear of upsetting the apple cart. Seek his opinion on simple matters and work your way toward more complex ones. It's all about discovering creative ways to help your partner have more self-confidence and self-esteem. Each time your partner succeeds in voicing his opinion, reinforce, reinforce, and reinforce some more!

Will Therapy Help?

If you plan to stay with a dependent partner in the long term, then by all means consider marital therapy. Undertaking professional counseling with your partner may be helpful to expand the set of healthy skills you need to make this relationship work. And here is some good news: Dependent persons are often more motivated to change than partners diagnosed with one of the other personality disorders. The prognosis for growth in therapy is moderately good. Your partner is likely to be upset by your distress regardingthe quality of your relationship and may be quite anxious or unhappy with herself as a result. This distress may motivate your partner to do the long and arduous work needed in therapy to eventually change her relational style and sense of self. A solid relationship with a professional may also afford your partner the consistent affirmation and attention she so desires so that once the therapy bond is formed, a dependent person requires little encouragement to continue. But there is a catch, sometimes dependent clients become too dependent on their therapists (remember the movie What about Bob?). It will be the professional's job to set firm boundaries and encourage increasing independence over time.

Although the prognosis for change in a dependent partner with adequate motivation is modestly good, therapy would not be a quick fix; consider it a long-term endeavor. Be certain to focus on yourself and your role during conjoint therapy with your partner. Through changing the way you interact with a sticky partner, you will be better positioned to change the dynamics in your relationship. Your partner must then either meet you in that new place or remain stuck. If your partner can't or won't rise to that challenge, you will be faced with a difficult decision about the future of your relationship.

When It's Time to Leave

As you must surely understand by now, leaving a dependent partner can be tough — gut wrenching even. Of course, leaving other personality-impaired lovers can be hard, but unlike the paranoid and antisocial partners who can be dangerous and unlike the schizoid partner who could care less that you are leaving, the dependent will appear emotionally shattered by your departure. If you are especially bothered by seeing another person — especially someone you care about — in this kind of distress, then leaving will be especially painful. Expect the sticky partner to beg you to stay, to cry uncontrollably, and to call or come by your place long after you have made it clear you need him to stop. Expect to feel guilty and ashamed of yourself, even when you have done everything in your power to be kind, fair, and gentle in the process of moving on. Leaving a dependent partner will require some genuine fortitude and determination on your part. Seek help and support from friends and family members. You need people around you to verify that you are not callous and cold hearted but rather that you have ended up in a relationship with someone who can never be a partner in the true sense of the word.

Summary

An adult with a Dependent Personality Disorder can be a perpetual black hole of emotional need. As a partner, this person will feel increasingly clingy, needy, and desperately demanding. Efforts to preserve some independence or create emotional breathing room will lead to anxiety or depression in this type. Over time, a relationship with a dependent person will feel obligatory and parental; what was once romantic and sweet may soon begin to feel stifling and exhausting. If you are seeking a genuinely mutual relationship with a partner who enjoys you without clinging for dear life, then the dependent type is not for you.

CHAPTER 14

THE RIGID PARTNER

The Obsessive-Compulsive Personality

Obsessive-Compulsive Personality Checklist

- ✔ He is so preoccupied with details, rules, lists, order, and schedules that the point of the activity or any enjoyment are lost.

- ✔ He is such a perfectionist that tasks don't get completed.

- ✔ He is excessively devoted to work and to productivity to the exclusion of relationships, fun, and leisure activities.

- ✔ He is overconscientious and inflexible about morality or ethical rules.

- ✔ He is unable to throw away old, worn-out, or worthless objects even when they have no sentimental value.

- ✔ He doesn't like to delegate tasks or work to others unless it is done precisely his way.

- ✔ He is a miserly spender on himself and others.

- ✔ He is rigid and stubborn and has a high need for control.

Are you attracted to uptight, serious, and controlling types? Psychologists refer to this kind of serious rigidity and inflexibility as **Obsessive-Compulsive Personality Disorder** (OCPD), which, as you will see, is quite distinct from Obsessive-Compulsive Disorder (OCD) — a severe anxiety disorder. The OCPD partner's life revolves around rules, order, and routine. Sound familiar? Life with a rigid partner can be mundane and joyless. You may begin to wonder when the rules for living life became more important than living itself. Keep reading to hear Liz's story and consider whether you have been under the control of a rigid personality type.

Liz's Story

I met George at a football game. We were both part of a large group of people who went to a tailgate party before the football game. It was a beautiful fall afternoon, the sun was out, and the leaves were beginning to turn colors. Everyone was having fun and joking — the spirit of the day was great. I remember being introduced to George and thinking to myself, "This is the man I am going to marry!" He was tall, handsome, and well dressed. He was easy to talk to and I remember being so impressed with how he seemed to have it all together. He told me he was a business major and that he wanted to go to law school. His father was a lawyer, as was his grandfather, and he knew he wanted to be an attorney when he was seven years old.

I found out he was in a fraternity and that he worked part time at his father's law office. He told me that this was the first football game he had gone to during college because he was usually so busy studying and working. His fraternity brothers had given him a hard time for not socializing with them on weekends (I later discovered that they had nicknamed him "the librarian" for his devotion to detail, order, and academic preparation), so eventually he caved and went to the football game. It was such a fun afternoon hanging out with George. He was polite and very nice — even if he did seem a little uncomfortable and distracted at times. I waited for him to call after that but finally decided to call him after a month. He was easy to talk to, but I could tell he was busy and distracted. He did ask me out though and we met for dinner the following Saturday night. I showed up a little late and he seemed ticked off; he was repeatedly checking his watch when I walked in. He told me he had arrived thirty minutes early and talked about how traffic patterns around campus in the afternoon necessitated careful planning. It was a nice evening, and he went out of his way to make sure everything went perfectly. It almost seemed that he had planned every detail from what to order to what to talk about.

We dated for a couple of years and things were pretty good. I got frustrated periodically that he didn't have much time for me, but I rationalized that it was because he was working so hard to make a good life for himself. It was great that he had goals and had a strong work ethic. I guess that pushed my own buttons from childhood. My father was a hard worker, and he created a nice, comfortable life for my mother, my brother, and me. My dad was a physician and his hours were long and dedicated to his patients. I remember wishing that he were around more and that he could attend my sporting events and plays and even some of my birthday parties. He was always busy at the hospital and even when he was home, it seemed his work was never done. My father could just never rest or let anyone else do something for him. On some level, I must have seen a lot of my father in George. He was even very traditional about our relationship and he would often get very uptight after our sexual relationship began, feeling very guilty and angry at both himself and me for "allowing things to go so far."

George and I moved in together after his first year of law school. I was in graduate school then too, so we were both busy and working hard. I really enjoyed being home with George when we could both find the time. We didn't have much money then, but it didn't matter. I was adjusting to being in graduate school and living with George and there were times when I felt really overwhelmed. George was stressed out with finishing school and trying to find a job. I noticed then that when he was stressed, George would work harder and harder, even though he never seemed to really get much more done. I'm not sure if it was a way of helping him feel more in control professionally or a way to avoid me and my demands on his time. When he was home, George was sometimes short tempered and judgmental — especially when I didn't abide by the way he thought things should be done. He spent a lot of time organizing the house and making lists of things for me to do. Every Sunday — one of our few days home alone together — turned into a spit-and-polish apartment cleaning day. It was outrageous! We had a small apartment but to clean the thing to George's standards would take three or four hours. But he didn't seem very willing to discuss alternatives or changes to his cleaning schedule. I kept thinking that he would be different and less pressured when he found a job. I was starting to walk on eggshells; I felt alone and isolated. It was at that time that I started to venture out. It seemed that I never laughed anymore or tried anything new. I joined a few clubs and met some other women. I volunteered at the library and joined a local women's running club. It was nice to socialize and have other women for support.

George was offered a job at a law firm and we were so relieved. We moved into a bigger apartment together but didn't make the commitment of marriage. George kept saying we would get married when he had a few years at a firm under his belt and was more secure financially. He even took me along to appointments with his financial planner to look at all kinds of graphs and pie charts showing our financial future and when the ideal time to "merge our assets" would be. He seemed really excited about all of these figures and careful planning, but honestly it began to erode any romance we had left — it sometimes seemed that George was more excited to see his financial planner than me. With George, everything had to be perfect before trying anything new.

George's hours kept worsening and his stress kept going up. Believe it or not, he became more difficult and judgmental than before. It wasn't just directed toward me; he was that way with his colleagues and his secretary too. We stopped having fun together and we rarely went out unless it was a work function he felt he had to attend. And on those occasions, I had to be on time and well prepared or I'd hear about it. As time went on I began to feel more and more single. My friendships with other women kept me going. George and I began to fight, and I can say that at that point we really didn't like each other.

George kept track of all the money I spent and it infuriated me when he would create pie charts on the computer comparing our spending — always showing that I "wasted" more than he. He even tried to set up a budget for me once; I got a monthly allowance to spend on bills and on groceries, but there was rarely any money left over for me. And a lot of it was my money! I finally saw that George was controlling me and forcing me into his own rigid mold.

George made all of the major decisions in our lives, usually without consulting me; I truly felt like the "little woman" at home without any of the luxuries of marriage or any of the true teamwork that seemed to characterize the relationships of other couples I knew. I wondered if this was how my mother felt. How did she put up with not having a partner involved and at home for all those years? I guess I didn't have the same patience as my mother because I couldn't do it anymore. I had enough of George's worry about everything, his inflexibility, his demand for complete control, and his judgmental anger whenever I didn't comply.

He wouldn't talk to me about our problems, at least not beyond his usual logical lecture, and he never disclosed anything emotional. I felt both alone and like I had completely lost any sense of joy about life. I finally moved out and began to start my life over again. I feel sad about our breakup, but I feel less tense now and like I have a lot more freedom to make decisions, be human, and be good enough without being perfect. I'm still amazed I hung in there with George for so long. And I'm now actually thankful that George didn't want to marry right away. I'm in counseling now, working on figuring out why I keep going after workaholic guys like my father.

The Rigid Personality

While it is important to have structure in our lives and to be mindful of and adhere to rules, laws, and regulations, there comes a point when one becomes overly preoccupied with orderliness, perfection, and details. The person with Obsessive-Compulsive Personality Disorder can literally have a hard time seeing the forest for the trees! She often gets so caught up in the minutia of life that she has a difficult time getting basic tasks accomplished. People with OCPD are difficult to have relationships with because their expectations are perfectionistic, not just for themselves, but also for everyone else in their lives. They work very hard, often too hard, to get their work done and their lists checked off, and it is not unusual for someone with this personality type to spend more time at work than at home. But it is also true that much of the rigid person's time is spent planning and organizing — getting ready to work — and that the actual amount of work accomplished may be modest at best. It is easy to see that inflexibility in all aspects of life drive the person with OCPD as she ultimately gets caught up in her own cycle of perfectionism.

Those with OCPD manage their lives with excessive structure and discipline. They are not comfortable with the gray areas of life and instead see things in black and white and make decisions that are cut and dried. They love to make lists and are scrupulous in following them. While lists and plans help to keep most of us organized, those with OCPD take it one step — OK, maybe two steps — further! They become so focused on lists, schedules, and minute details that these become more important than the original task! So, the OCPD college student may spend two hours arranging his desk and making multicolored study cards without leaving enough time to actually study. The paradoxical thing about people with OCPD is that they want to control their lives and surroundings so much that they inadvertently lose control over these very tasks; ultimately, the major point of the activity is lost. This happens at work, at home, and in relationships. They also fail to notice that their perfectionistic style drives the people in their lives crazy. It takes an inordinate amount of time for the person with OCPD to get anything done. Lists and protocols must be checked and rechecked, figures must be verified, and even the work delegated to others must be thoroughly reviewed and reworked. Sadly, this behavior leaves others feeling annoyed and undermined.

For the person with OCPD, time and effort are often misallocated so that the most important tasks get postponed until last. This is a little like saving your favorite thing to eat until the end of the meal and then not being hungry enough to eat it! Management of time and resources are not efficient, and this ultimately causes prolonged attention to small details that are often not important. This is due to perfectionism and extremely high and usually unrealistic standards for performance. They feel like they should be "perfect," and therefore, they spend an inordinate amount of time trying to achieve perfection at the expense of actually producing timely work. One of the authors once had a colleague who was placed on probation for failing to complete assigned tasks in a timely manner. Even though she was an outstanding writer, competent professional, and extremely intelligent, she could not seem to ever get past the details of preparing to work long enough to actually do some work! On her final weekend on the job, with a firm deadline for a written report due on Monday, she lived in the office around the clock. But instead of actually writing the report, she spent all weekend creating a template for writing the report on her computer. She was fired.

The rigid partner puts so much energy into order, precision, and productivity that relationships often suffer. As with most aspects of their lives, those with OCPD need to control relationships. They are rarely known to be warm and emotionally available; they maintain an emotional distance, and it is not uncommon for this to worsen as their devotion to work increases. They rarely take vacations, and when they do they take their work with them. A true OCPD person may even be unable to take ten minutes on the toilet without bringing along some work material. This is the person you see sitting on the beach while simultaneously returning emails on his blackberry, talking on a cell phone headset, and only occasionally glancing around at his surroundings. Yet, when he decides to truly engage in a leisurely activity (e.g., playing a sport), he tackles it like a work task that needs to be accomplished. For example, don't be surprised when the OCPD member of the office softball team provides weekly statistical breakdowns of each member's performance and detailed scouting reports of other teams.

Scrupulous attention to morals, values, and ethics are definitely important for someone with OCPD. As you are coming to understand, the person with OCPD does little in moderation. This holds true for his excessive conscientiousness and inflexible scruples. He can be quite judgmental of others and often enforces rigid moral codes at work and in relationships. Strict performance standards in relationships may offer little opportunity for flexibility or compromise. People with OCPD can be deferential to those with authority over them; however, they rarely extend grace to others. They also hold up, as the ultimate arbiter, the rules and regulations within which they work or live. The rigid partner cannot easily tolerate bending rules — either on the job or in his personal life. When pushed to be realistic or human in his approach, expect the OCPD person to respond defensively with something like: "Those are the rules!" He rigidly adheres to and enforces ethical codes and he does not refrain from "teaching lessons" in this regard. Unfortunately, this is often not helpful in establishing close and warm relationships. Colleagues and loved ones alike may find this aspect of the OCPD person's rigidity obnoxious.

People with OCPD are sometimes known to be hoarders or "pack rats." They don't like to throw items out, even when they have little sentimental value. They will hold on to worthless and worn out items and become furious if someone else attempts to discard them. It is not unusual to have this cause friction in their relationships; excessive space can be taken up as junk accumulates.

Inflexibility is additionally evident in the rigid partner's inability to trust or delegate tasks to others. She truly believes that her way is the only way, and she is not open to learning about or really considering someone else's ideas or thoughts. When she does delegate tasks — something that causes her anxiety — she will often leave detailed instructions for others and she expects strict compliance. She is likely to become annoyed and irritated if someone does not follow her instructions precisely. At the same time, if she is working on something and is behind schedule — a common phenomenon for the person with OCPD — she is likely to reject offers of help with the deeply held belief that only she can do the work correctly. This often causes low moral and a lack of confidence in subordinates or even in those who are in relationships with her. She does not mete out compliments or reinforcements often and can be rigidly judgmental and distant. She is miserly not just with kindness but frequently with her money as well. She often lives below her means, believing that money should be saved and controlled for the future. She becomes so wrapped up in her own need to organize, predict, and control life that she fails to recognize the consequences of this behavior for others. She is frequently described as stubborn and controlling. Even when she acknowledges difficulty or has some insight into her interaction style or into her rigid way of coping, she rationalizes it as being "necessary."

It is important to distinguish Obsessive-Compulsive Personality Disorder from Obsessive-Compulsive Disorder. These two terms are often confused, but while they sound similar, they actually signify two very different disorders. Those suffering from OCPD do not generally feel the need to repeatedly perform ritualistic actions (e.g., excessive hand washing) in order to control anxiety-provoking obsessions (e.g., being contaminated by germs). Keep in mind that people with OCPD have the personality traits perfectionism, control, order, rigidity, and stubbornness, but they are rarely overwhelmed by anxiety or plagued by disturbing thoughts.

In summary, OCPD is a disorder of control. Yet, the more control this person wields over his life, the more impaired he becomes. A negative cycle ensues, with the rigid person ultimately feeling out of control and then working overtime to regain control. The harder he works for perfect order and precision, the less efficient he becomes and the more out of control he feels. Eventually, the inability to achieve or sustain perfect order causes people with OCPD to feel exasperated and scared, thereby increasing their need for control and their commitment to work. But as you will see, the rigid person's relationships suffer mightily in this process.

What Makes a Rigid Personality?

How does someone become so controlling, rigid, and unaware of the perspective of others? What happened in this person's development that contributed to this style of perfectionism and inflexibility? As you probably already know from reading about some of the other personality disorders, there is likely to have been a host of events along with some inherent genetic predisposition that have coalesced to cause this personality style. The person with Obsessive-Compulsive Personality Disorder may have grown up in a home that was extremely chaotic and overwhelming. To compensate for feeling out of control in this turbulent home, OCPD children learned to control themselves and their immediate environment in order to lessen the anxiety and internal chaos they may have been feeling. Likewise, adhering rigidly to rules, schedules, and lists helped this child minimize the tumultuous and fuzzy boundaries that may have existed in her home. While this style may have helped this child deal with the internal and external chaos of her life, it has little long-term adaptive value.

Another common route to developing OCPD is evident in reports from children raised in homes where the parenting style was rigid and overcontrolled. These children were raised in excessively structured families where there were firm, unbendable rules and norms. Presenting a pristine and controlled appearance to the outside world was highly valued and expected; violating these rules or stepping out of line produced extreme consequences. With little warmth, flexibility, or toleration in the home, these children learned to be highly self-critical. When this perfectionism is carried into adulthood, it leads to excessive dedication to rule-based behavior and a powerful need to avoid perceived failure or mediocrity. OCPD is twice as likely to be diagnosed in males and first-born children.

The Obsessive-Compulsive as Partner

If you are in a relationship with someone who meets the criteria for Obsessive-Compulsive Personality Disorder, you are likely feeling unimportant, perhaps even disrespected. Feeling like an equal in your relationship becomes impossible as your partner exerts more control over you and your relationship. What at first appeared to be a relationship with a dedicated hard-working person now feels like a relationship with a controlling workaholic. When your partner isn't at work, he is at home running your life like a drill sergeant, dictating schedules, making lists, and enforcing order and rules. You may have learned to walk on eggshells so as not to trip your partner's short fuse, and all of this maneuvering and performing can be quite exhausting for you.

The rigid partner has a difficult time trusting others. Specifically, she may not trust you to accomplish tasks competently or according to her exacting standards. This can lead to feeling like your partner is looking over your shoulder all the time and that you are being forever micromanaged. Your partner is also not likely to give you kudos for a job well done and will instead critique your decisions and performance. Over time, this can erode your self-esteem. It may be quite hard for your partner to dictate to you without this behavior becoming onerous and obnoxious.

Unfortunately, you are not likely to get your emotional needs met or have much fun as long as your OCPD partner is allowed to run the show. Your partner is not tuned into your needs nor is he likely to be open to your perspectives. His work and need to be productive are likely to come before you and will leave you feeling like you constitute merely one among many competing priorities. Although he may rationalize excessive devotion to work as being responsible and necessary for success in life, you will notice that you spend more and more time getting your relational needs met outside your primary romantic relationship.

Your partner's rigid and inflexible traits and devotion to work and productivity may make spontaneity, relaxation, and playful fun all but impossible. "Fun" time would have to be scheduled, researched, and carried out with such detailed precision that somewhere along the way, the fun would be lost. You may find that your partner rejects going out or taking vacations as too expensive and extravagant when she can clearly afford such breaks. If you can actually convince your partner to go out for an evening or take a vacation, then you have successfully passed the first hurdle. But don't be surprised when she plans the vacation in minute detail and requires a thorough itinerary and orderly execution of each phase of the "plan." Your partner may have a difficult time truly relaxing and enjoying an activity. Leisure activities are almost painful for the rigid personality, and she either avoids them or attacks them as if they were a challenge to be tamed and mastered. Your partner can become obsessive in her desire to succeed at activities that should be purely for fun or pleasure. She may golf four times a week in order to become a scratch golfer or may get mired in the mechanics and physiology of tennis in order to beat all her friends at the game.

Even your sexual relationship may fall prey to your OCPD partner's rigid focus on order and planning. For instance, don't be surprised if your partner always wants to have sex at the same time and in much the same way. You might even notice that he is most comfortable with sexual encounters that are scheduled or planned in advance. And if you complain or ask for something new, expect your partner to get stuck focusing on the specific details or mechanics — not the larger message that you might be needing a different attitude and a more flexible/spontaneous approach to lovemaking.

Like many of the other personality disorders, you are likely to suffer more in this relationship than your partner. Your partner is able to get her needs met through work and dedication to productivity, while you are left with a relationship that can feel sterile as far as spontaneity, fun, and joy are concerned. If you are seeking a relationship with someone who is flexible, emotionally warm, and willing to spend fun time with you without excessive planning, you are likely to be frustrated with the OCPD partner; your needs and desires for intimacy and leisure time as a couple may go unfulfilled. Your partner may also lack the capacity to really understand your need for deeper connection and tolerance of human imperfection.

In summary, the Obsessive-Compulsive person has unreasonable expectations for himself as well as for his partner. These expectations are often unrealistic yet rigidly held. This person is excessively devoted to work and productivity at the expense of relationships and therefore has little capacity for fun or downtime. This person is known to be controlling and inflexible, unemotional, and overly moralistic. The partner of the person with OCPD ends up with unmet needs in the relationship, which ultimately causes unhappiness and despair. Unfortunately, the likelihood that your rigid partner will recognize the problem with his ironclad routine or have sufficient motivation to change this behavior is not very good.

Why Am I Attracted to Rigid Partners?

When things aren't going as expected in our love it is always useful to examine why. At times, we may contribute to a problem relationship dynamic. In the case of rigid partners, it is certainly worth examining whether you actually seek out this type. There may be something that attracts you to a partner who

- is preoccupied with details, rules, and order at the expense of your needs.
- is extremely perfectionistic.
- is more devoted to work than to enjoying time with you.
- is inflexible and overly moralistic and scrupulous.
- is a pack rat who refuses to throw things away.
- micromanages everything you do and is disapproving if you resist.
- is miserly and tight with money.
- is stubborn and rigid.

If we go back to our initial premise that one must evaluate her part in the relationship, what then, does this mean about you? Let's look at some of the reasons you may currently be, or have a tendency to be, attracted to rigid partners.

You may be attracted to this type of personality because you have grown up with the philosophy that in order to succeed in life one must work hard and that self-worth is based exclusively on achievements. Therefore, picking a mate who is extremely diligent and responsible, has a strong work ethic, and thoroughly observes all of society's rules and ethics may be appealing to you. You may have been raised to believe that this personality style epitomizes the American way of life. You yourself may have a tendency to work hard and to achieve. However, you may also value time spent with family and loved ones. You may value travel and slowing down periodically to enjoy life. But when you pick an OCPD partner whose work ethic, responsibility, and dedication was initially attractive, you also discover the traits of extreme perfectionism, inflexibility, and an inability to slow down to enjoy life. In order to avoid being perpetually lonely in these controlling relationships, you must learn to differentiate excellent organization and a strong work ethic from the extreme rigidity and perfectionism of OCPD. Certainly, there are many well-rounded partners who are reasonably organized and hard working.

Sometimes, we can be attracted to an OCPD partner's level of thoughtful planning and thorough attention to detail. This may be especially appealing if we ourselves struggle with disorganization and procrastination. Knowing this is a weakness, we may be too willing to allow an OCPD partner to take over domains of our life that are essential to independence, such as finances. By relinquishing control to a rigid partner, we automatically place ourselves in a position characterized by dependence and may feel that we have little choice but to "go along" with her perfectionistic agenda.

You may also have been captivated by a more traditional alliance where one person has more power within the relationship. Did you grow up in a home where one partner (typically the male) "wore the pants," in the house and was clearly the person who made major decisions and carried most of the power? It isn't unusual to pick relationships (sometimes very unconsciously) like those that were modeled for us at home. You may have initially felt comfortable with this style or arrangement but are now rethinking this preference and seeking something more mutual and less focused on life's details.

Living with an Obsessive-Compulsive Partner

If you recognize traits in your partner that suggest OCPD, you may feel both relieved to finally understand your partner's behavior and alarmed to discover he brings a psychological disorder to your relationship; either way, you probably have a host of questions and concerns. How do I continue to have a relationship with someone who will always be too focused on rules and routine to really enjoy me in the here and now? Can my partner learn to flex now and then so I can have some of my own needs met? Can I continue to walk on eggshells around this person to pacify his exacting routine and keep the peace? Can I continue to love someone who would rather spend time at work than come home to me and our family? As you must surely be aware, someone with OCPD is not easy to live with. Though you may have once been independent and confident, you may now be questioning your own competence and may feel punished for relatively minor deviations from your partner's home and relationship "protocols." What you once found attractive about your mate is now causing you grave unhappiness and despair as you realize that few of your needs and desires factor into your relationship. He is so emotionally constricted, so anxious about violating rules, and so negative about the idea of any change or novelty in your relationship that you may sense that you will have to either adopt your partner's OCPD approach to life or leave.

You may notice that much of your energy now goes into pacifying your mate and keeping the peace instead of enjoying a mutually satisfying relationship based on give and take. If you decide to stay in the relationship, you should be aware that most of the work required to improve the relationship will fall on your shoulders; after all, your mate is probably quite content with how things are going. Everything has its place, each activity is scheduled, and there are very few surprises. But some reading this chapter will decide that their love for an OCPD partner and the positive elements in the relationship outweigh the problems. Should you decide to stay in the relationship and attempt to work at living more happily with an OCPD partner, we now provide you with some hints on how to make your relationship a little more mutual and interesting.

Be Very Realistic about Your Expectations

People with personality disorders have fairly limited insight into themselves, their behavior, and their motives. They see the problems and deficiencies in their lives as originating outside of themselves. The person with OCPD truly cannot see that she has the problem. Rather, the problem is the fact that nobody else can be trusted to be as thorough or careful as she; even people close to the OCPD person seem strangely unappreciative of her willingness to keep things under control. The likelihood of profound change is small. However, if you can learn to live with your partner and possibly get certain emotional needs met elsewhere, you may come to find some balance in this relationship.

Sometimes we enter into intimate relationships with the expectation that our partner will be free of any quirk or weakness, and we want our partner to be our best friend, confidant, and lover. But how realistic is this expectation and how often can one person meet all of our needs? It is probably an unfair expectation. We are much more likely to have success living with an OCPD partner when we engage other people in our support system to get some of our important emotional and social needs met. Friends, family, co-workers, workout partners, support group members, and travel buddies can all be effective sounding boards, emotional supports, and connected confidants.

You happen to be in a relationship with a partner who, to some extent, will continue to be controlled, perfectionistic, conforming, demanding, anxious, and utterly preoccupied with routine and order. Freud would have called your partner *anal retentive*. The questions for you now are whether you can find enough in this relationship to sustain you and whether you can come to accept your partner's limited capacity to rise above these strong personality traits.

Help Your Partner See the Bigger Picture

People with Obsessive-Compulsive Personality Disorder often get so caught up in the minutia that they miss the bigger picture — the whole point of being alive. Reminding your partner what matters most to you may be helpful as long as this is done gently and without condemnation of your partner's tunnel vision. Remind your partner how nice it can be to stop and smell the roses, to hold hands and sit quietly together, to take a walk at sunset, to sleep in late and cuddle. And when your partner consents to slow down, take a night off, and let you guide him into some new relational territory, reinforce this behavior so that it is likely to reoccur.

Although it may feel hopeless to you at times, continue to plan those date nights and vacations. You need them, and your partner definitely needs them! The ability to set limits on work and to relax is difficult for your partner, so encouraging him to have some downtime without demanding it can make a difference. If you maintain realistic, expectations for enjoying periodic leisure time, hopefully your partner will rise to meet them. Finally, we recommend that you be a careful and thoughtful model of living a balanced lifestyle by exercising, eating well, having a nice support system, and enjoying the small things in life. Over time, some of these habits may just rub off on your partner and help him realize there is more to life than work and perhaps less danger in letting go of some control than he previously imagined.

Help Your Partner with Empathy

Adults with OCPD are often out of touch with their own feelings, and they genuinely struggle when it comes to detecting the feelings of others. They may be so focused on what needs to get done and whether things are being done the right way that they are simply not tuned into feelings — yours or their own. Over time, they have failed to master the subtle cues needed to be empathetic. Partners with OCPD are often constricted when it comes to understanding and expressing internal emotional states. What can you do? You can gently and consistently express your own emotional experience in the relationship and kindly ask your partner to articulate hers. Because obsessive-compulsive partners may have little experience with the dictionary of emotions, they may not have the words to accurately describe how they feel; you may need to offer guesses or possibilities from among which they can choose. Any time your partner does express emotional experience, be sure to reinforce this with praise and attention.

Capitalize on Your Partner's Strengths

Let's face it, your partner is extremely organized. Instead of fighting and resisting your partner's efforts at control and order in every area, why not "go with the flow" so to speak in areas where this structure may actually prove to be a real asset in your relationship? Why not carve out areas in which your partner can "take command?" For example, you may struggle with organization and planning in the area of finances, home maintenance, or vacation planning. Can you go to your partner and ask him to be in charge of these things? We suspect he will happily rise to the challenge and begin creating spreadsheets and long-term schedules immediately!

By giving up some terrain willingly, it may then be more palatable and reasonable to your OCPD partner when you carve out areas in which you will NOT relinquish control or allow your partner to dictate. For example, you may have to build a veritable fortress around items such as meal planning, leisure time, or your children's schedules. When your partner tries — and she will — to slowly intrude on these domains with rigid routine and order, you will have to remain kind but resolute in explaining that you are in command of those things. Be clear and unyielding about those areas in which you will not tolerate obsessive-compulsive control.

Therapy Probably Won't Hurt

True, psychotherapy generally does not cure personality pathology. But counseling and therapy may be more likely to help someone with OCPD than many of the other personality disorders we describe in this guide. One of the secrets to making positive gains in treatment will be framing therapy as a "task" or "job." Help your partner see that you are counting on him to use treatment to become more emotionally skilled and less uptight about things so that your relationship can thrive. If your partner can apply his perfectionistic efforts and attention to detail to trying to reduce some of the most problematic obsessive-compulsive traits, change might be facilitated. It may even help to frame participation in therapy as an opportunity to save your relationship. Of course, it is then important that you be willing to participate fully as well and that you praise and reinforce even modest gains and small improvements profusely.

When It's Time to Leave

If you come to the conclusion that this relationship is not working for you and that it is time to move on, it may help to know that your partner, if she truly has OCPD, may experience less distress about the end of the relationship than some other types covered in this guide. The primary reason for this is the OCPD person's emotional constriction and pattern of detachment. Your partner may pour herself even further into routine and work following your departure, but this may actually have some adaptive value. Your partner may also complain loudly that you are being unfair and failing to play by the "rules" of relationships or marriage, and she may point out adamantly that you have a contractual obligation to stay. Remember, the obsessive-compulsive person's primary defense will be order, focus on rules, and extreme attention to laws and moral requirements. Your partner may or may not have any insight about why you are finally leaving and may not be able to really appreciate how her rigid devotion to work and routine were part of the problem. Finally, your partner may indeed be suffering emotionally at the news of your leaving yet will probably not be able to express this very effectively.

Summary

To think more about life with an obsessive-compulsive partner, rent the classic movie *The Odd Couple* with Jack Lemon playing the OCPD character, Felix. As you watch the movie, ask yourself: Could I really live with that kind of partner? Can I really tolerate the rigidity, order, routine, and constant low-level anxiety? Is there something I find strangely attractive about the obsessive-compulsive type? Life with a rigid partner will be constrained, emotionally muffled, and the exact opposite of spontaneous. Be careful about handing over control of your life to an OCPD partner.

CHAPTER 15

THE GLUM PARTNER
The Depressive Personality

Depressive Personality Checklist

- His overall demeanor is defined by gloominess, cheerlessness, and unhappiness.
- His sense of self is defined by feelings of inadequacy, worthlessness, and low self-esteem.
- He is critical, blaming, and negative toward himself.
- He tends to brood and worry.
- He is negative, critical, and judgmental to you and others.
- He is pessimistic about almost everything.
- He tends to feel guilty and remorseful.

Have you dated someone with these personality features? Are you involved with an unhappy, pessimistic, and judgmental person? While all of us have moments of sadness and periodic blue spells, the glum partner has an ongoing, pervasively negative demeanor. Psychologists term this style of personality **Depressive Personality Disorder**. While not a serious mood disorder (like major depression or bipolar disorder), the depressive person has symptoms that mimic those of someone who is chronically depressed. He enjoys little and there isn't much you can do to bring him out of his funk. We encourage you to read Sadie's story and to consider whether you have been attracted to a person of the glum variety.

Sadie's Story

Steve's cool, quiet demeanor really attracted me. He seemed sort of dark and mysterious and I totally fell head over heals for him.

208 Crazy Love page

He had a dry sense of humor and wasn't like the other guys I had known. I was working in my first job after I graduated and, like most new graduates, was trying to find my way. Steve had been working in my building for a while, but can you believe I never noticed him at work? I actually met him at the gym after eyeing him for a few months. I used to work out on the treadmill a few over from the one he used, but he never noticed me. One day, I worked up the courage to move to the machine next to his. He didn't even notice me then! I think he was in his own world, but he was so good looking and his aloof thing kind of interested me. Although most of the guys I've dated have been more outgoing, for some reason I was drawn to Steve.

I struck up a conversation with him that ended up being nice. He didn't ask for my number or anything, but we did discover that we worked in the same building. I didn't run into him again until one day I saw him outside our building in the courtyard. Of course, I was the one who struck up a conversation, again. He always seemed really open to talking to me, but he obviously wasn't going to initiate anything. He had this very calm, slow manner of speaking, which I really liked. He seemed to be introspective and to be a realist. He was really good looking and smart but wasn't overly into himself. He actually seemed to be quite humble and to have very high expectations for himself. He hadn't been in a relationship in a while because, he said, he hadn't met anyone who had the qualities he was looking for in a mate. He also admitted that he thought most women wouldn't be interested in him. I noticed that he blamed himself for his last breakup; he noted that his girlfriend didn't think his career was very promising. Since we seemed to have a connection, I felt good knowing that he was humble and willing to take responsibility for things.

I asked him out for coffee and he seemed very willing, if not cheerful on the outside. We had a nice time, and we both seemed comfortable. He actually asked me out from there and we started dating each other. He complimented me, my looks, and my intellect. He seemed to think we were a good fit, and I thought so too. I was super attracted to him, and physically we hit it off. He was always nervous about whether I was OK, whether I was having a good time, whether I found him attractive. He was constantly worried that everything go off alright, and he seemed to spend a lot of time evaluating our time together. I remember thinking that I wished he would just relax and enjoy himself, but he never seemed to. Steve also tended to down himself all the time. Everything was his fault, and it just seemed that he carried an invisible burden around on his shoulders all day.

I knew he liked being with me and wanted to hang out with me because he called a lot and asked to do things. Funny, he seemed to always expect me to say no and was genuinely surprised when I didn't. Then, when we'd get together, he seemed a little bummed and maybe pessimistic about whether I was really having fun. The weird thing was that then I'd start questioning things and I'd try harder to be more fun and lively. I worked pretty hard to make sure we had a fun time together, but I never left feeling like it was relaxing or fun for Steve. There was always a subtle undertone of heaviness and almost painful self-doubt for the guy. One day, it dawned on me who Steve reminded me of: Eeyore! When I realized this, I burst out laughing. But when I shared this connection with him, he didn't see the humor and just kind of hung his head (like Eeyore . . .) and said a kid in school used to call him the same thing. I felt awful.

We got more serious despite this sort of depressive fog hovering over our relationship. I felt like I was getting to know him better and I worked hard to show him that our relationship was making me happy. Even though Steve usually gave me very nice compliments, at times he would become critical — not just about me, he was terribly hard on himself too — and over time, I began to feel evaluated in a subtle sort of way. Steve had high expectations for himself and worked hard to achieve them, but I knew he always felt that he fell short. The problem was that sometimes his expectations for me also felt impossible to meet. I could tell he spent a lot of time ruminating about these things, and this would always leave him in a quiet, negative kind of mood.

Although I had gotten to know Steve better, the dark mysterious guy I found so attractive early on was still mysterious to me. I never got the feeling that he was happy or really enjoyed things in life. He didn't seem to take much pleasure or even notice some of the simple things around us. One weekend we went for a hike and it was a beautiful day with breathtaking views of the mountains. The natural exquisiteness of our surroundings flooded me with delight, but Steve couldn't enjoy it and I don't even think he really noticed it. Instead, he was critical about our choice of location for the hike, said that we should have loaded our packs differently, and thought that we took too much food. It was exactly like trying to enjoy a hike in the woods with Eeyore in tow! When I reflect on Steve, it isn't so much that he was a perfectionist but that he didn't even have the ability to enjoy where he was in the moment. It almost felt like he preferred to be miserable and fixate on the dark side of things rather than attempt to have fun. He was definitely a glass half empty guy.

Steve's negative traits became more noticeable over time. I got to the point where I didn't want to plan things anymore because whatever I tried wasn't ever quite right. When we stayed in, he was often quiet and sullen. He was always down on himself too. Even our sex life sort of dwindled. He didn't think he was good at things, and he made negative comments about himself as a lover, as an employee, as a person in general. At first, I couldn't tell if he was just humble or if he was fishing for compliments. I used to try and pump him up, but it never worked. It took me a while to figure out that it didn't matter what I said, deep down he didn't believe it. He had really low self-esteem and I just couldn't fix it for him. When I would get annoyed with how difficult and tense he made everything, he would start to feel guilty and sad. Then he would try to make it up to me, all the time talking about how he always "screwed things up." I, of course, would try to smooth things over and try to make Steve feel better because ultimately I felt guilty. This cycle occurred over and over, and I couldn't seem to change it.

For a while I thought Steve was just depressed, and I really urged him to see his doctor. He went to his internist, who told him he didn't really meet the criteria for depression. She put Steve on an antidepressant medicine for a while, but neither Steve nor I noticed much change. I have to admit that I never saw Steve get really depressed or suicidal or anything, it was just a constant low mood and sad appearance that colored everything we did together. After knowing Steve for a couple of years I realized that it was just who he was, but it didn't feel good to me. He was dark and mysterious for a reason, and it wasn't as attractive to me anymore. I started to feel this constant gloominess too, and my own self-esteem started to wither. I loved Steve but knew that I could never be happy with him. Leaving him was one of the hardest decisions I've ever made, but I felt I had to in order to feel like myself again.

The Glum Personality

As is human nature, we all have days or even weeks where we might feel down. With time and everyday fluctuations we usually go back to "feeling like ourselves." We explain these jags of low mood away as "just a bad day," fatigue, or perhaps a normal response to an upsetting situation. These minor occurrences are a part of life, and we have learned to expect these setbacks from time to time. However, when we discuss the glum or depressive personality, we are talking about something much more enduring and pervasive. We think of this personality style as the **Eeyore Syndrome**. Remember the children's books about Winnie the Pooh and his friends? Eeyore was the donkey who was perpetually pessimistic and glum. When good things happened to him, he expected bad things to follow. Even his voice sounded flat and unemotional. He didn't get excited about much and didn't anticipate life ever being much different. Eeyore is our mascot for the glum personality; he beautifully typifies this personality syndrome.

Being in a relationship with a glum personality may feel like a vortex of joylessness. In our clinical experience, the person with a glum personality has a fairly limited spectrum of emotions. When asked what she is feeling or experiencing, this personality type has a difficult time. When asked what it feels like to be happy, she has a hard time finding the words to describe it. If asked to describe what brings her joy, she seems to struggle for an answer. Asking this person to make a list of twenty things that bring her happiness or delight is like asking someone to run a marathon in bare feet! So, not only does she have a very restricted range of feelings — except for many shades of sadness and melancholy — it is also difficult for her express these emotions.

This person's joyless and glum experience is deeply entrenched in a profound sense of personal unworthiness. The glum partner feels inadequate, and this gets projected onto others, the environment, and the future. It is difficult to feel joy when one feels pervasively incompetent. The glum person endures a deep and abiding deficit in both esteem and joy.

Consequently, the glum personality's feelings of inadequacy and low self-concept get translated into critical, judgmental, and blaming behavior. This negativity is usually self-directed and the glum person usually isn't shy about putting herself down. A compliment or kind gesture will be dismissed and instead will often be turned around and used as evidence of low worth. Depressive types' tendency to be self-downing and derogatory can be harsh and leave those around them constantly feeling compelled to rush in and dispute these jags of depressing negativity. This partner exudes negative energy and will suck the joy out of any gathering — sometimes in a very subtle way.

In order to fully understand the glum personality, one must also be aware that the judgmental, critical attitudes and behavior emanating from this partner may also be directed outward. People in the life of a glum partner will experience, firsthand, the same sort of harsh expectation and critique that the glum person directs toward himself. Nothing will be "good enough" or "right" in this person's eyes. A poor capacity for grace is so deeply entrenched that it is exuded persistently in words, attitudes, and demeanor. Even when subtle, this negativity can be oppressive in the glum personality. More often than not, though, the criticism expressed by a glum partner is overt and candid. Tact may not be a notable trait for the glum person. While he may explain or defend himself as being "realistic," others interpret him as pessimistic and callous.

A person with a glum personality spends a great deal of time and emotional energy dwelling, brooding, stewing, and agonizing over the negative, over perceived failures, over apparent shortcomings, over mistakes, and over chronic regrets. She is naturally pessimistic about the future and broods over the outcome of events small and large. This ruminating, along with her general unhappiness, causes her to give off a potent air of dejection and gloom. Of course, such profound negativity and depression turn other people off and send them scurrying elsewhere for fresh air and emotional sunshine. This cyclical pattern continues as the depressive's notions of unworthiness are reinforced by the rejecting behavior of others.

What Makes a Glum Personality?

Depressive symptoms certainly exist on a continuum of severity. On one end of the spectrum is a severe mood disorder — major depression — that can be thoroughly debilitating and even place the person suffering with it at risk for suicidal thinking and behavior. On the other end of the spectrum is normal mood functioning or no depression. The depressive personality falls someplace in the middle of this continuum. Although rarely immobilized with depressive symptoms, this person's mood is simply always glum, brooding, negative, and pessimistic. But the depressive type has become so acclimated to this mood state that these symptoms no longer feel acute or distressing. The depressive is inclined to say, "That's just the way I am!" Believe it or not, these people have become so familiar with this chronic low-level depression that it no longer seems odd to them.

Although research on this personality type is still underway, we do know that it is diagnosed more often in people whose first-degree relatives (e.g., parents, siblings) have been diagnosed with mood disorders (e.g., Major Depression and Bipolar Disorder). From this evidence, we can surmise that there is a strong genetic predisposition toward depressive personality features. Both men and women can suffer from the depressive personality syndrome.

Beyond genes, however, children with depressed parents are at risk for becoming depressive for other reasons. It is very difficult to be exposed to a depressed caregiver and not learn depressive approaches to viewing the world and evaluating self and others. One fascinating strand of research in early child development shows that even the youngest infants can detect depression in adults' faces. In experimental studies, infants turn their heads away from depressed faces and always choose happier adult faces when they are available (Radke-Yarrow, 1998). But when a child has only depressed models at home who demonstrate only depressed mood, these kids have less opportunity to learn a range of emotional expression. They may become expert with all the nuances of depressed mood without ever learning much about what joy, happiness, and pleasure look like. In essence, the parent's joyless modeling becomes integrated into the child's core personality style. Finally, evidence indicates that adults with depressive personalities are more prone to actually becoming seriously depressed at times. When this occurs, it is referred to as a *double depression* and may require medication and therapy to address the severe mood problem.

The Depressive as Partner

The depressive person will be a sad and woeful partner; this will make for a joyless relationship. The solemn, mysterious, self-deprecating traits that may have attracted you to your partner originally will probably be the traits that prove to be the most difficult for you in your relationship. The depressive personality's interpersonal style is based on his deep feelings of inadequacy and low self-esteem. Therefore, the way this person perceives himself, the world, the future, and all of his relationships is seen through the darkened lens of unworthiness and deep-seated unhappiness.

Getting involved with a depressive partner may actually cause you to start to feel depressed yourself. This vicarious spreading of depressed mood and a jaundiced outlook on life is one of the reasons mental health professionals are cautious about taking on too many mood-disordered patients — it can just become depressing! Your own low mood may come from several sources. Being critiqued and judged by your partner may take a toll; acutely aware of their failings, depressive partners become hyperaware of their partner's as well. The depressive will often make a good faith effort to express gratitude to a partner, but her pessimism, prickly negativity, and gloom will color even these expressions. When confronted about this tendency or when faced with your hurt feelings about being judged, the depressive partner will often feel guilty and remorseful — maybe engaging in a round of self-flagellation — making you feel guilty for ever bringing it up. You may find yourself starting to have a difficult time making decisions and letting your guard down for fear of your partner's harsh and tactless feedback. You may also find that your feelings are hurt more often than not and that you are helping your partner carry her burden of insecurity.

Perhaps more troubling is the reality that your partner spends an inordinate amount of time brooding and worrying about everything under the sun. Molehills are made into Himalayan mountains, and even the small relationship hassles that most couples experience will be catastrophic to your partner. You might be feeling that you are forever dealing with "huge" relationship issues with your partner and repeatedly assuring him that everything is OK. Ask yourself these questions: Are you constantly reassuring your partner that things really aren't so bad? Are you avoiding the mention of things that bother you? Do you fail to ask for what you need from the relationship for fear your partner will become even more sullen, brooding, and self-downing?

If you were hoping to be in a relationship with an assertive, confident partner, you will notice that your partner is the antithesis of the optimistic self-assured type. What you may have interpreted to be humility is actually a case of terrible self-esteem and a sense of utter worthlessness.

Here is a paradox: The depressive partner needs a lot of reassurance yet is not likely to believe it when you deliver. Perhaps you have gotten to a place where you notice that you are doing the majority of the relationship work? The partner of the depressive person ends up working overtime to find activities, topics, and approaches to interacting that reassure and reinforce the depressive's fragile sense of self.

It is hard for nearly all healthy adults to be in the company of a person who consistently radiates a gloomy and pessimistic aura. When we are around someone who is blue, it is natural to try and bring that person out of her funk. The deeper the funk, the more adamantly people around the person try to help her feel better. For some wise counsel on this matter, we now return to our earlier example of Eeyore. It didn't matter how hard Pooh worked to convince Eeyore that tomorrow was going to be a beautiful day with much to offer; Eeyore always assumed it would rain. Eeyore actually had a personal rain cloud that followed him around 24/7. And poor Eeyore always ate his honey with prickly thistles — a nice image of the bittersweet way the depressive personality experiences the world. When Eeyore's tail fell off, recall that his chums went out of their way to get it reattached for him, but Eeyore couldn't manage any joy or delight at this. He remained gloomy and cheerlessly waited for something else to go awry.

Why Am I Attracted to Depressive Partners?

So what is it about you that leads you to be attracted to the depressive personality type? Your attraction to the depressive style means that you are drawn to a partner who most likely

- has a consistently gloomy, dejected, and unhappy mood.
- is consumed with feelings of inadequacy and unworthiness.
- is self-critical and self-judgmental.
- is also critical, judgmental, and harsh toward you.
- broods and worries.
- is pessimistic about most things, including you.
- is remorseful and feels guilty and constantly regretful.

What does all of this say about you?

There may be several facets of the depressive's initial demeanor that attracted you. Some of these traits might continue to attract you, especially if you have hung in there with a depressive partner for some time. Your partner may seem responsible, which may continue to be very appealing on some level. The sobriety with which this partner faces life may make him appear more serious and conservative. Also, your partner's tendency to be self-downing may endear him to you as humble and unpretentious.

Perhaps you have the propensity to be drawn to partners who seem to need you to "save" or "help" them. Looking back over your own love history, you may discover that you consistently wind up in relationships with partners who exude a deficit of some sort — in this case a glaring deficit in self-esteem and basic happiness. What really ropes you in is the challenge of making this partner feels better — of curing her of the depressive features so core to your partner's personality. You may realize that you began taking on this role even as child. Being a "helper," or "rescuer," isn't necessarily a terrible thing — unless you are trying to save a PDP. If you harbor illusions of rescuing or curing a depressive PDP, it will certainly be an uphill battle.

A final consideration when thinking about what leads you to be attracted to depressive partners has to do with the balance of power within your relationships. Your serious, quiet, partner may be the more passive and submissive partner in your relationship, and you may like being the person who calls the shots. Although many relationships are characterized by an unequal distribution of power between partners, you may find that you are most comfortable or most in your element when making most of the decisions. You may also be more comfortable when parenting or caretaking; beyond a desire to help, this may have something to do with your need to manage, direct, and "cure" someone else. Of course, the paradox of this kind of power arrangement with a depressive partner is that you may inadvertently be reinforcing your partner's poor self-esteem and tendency to see himself as incompetent. It is worth asking yourself whether your partner's ongoing depressive mood is comfortable to you on some level.

Living with a Depressive Partner

For better or worse, you find yourself in a relationship with a depressive personality type. Can this relationship ever give you what you'd hoped for at the outset? Does your partner have the capacity for change? Can you ever hope to see your partner smile on a consistent basis, let alone become fun loving and spontaneous? Although we are loath to sound like tired pessimists ourselves, we must state clearly that expectations of marked change in the depressive behavior of this partner type are probably unreasonable. The glum person has formed a lifelong pattern of emotional experience and thinking that casts everything and everybody in the gray light of depression and gloomy pessimism. You may only now be fully appreciating that your partner's depressive demeanor is rubbing off on you and coloring your own outlook on the relationship, if not life in general. Being with a depressive partner can feel a bit like being stuck in emotional quicksand.

Although your depressive partner will probably continue to struggle with depression over the course of your relationship, you may be preparing to stay for the long haul. Perhaps you will be content with even small improvements or glimmers of happiness. If you are planning to hang in there, here are several suggestions for increasing the probability that your relationship will go smoothly.

Anticipate Small Changes

Personality change is difficult business, and even healthy adults rarely demonstrate dramatic changes in personality style. For people with personality disorders, resistance to change will be exacerbated by the very rigidity that characterizes these problems. So what does this mean for you? It will be helpful for you to have very modest expectations for your glum partner; change will occur in tiny increments. Helping your partner to less frequently verbalize self-downing thoughts or to actually enjoy short stretches of time might be huge victories in the long run. Also, keep in mind that change requires motivation. Is your depressive partner genuinely discontent with her mood state and brooding behavior? If your partner is not particularly discontent with herself, the likelihood of change is quite slim.

Be Aware of Your Role in Reinforcing Your Partner's Behavior

What is your role in perpetuating your partner's current depressive behavior? Are you inadvertently reinforcing some of the very behaviors you find noxious in your glum partner? For example, each time your partner becomes particularly morose and moody, do you race in with worried caretaking behavior? Do you shower your partner with concerned attention and beg her to talk to you? Do you unconsciously excuse your partner from responsibility around the house or in your relationship because you worry she is too sad or too fragile? When your partner becomes overtly self-depreciating, do you rush in to sing her praises? You can see how caretaking types might inadvertently keep a partner wallowing in depressive behavior. Further, if you do all of the work to help "fix" your partner's depression, how will she ever get better? Most of us would like to be cared for rather than do the hard work of changing ourselves. Are you enabling this sort of disengagement? Finally, if you are currently taking on so many of your depressive partner's worries and burdens that you yourself have become distressed and depressed, then you are allowing your partner's personality to become contagious. It will be essential that you do a better job setting boundaries and supporting your depressive partner without reinforcing her depressive symptoms.

Teach Your Partner to Stop and Enjoy the Small Things in Life

The glum partner's general demeanor is serious and negative. This person is not typically the life of the party! Real relaxation and the ability to genuinely stop and savor a moment may be elusive experiences for the depressive. We know this sounds trite and easy; the reality, however, is that depressive people rarely find enjoyment in the passing moments and simple pleasures of life. By teaching your partner to slow down and savor things with you, you will be giving him permission to be content — even if briefly. And practicing this with your partner might simultaneously give you the opportunity to find peace and contentment in small ways. Practice relaxation with your partner and consider exercising together. With brain-induced endorphins on board, it may be tough for him not to enjoy some sense of well-being. Finally, if your partner has trouble not articulating a steady stream of depressing content about himself and the future, consider limiting this dialog to short periods during each day (e.g., "I will be happy to hear your concerns but only for ten minutes each day; after that, I expect you to work hard at describing yourself, me, and the future in more positive terms").

Simple activities with your partner, like making a list of all the places you would like to visit together, the books you would both enjoy reading, or the restaurants you would like to sample can generate fresh, optimistic ideas. Try to get unstuck by getting outside of your usual activities and routines. Try living outside of your usual world and take your partner along.

Engage in Cognitive Reframing

People who have depressive personalities tend to be chronically pessimistic and brooding. This form of thinking, or cognition, is not healthy and nearly always perpetuates a depressive style of thinking. Interpreting everything through a bleak lens of negativity is nearly guaranteed to lower self-esteem and diminish hope. Helping your partner develop multiple perspectives may be helpful. It is relatively easy to get stuck on one way of seeing things or one way of interpreting events. By pointing out alternative interpretations of events, you may encourage your partner to open her perspective and move beyond purely depressive understandings of situations. For example, when your partner has a disappointment at work, it may be helpful to challenge the assumption that it is a direct result of her incompetence or inherent worthlessness. Where is the evidence for this thinking? Where is it written that she must be perfect to be acceptable? So what if she made a mistake, how does that define her fundamental personhood?

Therapy May Be Useful

While therapy is not often efficacious with personality-disordered clients, partners with depressive personalities may experience occasional distress and turmoil. For example, your partner may begin to feel internal angst and an increase in negative symptoms and brooding if your relationship begins to deteriorate. Therapy may be a good place to begin to work on habitual styles that lead to self-downing and low mood. Like all PDPs, the depressive is prone to resist care and quickly revert back to old patterns. Therapy will need to be sustained, and your partner will need to have some genuine motivation to change. Also, there is some evidence that antidepressant medications can help some of the symptoms plaguing the depressive type. We recommend consultation with a psychiatrist to explore this possibility carefully.

When It's Time to Leave

We often hear people ask, Will I know when to leave? How will I know that I've tried everything? Is there really much chance that my partner's mood will improve enough to have a healthy and happy relationship? These are questions that cause anguish and despair. The answers are not always easy ones to come to grips with. Many PDPs do not feel the need to change. In our practice, we have noticed that it is sometimes harder for someone to leave a depressive partner because these partners are inherently sad and hopeless. It is much easier to leave an abusive, angry, or deceitful partner than someone who is passive, dejected, and gloomy. But the depressive partner can seriously diminish your quality of life, your mental health, and your sense of self. Taking good care of your own health must be a serious consideration as you struggle with the question about whether you can really commit to life with a depressive person. If your partner becomes more depressed or expresses a desire to hurt himself as you terminate the relationship, help your partner by notifying appropriate authorities (e.g., physicians, police) as well as family members or friends. By now you are keenly aware of how important a broad support system is when facing the end of a relationship.

Summary

Glum adults are chronically mildly depressed. They have poor self-esteem and exude a thick cloud of gloom, dejection, and angst. Expect this partner to be critical and negative about herself, you, the world, and the future. You should also expect to spend much of your time either working fruitlessly to cheer your partner up or escaping your partner's low mood through time with friends or solitary activities. Some adults are unusually resilient to the impact of a lover's emotional state. Most of us are not so fortunate and may find life with a depressive PDP to be intolerable.

SOME FINAL THOUGHTS

CHAPTER 16

WHAT IF I'M MARRIED TO A PERSONALITY-DISORDERED PARTNER?

Here is a familiar scenario from the office of any practicing couples therapist. A new couple enters therapy, and it quickly becomes crystal clear to the therapist that a large measure of the relationship dysfunction can be traced to a serious personality disorder in one member of the couple. Perhaps he is a raving narcissist with no capacity for empathy or even genuine interest in his wife's needs or experiences. Or, perhaps she is a severe histrionic who has had several affairs, is chronically flirtatious, and is difficult to predict emotionally. No matter the specific personality disorder, the therapist must cautiously decide if and when to apprise the nondisordered spouse of the nature of his or her lover's impairment. Should the therapist label this disorder immediately? Should the therapist refrain from labeling the disordered spouse and let his or her partner just figure it out? And once the healthier partner understands the nature of the disorder, should the therapist describe the bleak prognosis for change and recommend separation? These are very difficult questions.

Your situation is different. Having read this guide, you have probably already diagnosed one (or more) partners with a personality problem. The crazy-making emotions or behaviors you have been enduring may now make better sense. Quite often, partners find the process of realizing and accepting the fact that they are with a PDP to be complicated and emotionally draining. Although there is some genuine relief in knowing what's wrong with your partner, fighting through denial and accepting your partner's impairment may be no easy task. But where do you go from here? Can you live with this person indefinitely? Can you remain committed in spite of the endless cycle of distress and impairment you might have to endure? Do you want to? We believe that these are among the toughest questions you will have to ever ask yourself — particularly if you are married or in a long-term love relationship.

Although knowledge leads to freedom and power in relationships and although it is always best to know if your love mate is seriously impaired, you may now be asking yourself a whole host of questions about yourself, your judgment, and what your relational future might hold. Some of the most common questions in this vein include

- Why did I marry this person?
- How come I didn't see my partner's personality disturbance *before* we got this far?
- How did it go so wrong when I was so happy and in love at first?
- Am I partly to blame for my partner's personality problems?
- How can I really be sure my partner even has a personality disorder?
- If I were a better spouse, wouldn't my partner get better?
- Is there any way I can really make this work?
- How can I leave now that I've made a life commitment?
- If I leave, what will I do and how will my kids cope?
- Am I destined to always fall for PDPs?

These questions, and many more, are common and healthy. If you are reading this chapter, then you are probably in a long-term relationship, probably a marriage. We recognize that enduring and committed relationships are one of the real treasures in life, that they are associated with many health benefits for those who have them, and that kids generally do much better when their parents are together. No therapist worth his or her salt will take your relationship lightly or encourage you to exit a marriage over a few annoying habits or eccentricities. All of us have some personality quirks or even traits of some of the disorder types covered in this guide. But when an adult has a full-blown personality disorder, the landscape shifts and the prognosis for positive change and marital adjustment declines.

While we empathize with the roller coaster of emotions you are undoubtedly feeling at this point, we also believe firmly in the value of informed decision making. Before jumping to any sort of decision about what to do in your own case, let's take a moment to review the preeminent characteristics of adult personality disorders. Think about each of these in the context of your love relationship. As you mull over each characteristic, ask yourself Is this something I can endure in the long term? If your partner has a personality disorder, it means that she

- has distorted perceptions — particularly regarding herself and others — that lead to disturbed interpersonal functioning.
- has rigid personality traits that cannot be flexed or adjusted when needed and that nearly always cause emotional distress or relationship impairment.
- has a history of this personality rigidity dating back at least to adolescence and a profile of poor relationships.
- demonstrates her disturbance in a wide range of situations.
- has very little insight about her dysfunctional interpersonal style and may see the problem as yours.
- has very poor motivation to change herself but may be happy to change you.
- will be unlikely to make substantial change in her behavior over time and will often be a difficult therapy client — *if* she even participates.

There it is. What you see in your current partner is very likely what you will get from here on out. Although personality disorders tend to become less severe over time and even though some adults with personality disorders manage to improve in long-term psychotherapy, most personality disorder syndromes will linger and cause distress and disturbance for love partners.

The real question — and the one we simply cannot answer — is What will you do? Some reading this guide and coming to the grim realization that they are committed to a PDP will choose to stay in the relationship and try to make it work. Children may be involved, or you may decide that your partner's behavior is not as severe as those portrayed in this guide. Others will arrive at the painful conclusion that they have reached their limit or hit the proverbial relationship wall. You may have neither the energy nor the desire to remain in your marriage for another moment.

Whatever your ultimate decision, we recommend that you take your time making it and that you consider seeking professional help along the way. Also, please consider returning to the chapter in this guide that addresses your partner's personality disorder and reread the final sections. Those of you recommitting to stay in the relationship and wishing to try to make it more livable will find specific advice for making the journey less lonely and less jarring emotionally. Regardless of your partner's specific form of personality impairment, here are some general reminders about loving a personality-disordered person:

- Any change you discover in your partner's behavior will be slow, difficult, and painfully halting. People with personality disorders have little insight about their own personalities and can be quite defensive when the need for change is suggested. Change, if it occurs at all, will occur in baby steps. Make sure your expectations for change match this reality before deciding to stay.

- Your partner's behavior and responses are not about you. Remember, she had a personality disorder long before you met her. Just as you would be tolerant and patient with a family member diagnosed with a physical disorder, so too should you see your partner's behavior as a disability of the relational variety.

- Psychotherapy, medication, and superhuman effort on your part are not magic bullets. The secret is acclimating and taking care of yourself, not finding a "cure."

- Focus on your role in the current relationship turmoil. Yes, your partner may have a personality disorder, but how do you typically respond and does your response just make matters worse? For example, when your partner is suspicious and distrustful, do you become intentionally withholding and vague? Or, when your partner becomes clingy and dependent, do you push her away and threaten to leave? It may be that you are currently responding to your partner's pathology in ways that only make matters worse.

- Remind yourself often about the things that initially attracted you to your partner. Have these things truly evaporated altogether or have you become so preoccupied by the features of her personality problem that you scarcely notice these alluring features any longer?

- Take good care of yourself. Yes, you may live with a detached, antisocial, or avoidant person, but you can still socialize actively, exercise, attend support groups, and refuse to get sucked into silly conflicts with your partner.

- Reward your partner. Positive reinforcement is powerful medicine for any relationship problem. Constantly seek ways and opportunities to let your partner know what you like about her, what she is doing well, and that you have noticed even small changes in the right direction. Nothing will be more important when it comes to increasing the frequency of desired behaviors.

- Those of you who know you are on the way out the door should read the section on leaving a partner with that specific disorder. Some PDPs can become threatening, belligerent, and even violent. You should be prepared before you make the break. Leaving any relationship is difficult, leaving a PDP can make you feel ashamed, guilty, anxious, terrified, or just ambivalent. Consider seeking the assistance of a therapist, minister, family member, support group, or all of the above along the way.

Finally, be vigilant to signs of a pattern in your attraction to disordered personality types. Explore chapter 3 of this guide honestly and seek professional assistance as needed. It is unlikely to be mere chance that you have ended up in several relationships with personality-impaired souls. Consider the possibility that something about this type attracts you and then ask yourself why.

BIBLIOGRAPHY

American Psychiatric Association. (2000). *Diagnostic and statistical manual of mental disorders fourth edition-text revision*. Washington DC: author.

Beck, A., Freeman, A., & Associates. (1990). *Cognitive therapy of the personality disorders*. New York: Guilford Press.

Benjamin, L. S. (1996). *Interpersonal diagnosis and treatment of personality disorders*. New York: Guilford Press.

Brennan, K., & Shaver, P. (1998). Attachment styles and personality disorders: Their connection to each other and to parental divorce, parental death, and perceptions of parental caregiving. *Journal of Personality, 66*, 835–878.

Cameron, N. (1963). *Personality development and psychopathology*. Boston: Houghton Mifflin.

Coolidge, F. L., & Segal, D. L. (1998). Evolution of personality disorder diagnosis in the Diagnostic and Statistical Manual of Mental Disorders. *Clinical Psychology Review, 18*, 585–599.

Fong, M. L. (1995). Assessment of DSM-IV diagnosis of personality disorders: A primer for counselors. *Journal of Counseling and Development, 73*, 635–639.

Golomb, M., Fava, M., Abraham, M., & Rosenbaum, J. F. (1995). Gender differences in personality disorders. *American Journal of Psychiatry, 152*, 579–582.

Hare, R. D. (1993). *Without conscience: The disturbing world of the psychopaths among us*. New York: Pocket Books.

Joseph, S. (1997). *Personality disorders: New symptom-focused drug therapy*. New York: Haworth Medical Press.

Kernberg, O. F. (1984). *Severe personality disorders: Psychotherapeutic strategies*. New Haven, CT: Yale University Press.

Kernberg, O. F. (1985). *Borderline conditions and pathological narcissism*. Northvale, NJ: Aronson.

Kiesler, D. J. (1996). *Contemporary interpersonal theory and research: Personality, psychopathology, and psychotherapy*. New York: Wiley.

Linehan, M. (1993). *Cognitive-behavioral treatment for borderline personality disorder*. New York: Guilford Press.

Lykken, D. T. (1995). *The antisocial personalities*. Hillsdale, NJ: Erlbaum.

Masterson, J. F. (1976). *Psychotherapy of the borderline adult: A developmental approach*. New York: Brunner/Mazel.

Millon, T. (1996). *Disorders of personality: DSM-IV and beyond*. New York: Wiley.

Millon, T., & Davis, R. (2000). *Personality disorders in modern life*. New York: Wiley.

Myers, D.G. (2000). The funds, friends, and faith of happy people. *American Psychologist, 55*, 56–57.

National Institutes of Health. (2004). National epidemiologic survey on alcohol and related conditions. *Journal of Clinical Psychiatry, 65*, 948–958.

Radke-Yarrow, M. (1998). *Children of depressed mothers: From early childhood to maturiy*. Cambridge, England: Cambridge University Press.

Sebold, A. (1999). *Lucky: A Memoir*. New York: Scribner

Sebold, A.(2002) T*he Lovely Bones: A Novel*. New York: Little, Brown.

Shapiro, D. (1981). *Neurotic styles*. New York: Basic Books.

Sperry, L. (2003). *Handbook of diagnosis and treatment of DSM-IV-R personality disorders* (2nd ed.). New York: Brunner-Routledge.

Stone, M. H. (1993). *Abnormalities of personality: Within and beyond the realm of treatment*. New York: Norton.

Turkat, I. D. (1990). *The personality disorders: A psychological approach to clinical management*. New York: ̈Pergamon.

Widiger, T. A., & Costa, P. T. (1994). Personality and personality disorders. *Journal of Abnormal Psychology, 103*, 78–91. *Cognitive therapy*

Young, J. (1990). *Cognitive therapy for personality disorders: A schema-focused approach* (3rd ed.). Sarasota, FL: Professional Resources Exchange.

Index

A

abused children
  and borderline personalities, 96, 101
  and narcissistic personalities, 133
  and personality disorders, 9–10
American Psychiatric Association's
    diagnostic manual (DSM-IV), 10–11
anal retentive, 202
antisocial personalities
  described, 11–12, 77, 80–85
  living with, 90–93
avoidant personalities
  described, 161, 165–167
  living with, 171–174
  as partners, 168–169

B

behaviors of PDPs, 2–3, 10–11
bibliography, 220–230
Bipolar Disorder, 213
book, this
  how to use, 5–6
  purpose of, 4–5
borderline personalities
  See also stormy partners
  described, 13, 95–96, 98–102
  living with, 107–112
  as partners, 102–104
Bundy, Theodore, 84

C

checklists
  antisocial personality, 77
  avoidant personality, 161
  borderline personality, 95
  dependent partner, 175
  depressive personality, 207
  histrionic personality, 113
  narcissistic personality, 127–128
  obsessive-compulsive personalities,
    189
  paranoid personality, 31

checklists *(cont'd.)*
  passive-aggressive personality, 143
  schizoid, 45
  schizotypal personality, 61–62
childhood and roots of personality
    disorders, 8–10, 41
clusters of PDPs
  A—doubting, detached, and odd
    partners, 29
  B—dramatic, erratic, and dangerous
    partners, 75
  C—anxious, withdrawn, and needy
    partners, 159
cognitive reframing, 218–219
counseling. *See* therapy

D

dangerous personalities
  See also antisocial personalities
  attractiveness of, 87–90
  described, 77, 80–85, 94
dependent personalities
  See also sticky partners
  described, 175–176
depression, major, 213
depressive personalities
  attractiveness of, 215–216
  described, 207, 211–213
  as partners, 213–215
depressive personality disorder, 207
detached personalities
  See also paranoid personalities
  described, 45, 49–52
doubting partners. *See* paranoid
    personalities
drugs, 13

E

Eeyore Syndrome, 211, 215
entitlement, 132
environmental factors in personality
    disorders, 8–9

F
families, schizophrenia in, 51–52
first impressions, 22–23
Freud, Sigmund, 202

G
genes, and personality disorders, 8
glum partners
    See also depressive personalities
    described, 207, 211–213

H
Hippocrates, 7
histrionic personalities
    See also theatrical personalities
    described, 113, 116–118
    as partners, 119–121

L
Lovely Bones, The (Sebold), 69

M
marriage with PDPs, 223–227

N
narcissistic personalities
    See also self-absorbed personalities
    described, 127–128, 127–128,
        131–134
    living with, 137–142
    as partners, 134–135
National Institutes of Health survey on
    personality disorders, 3

O
obsessive-compulsive disorder, 196
obsessive-compulsive personalities
    See also rigid personalities
    attractiveness of, 199–201
    living with, 201–205
    as partners, 197–199
obsessive-compulsive personality
    disorder (OCPD), 189,
        193–197
odd partners. *See* schizotypal
    personalities

P
paranoid personality disorder, 7–8
paranoid personalities
    attractiveness of, 39–41
    described, 31, 35–37
    living with, 41–44
    as partners, 37–38
parents
    and children's personality disorders,
        8–10
    shared features with partners, 17, 24
partners
    antisocial personalities as, 85-87
    avoidant personalities as, 168–169
    borderline personalities as, 102–104
    Clusters A, B, C, 29, 75, 159
    dangerous, 77
    dependent personalities as, 181–182
    depressive personalities as, 213–215
    detached, 43
    narcissists as, 134–135
    obsessive-compulsive personalities as,
        197–199
    odd, 61–62
    paranoid, 37–38
    passive-aggressive personalities as,
        150–152
    personality-disordered. *See* PDPs
    rigid, 189
    schizoids as, 52–53
    schizotypal personalities as, 67–69
    shared features with parents, 17, 24
    theatrical, 113, 119–121
passive-aggressive personalities
    See also undermining personalities
    described, 143, 147–150
    living with, 154–157
    as partners, 150–152
past history, and personality disorders, 12
PDPs (personality-disordered partners)
    associated problems of, 13–14
    attractiveness of, 17, 22–28
    capacity for change, 14–15
    clusters, 29, 75, 159
    described, 1–2
    marriage with, 223–227

personality disorders
  See also specific disorder
  clusters of PDPs. *See* clusters of PDPs
  detecting, 2–4, 11–13
  introduction to, 7–10
  key features of, 10–11
  personality-disordered personalities.
    See PDPs
prognosis for PDPs, 14–15
projection, paranoids and, 38
psychotherapy. *See* therapy

R
reframing, cognitive, 218–219
Reagan, Ronald, 92
rejection by parents, 9–10
rigid partners
  See also obsessive-compulsive
    personalities
  described, 189, 193–197

S
scared personalities
  See also avoidant personalities
  attractiveness of, 169–171
schizoid personality disorder, 9,
  49–52
schizoids
  See also detached partners
  living with, 56–59
  as partners, 52–53
schizotypal personalities
  attractiveness of, 69–71
  described, 61–62, 64–67
  living with, 71–74
  as partners, 67–69
Sebold, Alice, 69
self-absorbed personalities
  See also narcissistic personalities
  attractiveness of, 135–137

self-worth, and love, 25–26
Skinner, B.F., 58
stalking, 43
sticky partners
  See also dependent personalities
  described, 175–176, 178–181
stormy partners
  See also borderline personalities
  attractiveness of, 104–107

T
temperament and behavior, 7
theatrical personalities
  See also histrionic personalities
  attractiveness of, 121–123
  described, 113, 116–118
  living with, 123–126
therapy
  for avoidant personalities, 173
  for borderline personalities, 108–109
  for dependent personalities, 187
  for depressive personality disorder,
    219
  for narcissistic personalities, 141–142
  for obsessive-compulsive personalities,
    204
  for paranoids, 43
  for passive-aggressive personalities,
    155–156
  for PDPs, 14–15
  for schizoids, 58–59

U
undermining personalities
  See also passive-aggressive
    personalities
  attractiveness of, 152–154

V
verbal holding strategy, 42

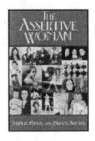